CHALLENGE AND DECISION

CHALLENGE AND DECISION

POLITICAL ISSUES OF OUR TIME

FIFTH EDITION

Reo M. Christenson

Miami University (Ohio)

Harper & Row, Publishers

New York, Hagerstown, San Francisco, London

Acknowledgment

Edward S. Banfield, *The Unheavenly City,* Boston: Little, Brown, 1968, p. 47.
Reprinted with permission.

Sponsoring Editor: Dale Tharp
Project Editor: Karla B. Philip
Designer: T. R. Funderburk
Production Supervisor: Will C. Jomarrón
Compositor: American Book–Stratford Press, Inc.
Printer and Binder: The Murray Printing Company

CHALLENGE AND DECISION: Political Issues of Our Time, Fifth Edition

Copyright © 1964, 1967, 1970, 1973, 1976 by Reo M. Christenson

Library of Congress Cataloging in Publication Data

Christenson, Reo Millard, Date –
  Challenge and decision.
  Bibliography: p.
  Includes index.
   1. United States—Social conditions—1960–
2. United States—Economic conditions—1961–
3. United States—Politics and government—1945–
I. Title.
HN65.C49 1976   309.1′73′092   76–10339
ISBN 0–06–041267–4

TO CANDY,
THANKS TO DON AND PEGGY

CONTENTS

Foreword by Morris K. Udall

In the last half dozen years, Americans have come face to face with a new reality so strange, so alien to the premises on which we built our nation, that its real import is not yet perceived by many—including far too many national leaders.

Quite simply, we have always acted on the assumptions of the frontier —that new, cheap and plentiful resources, both human and natural, could always be found and exploited.

Though our geographic frontier closed at the turn of the century, this frontier mentality stayed with us. And it served us well in many ways, while the assumptions still worked: *biggest* and *best, newest* and *fastest* were virtually American trademarks. In the last 30 years, especially, we experienced a booming growth unparalleled in human history.

And then a series of events—unforeseen by most of us—sent shockwaves through our nation: Vietnam, the failure of our grand social experiments of the 1960s; energy shortages; environmental decay; and, the moral/ political crisis of Watergate. Like an earthquake, these tremors cracked the foundation of our society and economy, leaving the structure intact, but precariously unsteady.

Like an earthquake, too, was their effect on the minds of our people. Doctors tell us that those who live through big quakes often suffer severe psychological reactions, for the fundamental premise of our relation to the physical world—the stability of the earth beneath our feet—has been destroyed. We see a similar syndrome in our political debates, in the polls, and in our personal lives.

We enter this new and different era, not by choice, but because circumstances have changed so drastically. The story of the last quarter of the twentieth century will be how we adapt to these changes, whether we make the hard choices that these hard times demand or drift along trying to answer today's problems with yesterday's answers.

It is clear, for instance, that we can no longer count on an ever-expanding economic pie to continue bringing more and more people out of poverty; we must either be content to consign millions of our fellow citizens to a permanent economic and social underclass, or we must take positive action to redistribute some of the bounty now concentrated at the top and to deal with the personal dysfunctions wrought by generations of deprivation. It is clear that energy resources will become increasingly more difficult to find and exploit; we have to make tough choices about how we make use of what we have—choices about price, technology, and distribution—and, whatever decisions we make, some belts will have to be tightened more than others. It is also clear that at all levels of government our resources will be strained and our choices will be more difficult; both the Pentagon and HEW have seemingly infinite capacities for absorbing money, and the people must force their representatives to be increasingly selective and precise in their decisions.

The book you are about to read brings these problems, and the difficult choices we must make in trying to solve them, into sharp focus. Professor Christenson is a man of strong opinions—opinions I don't always share—and he makes no attempt to hide them. Rather, he goes out of his way to make his biases clear, and to provoke the reader into thinking about and challenging his arguments. The method is as old as Socrates; the issues are as current as this morning's newspaper; the implications will shape the rest of our lives.

PREFACE

Since the fourth edition of *Challenge and Decision* (1973), America has, for the most part, marked time on the major issues discussed in that volume. Cavalierly disregarding all of my helpful hints on tax reform, poverty, national health insurance, crime prevention, and pollution, Washington has neither solved nor greatly ameliorated these problems. They continue, therefore, to be discussed in this edition. Their treatment, however, has been substantially altered. These alterations, plus new chapters on energy, inflation and recession, the federal budget, the feminist movement, and pornography, give the fifth edition a content that is over 60 percent new.

As with previous editions, I have drawn heavily on leading contemporary magazines concerned with public affairs. Personal opinions are often evident, sometimes with trumpets blaring, but it has been my experience that college students welcome the expression of opinion by their professors as long as they are intended to stimulate thought and discussion.

I am especially indebted to Professor James Q. Wilson of Harvard; Professor Robert Lampman of the University of Wisconsin; and Barry Commoner, whose writings proved particularly helpful in the chapters on crime, poverty, and pollution. My sincere thanks to economist Wally Edwards of Miami University for judicious advice on several chapters, and to Susan Kay and Alan and Sondra Engel for valuable comments on Chapter 8. My appreciation also goes to Alice Lafuze, a superb typist and a most engaging person; to Lisa Palmer, my trusted and discerning assistant; and finally, a tip of the hat to Dale Tharp and Karla B. Philip of Harper & Row.

My wife Helen's contribution to the volume should also be acknowledged. Whenever I wrote a passage that seemed to come off rather well, she obligingly let me read it to her and made the proper approving noises. She was also invaluable, as always, during the last days' frenzied efforts to meet the cruel deadline.

If there are any errors of fact or judgment in the book, I will be simply flabbergasted.

Reo M. Christenson

ONE
Pollution: The Issue Is Survival

America bristles with problems: poverty, unemployment, inflation, high taxes, tax loopholes for the rich, maldistribution of income, a staggering crime rate, expensive and/or inadequate health care, scandalous nursing homes, congressional malfunctioning, corruption in high places, threats to privacy, schools that can't teach, prisons that can't rehabilitate, a plea-bargaining system that perverts justice, a messy welfare system, minority unrest, radio and television programs drowning in (often tasteless) ads, a gun-happy populace endlessly entertained by media portrayals of violence, 9 million alcoholics, an estimated 45,000 annual auto fatalities, an irresponsible entertainment industry, a chaos of moral values, a loss of national élan and self-confidence—the list could go on and on.

But while all of these are important, none of them imperil the species. Only pollution does that. Only pollution threatens our soil, our water, our air—even the ozone—so gravely that scientists wonder if mankind will render this planet uninhabitable. Or, if not uninhabitable, at least a far less inviting place in which to live.

Pollution is, of course, closely related to the energy problem. The way we power our machinery and the way we dispose of our energy wastes may largely determine man's future on earth. If we plunge headlong into tomorrow, heedless of the risks created by productive processes whose long-range effects are ill understood, we may do irreversible and tragic damage to our world and the world our children inherit.

On every hand, we read of this or that product or substance that can jeopardize our health or our environment. The flow of ominous information and speculation is so continuous that we are often tempted to throw up our hands in dismay (or disbelief), concede that this is a world of infinite danger, and go on living as we wish, come what may. An understandable attitude but hardly a responsible one. Certainly the government must constantly weigh the evidence, assess the relative hazards in light of our imperfect knowledge, and make the best judgments it can. Even when the government acts responsibly, our massive ignorance may bring us to grief. But the absence of the most prudent policies we can devise would surely represent inexcusable negligence.

What is the evidence that pollution is really that serious? If the evidence is persuasive, what can we do about it? What are the political implications of the choices that face us?

All life in the ocean, distinguished Swiss oceanographer Jacques Piccard warns, will be destroyed in a generation if present rates of pollution continue.[1] Jacques Cousteau declares that 40 percent of the life in the ocean has already been wiped out by overfishing and pollution. Cousteau regards the problem as extremely grave because "every chemical, whether in the air or on land, will end up in the ocean."[2] A 1974 report of the U.S. National Oceanic and Atmospheric Administration observes that wastes deposited by East Coast cities, along with oil tanker discharges and spillages, have created a million square mile sludge of oil and plastics in the Atlantic and Caribbean.[3] Pollution in the Mediterranean has almost eradicated its marine life. The Marine Affairs Provost at the University of Rhode Island says that "if the oceans become polluted, they will probably remain polluted on any time scale meaningful to man."[4]

If the danger to oceanic life were the only threat pollution posed, this alone would warrant giving it first rank among our national (and international) priorities. But the threat is greater than this. World-renowned ecologist Barry Commoner sees it this way: "The environment is a complex, subtly balanced system and it is this integrated whole which receives the impact of all the separate insults inflicted by the pollutants. Never before in the history of this planet has its thin, life-supporting surface been subjected to such diverse, novel and potent agents. I believe the cumulative effects of these pollutants, their interactions and amplifications, can be fatal to the complex fabric of the biosphere."[5]

Economist and noted author Robert Heilbroner, a lifelong optimist recently turned pessimist, fears continued industrial growth on a worldwide scale; he warns that the fuel consumption involved generates enormous amounts of heat and carbon dioxide that will either raise the earth's temperature in three or four generations to an unlivable level or radically alter life on this planet.[6]

Others see the opposite happening. They fear that as dust, fumes, and water vapor pour into the air from industrial chimneys, jet aircraft, automobiles, and so on, these pollutants may collect in the outer atmosphere, prevent the normal quota of sunlight from reaching the earth, and lead to a cooling of the earth's temperature. The result could be a new ice age, with glaciers once again moving far down into the temperate zone. (At least temporarily, however, earth temperatures are going down, glaciers are advancing and heat-loving animals are migrating southward. Whether this is a short-term cyclical development or the beginning of a long-term trend vindicating the ''earth-cooling'' prophets is not yet known.)

A final menace that we should note is the report of various scientists that aerosol contains gases that drift into the stratosphere. These gases destroy a significant amount of the ozone, which filters out intense ultraviolet light waves that are dangerous to man in high concentrations. America produced about 3 billion cans of aerosol in 1974; added to the aerosol produced abroad, this could obliterate 20 to 40 percent of our ozone layer in several generations.[7] Although scientists disagree on the issue, aerosol's possible hazards vividly remind us of the perils a dynamic technological society faces as it introduces some 500 new chemicals into the environment annually.

Perhaps none of these dangers will materialize. Perhaps the doomsayers lack proper respect for man's capacity to cope with his problems once their gravity is clearly discerned. Perhaps the dangers themselves are greatly exaggerated. No one can say. We can say, however, that the potential for human catastrophe was never so great or many-sided as it is today.

Pollution is not a new phenomenon. Since nomads first used fire to drive animals from the forest to facilitate their slaughter, pollution has attended man's efforts to survive. The rich Tigris and Euphrates valleys were devastated by soil erosion following the destruction of the natural forests and the ill-advised use of irrigation. The Romans complained about smoke hanging over their cities; their drinking water was polluted before the first century A.D. During the Middle Ages urban inhabitants dumped their garbage into the streets and into rivers winding through their cities, producing epidemics of massive proportions. In the early fourteenth century a royal proclamation forbade the burning of coal in London; a rebellious manufacturer who ignored the king's command was beheaded in the interest of cleaner air. Contamination of rivers from mining is as old as mining itself; black lung disease has afflicted miners for as long as men have dug coal beneath the earth's surface. In addition, poor agricultural practices produced much of the Sahara Desert, which still advances a mile each year.

Pollution first attracted major national attention in the United States in 1962 when Rachel Carson published her historic volume, *Silent*

Spring.[8] Warning of the effects of DDT and other pesticides, Carson foresaw widespread destruction of birds and other wildlife from our indiscriminate use of these highly lethal poisons. Her book was greeted respectfully by many reviewers and angrily by others who charged her with careless research and sensationalism. The U.S. Department of Agriculture and spokesmen for the chemical industry refused to acknowledge the validity of her indictment. Further research, however, tended to confirm Carson's attacks, and a renewed wave of interest in pollution surfaced in 1970, an interest that has been maintained at a high level, although diminished somewhat by the economic problems associated with the post-Vietnam recession.

Currently we are dumping over 200 million tons of pollutants into the atmosphere, with the heaviest concentration over our major cities. Over 40 million Americans are said to live in areas with major air pollution: The most polluted cities include New York, Los Angeles, Philadelphia, Detroit, Cincinnati, St. Louis, Buffalo, Wheeling, and Chicago. Breathing New York air is equivalent, it is said, to smoking two packages of cigarettes a day.

Hundreds of millions of people around the world do not really know what clear air or sunlight is. Even Hawaii, which has some of the clearest air in the world, is experiencing an increasing amount of pollution haze. Although rainfall is nature's method of purifying air, much aerial pollution circulates at levels above that at which rainfall forms; at these levels, pollution steadily accumulates as automobiles multiply and industrial production grows.

Snow samples taken from the North Pole reveal that there is ten times more lead in the air than was present 200 years ago. Skeletal comparisons indicate that our bodies also contain ten times as much lead as they did centuries ago.

WHO ARE THE VILLAINS?

Let us take a closer look at the causes, extent, and costs of pollution today. Transportation, with more than 120 million cars and trucks leading the way, accounts for over 40 percent of air pollution. (Jet aircraft cause only about 1 percent of total pollution, although the pollution index near airports is very high.)

Manufacturing and electric power generating plants contribute only slightly less pollution than does transportation. Some of their most dangerous emissions—such as sulfur dioxide and nitrogen oxide—are, unfortunately, invisible. In this connection, René Dubos notes that "some 70 percent of the particulate contaminants in urban air are still unidentified. Their biological effects are unknown."[9]

Barry Commoner argues that it is not technology per se but the *kind* of technology that industry found profitable after World War II that has produced most of our pollution and enviromental damage. Heavy, high-powered cars, leaded gas, synthetic tires, and the use of detergents instead of old-fashioned soap, commercial fertilizer instead of manure, plastics and plastic wrappers instead of wood and metal products, synthetic fibers instead of wool and cotton, aluminum instead of steel or lumber, trucks instead of trains, and nonreturnable cans and bottles are among the major villains. Commoner contends that the increase in population accounts for less than 20 percent of increased pollution since 1946, and greater affluence (leading to the consumption of more goods per capita) accounts for less than 5 percent (transportation excepted), while changing production patterns account for most of our pollution.[10] In each instance he demonstrates that greater profitability per investment dollar, without regard for environmental impact, has produced the technology shifts that have brought us to grief.[11] And finally, solid waste disposal contributes almost 5 percent of our pollution, while miscellaneous sources (including forest fires) account for over 15 percent.

The direct economic costs of air pollution are estimated at about $14 billion a year. This is brought about by declining real estate values in highly polluted areas, increased dry-cleaning costs, the deterioration of clothing and house furnishings from the penetration of destructive pollutants, and the impact of pollution on paint, rubber, leather goods, construction stones, and certain metals. Moreover, vegetation grows from 10 to 20 percent less in urban areas than in rural areas because of polluted air.

Health costs produced by pollution are estimated at about $35 billion a year. The incidence of cancer progressively increases from rural areas to small cities to larger cities, with inner-city areas suffering from the highest rates. In London, for example, it is estimated that about half of the lung cancer is the result of smoking cigarettes and one-third the result of air pollution. Respiratory diseases (led by emphysema and bronchitis) are rising rapidly in the United States. A Los Angeles pathologist contends that he finds no lungs undamaged in persons over twelve years of age.

Bad as air pollution is, it could get worse. The nation plans to rely more heavily on coal as an alternative to oil, even though we seem not to have mastered the art of removing dangerous contaminants from coal smoke in an economically feasible fashion. (There is conflicting evidence on this, however.) Most of the cars on the highway have no emission controls or quite inadequate ones. The catalytic converter of the mid 1970s, which along with other devices was supposed to reduce major auto exhaust pollutants 83 percent by 1975, is still a question mark. Because the converter unexpectedly increased other dangerous emissions (sulfuric acid mists and acid sulfate), the entire auto emission program was in a state of uncertainty. Although national air quality measuring devices indicated that air pollution was improving in 1974 (largely because of significant declines in sulfur dioxide and particulate matter), this happy state of affairs might be reversed as the nation returns to a greater reliance on coal.[12] President Ford asked, moreover, for a prolonged moratorium on sulfur emission controls to facilitate utility plant conversion from oil to coal. And, pollution control has lost its priority to economic growth, jeopardizing the work of the Environmental Protection Agency.

The most serious source of water pollution is industrial waste. Total industrial pollution is about the equivalent of over 100 million people dumping their wastes directly into our lakes and streams. One form of industrial pollution involves the return of heated water (used for cooling purposes) to rivers and lakes. This, too, affects the forms of life that can survive in these waters. Since atomic energy plants require enormous amounts of water for cooling purposes, thermal pollution can be an important problem here.

About half as much water pollution comes from municipal sewage as from industrial wastes. Over 1500 communities still deposit untreated sewage into our waters. Nearly 50 million people in other communities rely on primary sewage treatment plants; these cause solids to settle to the bottom but accomplish little else. Most communities have secondary sewage treatment facilities that convert organic wastes into inorganic compounds. Pesticides, dyes, chemical compounds, and some acids are unaffected by secondary treatment, but the most serious deficiency of these plants is that inorganic wastes usually contain large amounts of nitrogen and phosphates (derived in considerable measure from detergents). These fertilizers have major effects on marine vegetation. When introduced into lakes and rivers, they increase the growth of algae and other forms of aquatic life. In small quantities and under certain circumstances, additional fertilizers may improve the quality of water and hence of the life which survives in them; in excessive quantities they can have disastrous effects. One pound of phosphate, for example, can produce 700 pounds of algae. When heavy growth of algae occurs, the process of decay consumes large quantities of dissolved oxygen. As the amount of dissolved oxygen in the water falls, a process called *eutrophication* takes place. The water becomes foul and brackish, the better varieties of fish cannot survive, and the water becomes "dead." The introduction of large amounts of fertilizer into Lake Erie is the principal reason that body of water deteriorated so alarmingly.

Septic tanks service about 70 million Americans. These receptacles provide no sewage treatment whatever. When situated near resort lakes, their underground runoff flows into these lakes, depositing fertilizer and other deleterious substances and preparing the way for eutrophy.

It is not just the inadequacy or absence of sewage treatment plants that accounts for eutrophication. Commercial fertilizer runoff from farms also plays a very significant role. American farmers use astronomical amounts of commercial fertilizer (mostly nitrogen and phosphorus) to maximize production. Between 1949 and 1969 the use of nitrogen for agricultural purposes increased 648 percent, an application largely responsible for the remarkable increases in acreage yields of corn and other crops. Although some of this fertilizer is consumed by crops or remains in the soil, substantial portions filter down into the subsoil and from there into streams and lakes. It has precisely the same effect on the water as fertilizer from municipal sewage. Few more intractable problems face this nation than that of coping with this development.

Nitrogen entering the atmosphere from automobile exhaust further intensifies the water pollution problem. Rainfall returns this fertilizer to the soil, adding a volume of nitrogen equal to one-third of all commercial nitrogen applications. Not even the most remote lake is immune to this fallout, which adds to the eutrophication potential of otherwise unpolluted bodies of water.

Massive usage of pesticides also contributes heavily to water pollution. About 30,000 pesticides are registered with the Environmental Protection Agency. We are using almost 500 million pounds per year, and consumption of pesticides has been increasing steadily. A considerable portion of pesticide spray remains in the air and is then carried by the winds until it falls into the oceans, lakes, and rivers, or onto the land.

What pesticides are doing to the delicate ecological balance of our planet is not well understood. Although the United States and some other countries have banned DDT (a nonbiodegradable insecticide) as well as some other dangerous sprays, the long-range effects of their substitutes on insect life and the environment currently cannot be known. Ecologists warn that the wholesale destruction of various kinds of insects may have ultimate adverse effects that we cannot predict. The World Health Organization states that over 200 species of insects have developed resistance to insecticides that were once fatal to them.[13] As older insecticides lose their effectiveness, newer ones are being discovered. Will insects eventually develop strains immune to almost any poisons that can be found (as seems to be true of certain rats), confronting mankind with a more ominous threat than any he has yet known from the insect world? Science fiction? Perhaps, but entomologists are not sure that man's inventive genius will always keep pace with Nature's cunning.

We should be aware of other contributors to water pollution. Feedlots, in which livestock are confined prior to slaughter, now account for more organic waste than all the sewage from American cities. Because it is currently uneconomical to return this fertilizer to the land, it often accumulates in huge piles, which, as runoff takes place, poison the soil and the water supply in the area. Reasonable amounts of animal or human fertilizer have a tonic effect on soil productivity, but excessive amounts are destructive.

Abandoned coal mines, especially in Appalachia, release copious quantities of sulfuric acid into the waterways. It is estimated that about 12,000 miles of Appalachian streams have been seriously polluted by this runoff.

Runoff from uranium mines has raised the level of radioactivity in the waters of many southwestern areas to dangerous levels. In the far west, large areas (especially in the Imperial Valley) have been ruined by salt water seeping underground; as water tables fall, due to the heavy consumption of water for industrial and other purposes, salt water forces its way in.

Last but no means least, oil pollution takes place on a major scale. Approximately 10 million tons of oil flow into rivers, lakes, and oceans each year. Perhaps 1 million tons come from the wreckage of about five oil tankers a year, and leaks spring from a dozen more. Leaks from offshore oil wells add an undetermined amount. Although these often lead to major news stories that capture public attention, a steady flow of oil moves into our lakes and rivers, and eventually into the ocean, from more prosaic sources. About 30 percent of the 10 million tons comes from crankcase oil dumped into sewer lines from garages and filling stations. After centuries of tanker accidents and spillage at sea, the situation is such that Thor Heyerdahl sighted hunks of hardened oil throughout much of his 1970 voyage across the Atlantic in a papyrus raft. Oil, we should note, has detrimental effects on both vegetable and animal marine life.

Since some 50 million tons of solid wastes are dumped directly offshore in various coastal areas, oceanic pollution is much more serious in some areas (such as San Francisco Bay) than in others. Since 90 percent of all marine life exists in the 4 percent of the ocean adjoining land, the fact that pollution is concentrated most heavily offshore tends to produce the greatest damage to ocean life.

In "How To Kill An Ocean," (*Saturday Review,* November 29, 1975), Heyerdahl observes that almost every creek or river in the world carries pollutants into this vulnerable part of the ocean. Almost every large city on the planet, he adds, "makes use of the ocean as mankind's common sink." The result, he warns, threatens the microscopic forms of ocean life—the phytoplankton—which supply much of the earth's oxygen. Unless people change their ways, "a dead ocean means a dead planet."

An additional source of pollution derives from solid waste disposal. As the most affluent nation in the world, America produces a phenomenal amount of garbage—twice as much per capita as in 1920. Plastics are particularly exasperating to environmentally concerned persons, since they do not decay. In all, we dispose of nearly 5 billion tons of solid wastes a year and spend about $5 billion a year collecting and disposing of our garbage.

If sheer volume presents a problem, the wastes generated by atomic reactors are perhaps even more worrisome and potentially far more dangerous. Writing in *Foreign Affairs,* Lord Ritchie-Calder noted that atomic wastes are buried in a 650-acre tract near Hanford, Washington. "There, in the twentieth-century Giza, it has cost more, much more, to bury live atoms than it cost to entomb the sun-god Kings of Egypt." The wastes are stored in million-gallon carbon-steel tanks, and "their radioactive vitality keeps the accompanying acids boiling like a witch's cauldron." Because these acids erode the most durable containers, the containers "will not endure as long as the pyramids" and nowhere near the hundreds of thousands of years the atoms will remain dangerous.

Lord Ritchie-Calder warned that by the year 2000 we may have several thousand "nuclear hearses" en route to their "burial grounds" on any given day, carrying the equivalent of a billion curies—"which is a mighty lot of curies to be roaming around a populated country. . . ."[14]

There is talk of sending atomic wastes to the sun by rocket, or of dropping them into extinct volcanoes, or of burying them under polar ice caps. Each of these has scary aspects, however. More probably, the government will try to store them in deep underground salt mines in areas in which the geologic formations are believed to be exceptionally stable. Unhappily, no one knows for sure just *where* they can be safely stored.

Excessive noise is among the various forms of pollution to which modern industrialized man is subject. The average level of noise in a modern city has been rising, and it has reached a point injurious not only to hearing but to other aspects of physical well-being. Laboratory rats develop hypertension when exposed to prolonged loud noise; their adrenalin supply becomes depleted, their lymph tissues shrink, and they may develop bleeding ulcers. Unborn babies respond violently to loud noise. Employees working in unusually noisy surroundings have poorer health than those in quieter surroundings. Experiments reveal that the sound level generated by some rock groups can be fatal to rats. Theodore Berland, author of *The Fight for Quiet,* cites an authority who fears that hard rock "may be producing a nation of teenagers who will be hard-of-hearing before they are [thirty]."[15] His warning is reinforced by the Environmental Protection Agency, which predicts that this generation will experience a highly abnormal incidence of hearing problems. Already 16 million Americans have suffered hearing loss because of excessive noise. Steady exposure to the noise level of the typical big city (70 decibels) can damage the average ear over a period of years. (New Yorkers have 180 percent more hearing problems than the national average).[16] Exposure to even one day-long ride in a snowmobile (115 decibels) can injure one's hearing. Persons living near airports not only have more hearing difficulties but a higher percentage of other physical maladies as well.[17]

What has America done about pollution up to this point? A great deal from the viewpoint of many observers, but not nearly enough from the viewpoint of others. Here are the major steps that have been taken:

In 1899, a refuse act was passed that forbade the dumping of oil or refuse in navigable streams without a permit from the federal government. After gathering dust for decades, it is now being used (along with recent legislation) as the legal basis for an increasing number of suits against violators.

The Federal Oil Pollution Act passed in 1924 forbidding the dumping of oil into navigable waters was ineffective also, partly because of lax enforcement and partly because the law was loosely worded. No further steps were taken to control pollution until 1948, when the first federal water pollution act was passed, authorizing federal loans for constructing local sewage treatment plants and giving Washington a minor role, subordinate to the states, in controlling pollution. The act had little practical effect; Congress declined to appropriate even the modest funds allocated by the law. In 1956, over President Eisenhower's objections, Congress authorized $500 million over a ten-year period to help finance waste treatment plants.

A major step followed in 1963 when President Kennedy won approval of the Test Ban Treaty binding the United States and the Soviet Union to discontinue atmospheric testing of atom bombs. Underground tests have continued, but these do not contaminate the atmosphere.

In 1972 Congress passed the Water Pollution Act authorizing the expenditure of nearly $18 billion over a three-year period, mostly to improve our wholly inadequate municipal sewage systems. Money was allotted for the removal of toxic sludge from river and lake bottoms; other funds would enable business to obtain low-interest loans for installing "the best practicable" antipollution equipment by 1977 and the "best available" equipment by 1983. The goal was to end water pollution from municipal and industrial sources by 1984.

In 1963, the Clean Air Act authorized federal aid to state and local governments to encourage and support local pollution control programs. It also empowered the Department of Health, Education, and Welfare (HEW) to hold public meetings on air pollution within states that requested such hearings. If polluters failed to meet certain minimum requirements, HEW was authorized to take them to court.

Thermal inversion takes place when a stagnant body of cool air prevents warm air from escaping, thus allowing urban pollution to build up to noxious levels. After this phenomenon allegedly killed 80 persons in New York City in 1966, Congress passed the Air Quality Act of 1967.

More money was appropriated for research and for state vehicle inspection; HEW was empowered to designate air quality control regions, to establish emission criteria, and to recommend control programs to the states.

In 1970, Congress established the Council on Environmental Quality. This agency was instructed to study pollution developments and problems, advise the president, and prepare an annual report on the environment. The Environmental Protection Agency (EPA) was created the same year to coordinate and integrate the entire range of federal programs dealing with air and water pollution, solid waste disposal, pesticides, radiation, and noise. Both the Federal Water Quality Administration and the National Air Pollution Control Administration were placed under EPA's jurisdiction.

EPA sets emission standards for industry and government, helps enforce those standards, assists state and local governments with their pollution control programs, engages in and sponsors research, promotes the training of personnel to combat environmental problems, and disseminates information on pollution.

Among its major responsibilities is enforcing the statutory requirements that all federal and private agencies holding federal contracts prepare an "environmental impact statement" before proceeding with projects having environmental significance. This statement must set forth the probable effect an undertaking will have upon the environment and seek to justify its mission. EPA must then review the statement and refer any that are found unsatisfactory to the Council of Environmental Quality. Since the statement is made public, private citizens may seek a court order restraining the proposed action if they believe it violates national standards. Thus far the courts have proved staunch allies of the environmentalists when cases involving the interpretation of environmental laws have been brought before them.[18]

The Clean Air Act of 1970 was one of the cardinal pieces of pollution legislation enacted by Congress. Automobile manufacturers were ordered, by 1976, to reduce exhaust emissions of hydrocarbons, carbon monoxide, and nitrogen oxide to less than 10 percent of the levels prevailing in 1970.

As the recession of the mid 1970s set in, however, with pollution control losing precedence to economic recovery and with technical problems continuing to arise, the deadlines have been repeatedly extended.

THE FUTURE: ISSUES AND QUESTIONS

Where, then, do we stand and what remains to be done? What are the chances that we will do it—in time?

Some progress seems to be taking place in the Great Lakes. The United States and Canada signed a treaty in 1972 agreeing to take the necessary steps to reverse the alarming pollution in these largest of the world's fresh-water lakes. Lake Erie, particularly, had been labeled a "dying lake," with beaches closed, fish life sharply declining and eutrophication affecting a substantial portion of the lake. Since 1972 both nations have spent large sums to arrest and reverse this trend. Mercury discharges have been largely eliminated, phosphorus inflows (mostly from detergents) have been greatly reduced, and industries depositing wastes into rivers entering the Great Lakes have been more tightly regulated. While the improvement is not dramatic, it is solid and heartening.[19]

The Environmental Protection Agency estimates that pollution abatement expenditures from 1974 to 1983 will run to about $380 billion. Per person spending, which is now about $50 per person, will rise to almost $100 per person by 1983. Currently, business antipollution spending exceeds government spending by about 80 percent.

Internationally, some modest gains have been made. In 1972 seventy-one nations agreed to: (1) prohibit dumping plastics and certain very harmful chemicals in the ocean, while regulating the discharge of somewhat less harmful substances, (2) construct facilities for collecting waste oil and chemicals at all major ports, (3) forbid tankers to wash out their holds at sea, and (4) require oil tankers to maintain segregated compartments that will minimize oil spillage in case of shipwreck.

The less-developed countries, however, are generally much less interested in pollution control than in speedy economic development. While the more affluent nations can afford the heavy costs involving in curbing pollution, the less affluent believe they must devote their limited resources to the most rapid expansion of their industry; they will worry about pollution later, just as the more prosperous countries have done. An understandable posture, again, but not one conducive to effectively meeting a worldwide problem requiring the cooperation of all nations.

Considerable gains seem to have been made in industrial pollution abatement, even though the job is far from completed. Steady advances have also been made in the construction of secondary sewage treatment facilities for handling municipal wastes. Even taking account of the uncertainties surrounding auto emission control devices, new cars emit far less hydrocarbons and carbon monoxide than do the older models. These developments may not be improving the overall quality of our water and air, but they may have arrested the deterioration of these vital resources. This is no trivial accomplishment.

Still, the EPA says that about three-fourths of the population lives in areas where the levels of sulfur dioxide, particulates, or both remain higher than is safe. Water pollution remains almost as serious a problem as ever. Whether the internal combustion engine will ever be able to consume gas in a manner that reduces dangerous emissions to a safe level remains to be seen. Various competitive engines have claimed public attention, only to fade as engineers took a closer look at them. If some students are correct, however, Honda's new carburetor could come close to solving the problem. The Honda uses a double carburetor with a small chamber that explodes a fairly rich mixture of gas and air while a larger one handles a lean mixture. Requiring no pollution control gadgets, it meets the most stringent EPA standards, while getting excellent mileage. The major U.S. companies are said to be taking a lively interest in it. If it, or some alternative system, is able to conquer the auto emission problem, it will be one of the historic events of modern times. With automotive engineers in many countries, capitalist and otherwise, devoting their best efforts to dealing with pollution control and efficient gasoline consumption, it will be surprising if an answer is not found; especially now that high gas prices are forcing consumers to opt for the smaller cars, which are best adapted to making maximum use of antipollution technology. In an age cheated of optimism, this is one area where optimism seems warranted.

Industries in the nonautomotive field are also highly pollution conscious these days. Many of them are making sizable investments in pollution control machinery and processes. However, a preoccupation with the mid 1970s recession and with achieving economic recovery strengthened industry's resistance to EPA pressures for further progress. As a result, the current regulatory program may prove less effective than a pollution emission tax. In *Pollution, Prices and Public Policy*,[20] economists Allen V. Kneese and Charles L. Schultze make an impressive case for the imposition of this tax.

Kneese and Schultze note that about 55,000 corporations have a significant impact on pollution. Current law requires these corporations to use the "best practicable technology" by 1977 and the "best available technology economically achievable" by 1983. But the law also requires that the "best practicable" be weighed against the cost of pollution control, the size and age of the industrial facility, the process used, the energy requirements, and the nonwater quality impact of the controls.[21] This, say the authors, "if taken literally would imply tailoring effluent standards individually to virtually every plant in the nation. . . . There seems to us no realistic way for the administrator to avoid negotiating and bargaining with virtually every individual source of waste discharge of any size."[22]

They further argue that "the regulatory approach suffers from an inescapable dilemma. If the system is simple enough to be handled by a central bureaucracy . . . it is bound to be very inefficient. But if it seeks to accommodate the tremendous diversity of the economy, and tries to devise effluent standards that minimize costs, the regulatory task becomes insurmountable."[23]

Broad general standards like "best practicable technology" invite administrators to devise explanatory and ever more detailed regulations for guiding plant managers. Each new set of regulations creates unsuspected problems that lead to the proposal of still more refined rules, calling for additional hearings at which industry presents its objections. Meanwhile, endless litigation accompanies bureaucratic decisions having specific application to individual plants, since corporations often regard these decisions as "arbitrary" or "unreasonable" and hence beyond the authority of the agency involved. Cases are processed, judicial rulings are appealed, and proceedings drag on for years.

Kneese and Schultze deplore the fact that once a company meets the standards imposed there is no incentive for it to improve that effort, even if it might be economically feasible in particular instances. Why do more than is minimally required?

They further observe that it is the almost universal experience of regulatory agencies to gradually become captives of the industries they are supposed to control.[24] Regular contact with industry representatives and little contact with representatives of the public interest, heavy pressure to be "fair" to those industries, developing expertise that might qualify them for lucrative positions within these same industries once their terms of office expire—these factors cause agency officials to gradually adopt a "mothering" and protective role sharply at odds with the intentions of Congress when the law establishing the regulatory agency was created. Congress, meanwhile, is preoccupied with a thousand other matters, leaving little time for legislative supervision of the agencies it spawns.

Meeting the standards specified in the antipollution laws of 1970 and 1972 will soon be costing the nation $60 billion a year, Kneese and Schultze add.[25]

Concluding that any problem involving such enormous complexity, requiring such technical expertise, and covering scores of thousands of firms is ill adapted to the conventional regulatory approach, the economists go on to point out the merits of levying an *effluent tax* which penalizes firms in direct relation to the amount of pollution they discharge into the air or water. Not only would firms pay in proportion to the damage they inflict on the environment, but they would also have a direct economic stake in reducing that pollution to the maximum degree practicable so that their taxes would be lightened.

Such a policy would harness corporate self-interest to desirable public ends. Noting that the 55,000 major corporations make millions of decisions each year that affect the environment, Kneese and Schultze contend that bureaucrats simply cannot do a good job of policing these decisions, while plant managers and technicians *can* do that job well if their decisions are disciplined by the ever-present necessity to reduce pollution in the interests of cutting corporate costs.

The bureaucratic apparatus and process would be enormously simplified by the substitution of such an emissions tax. The agency in charge would require each firm to install metering devices at appropriate points. These would then be read from time to time and the proper tax calculated. In contrast to the infinite complexities of the current system, this approach would be simplicity itself. And instead of taking substantial sums from the federal treasury to finance the administrative costs, the revenues raised from the tax would far more than meet the minor administrative expenses entailed. Hopefully, of course, tax revenues would steadily fall as industry found it profitable to cut its pollution discharges to a minimum.

Litigation, while not eliminated, would be minimized, as would the administrative complications associated with the establishment of pollution standards.

To this writer, Kneese and Schultze's case seems cogent. Why Congress fails to pursue this course (favored by most economists) is somewhat of a mystery. Perhaps the heavy legislative investment of time and energy in the current system, a desire for vindication by those responsible for instituting that system, a reluctance to upset the status quo in the absence of a clamor for change, plus the predilection of lawyers (who predominate in Washington) for a legalistic remedy rather than a solution based on economic self-interest[26] may explain Congress' seeming indifference to so rational an approach. Still, with Democrats not averse to taxing business, Republicans disliking excessive bureaucracy and waste, and both parties presumably interested in reducing pollution as rapidly as feasible, the basis for bipartisan support of an emissions tax would seem to be present.

Can necessary antipollution legislation plus firm enforcement measures restrain pollution in a capitalistic society in which business interests are endowed with great political power?

Many writers have noted that the communist countries and even the democratic socialist nations have developed pollution problems akin to those of the United States. Nor have they dealt much more effectively with the problems, since they, too, have been preoccupied with improving the standard of living of their people. In the United States the principal recurring question seems to be the level of public concern. When a significant proportion of the articulate public has been genuinely aroused, Congress has not permitted industrial objections to stymie strong legislation. And when public concern remains high, administrators and courts generally act in response to the public welfare rather than to organized business pressures. When the public's attention subsides, however, the normal phenomenon of organized pressures outweighing a weakly supported public interest reasserts itself—which is an excellent reason for instituting a permanent pollution abatement system that relies on the economic self-interest of American business rather than on a regulatory system that depends so heavily on transient bursts of public alarm to give it political muscle.

Large stretches of the environment, as previously mentioned, have been grievously ravaged by strip mining. In addition to the poisonous runoffs from abandoned coal mines, land gouged open by the strip-mine process is not only depressingly unsightly but is often incapable of sustaining vegetation. A long-time champion of conservation and of respect for the environment, Representative Morris Udall of Arizona, spent years drawing up, perfecting, and rallying support for a strip-mining bill that would:

1. forbid strip mining where the land cannot be restored to relatively normal condition after the coal is extracted;
2. require the restoration of the land by companies engaging in permissible strip mining;
3. impose a tax on strip-mined coal to finance the restoration of land previously despoiled by such mining; and
4. give the states primary responsibility for regulating strip mining but permit the secretary of the interior to establish an overriding federal program when the states fail to meet minimum standards.

Although the measure passed both houses of Congress by heavy majorities in 1975, Congress failed to override President Ford's veto. The president insisted that the bill would saddle the strip-mining industry with such heavy burdens that coal production would slow down at a time when the energy shortage required a speedup instead. Since coal production was becoming highly profitable, as coal prices reflected the price of oil, the president's case was not convincing. But during the Great Recession, charges that the Udall program would lead to unemployed coal miners apparently had its effect on some legislators. Partisan appeals and sympathies were also a factor, unfortunately for the environmentalists.

An encouraging note is being sounded on the garbage front, however. The awesome accumulation of garbage in America had been causing many mayors to worry that their cities would run out of dumping grounds within accessible reach. In St. Louis, however, a private utility collects the city garbage for a reasonable fee, sorts out recyclable metals for resale, sets aside plastic materials for burial, and burns the rest in its power plants at a ratio of one part garbage to four parts coal. The operation has proved profitable for both the utility company and the city.[27] Connecticut plans to convert all of its combustible garbage into fuel for generating electricity. El Cajon, California, claims to be producing a barrel of oil from each ton of garbage; if done nationwide, it is said, garbage could supply 8 to 15 percent of our energy requirements.[28] So at least one problem which alarmed us a few years ago may be on its way to resolution. (Now—if only the plastics industry could be banished to a remote and barren island and all communications with that island could be severed . . . or will a biodegradable plastic really be found?)

Another modestly hopeful development is the discovery that reeds and bulrushes (yes, the kind of bulrushes in which Moses was hidden) have a remarkable capacity to cleanse polluted water. European experiments demonstrate that "these hardy biblical plants prefer clear water so much that they actually *create* clear water by a metabolic process that devours organic and inorganic pollutants."[29] Unfortunately, these plants require a lot of land, and they seem better suited for rural than large-scale urban water-purification projects.

As long as the world's economy is heavily dependent on oil and the volume of oil shipped by tankers rises steadily, tanker accidents and other oil spills will continue to plague us. The new and gigantic million-ton supertankers will not add to our peace of mind. As Noel Mostert reminds us in *Supership*,[30] these tanks are more fragile than is realized and are often operated with poorly trained crews. Because of the high accident rate of tankers in general, insurance rates have been rising alarmingly. Mostert may be wrong when he says life in the seas cannot be expected to survive the growing fleet of tankers, but certainly every conceivable precaution should be taken to minimize accidents and spillage.

No problem currently appears more insoluble than that produced by our massive reliance on commercial fertilizer. The use of such fertilizer can hardly be expected to decrease, thus insuring that fertilizer runoff will continue to impair our drinking water and add to the eutrophy of our lakes and streams. Barry Commoner has noted, moreover, that the continued heavy use of commercial fertilizer may destroy the soil microbes that naturally fix nitrogen in the soil when legumes are planted.[31] If these fears are well founded, the danger of permanently altering the soil's corrective and rehabilitative processes cannot be exaggerated.

It is significant that neither the president nor the Congress even wants to discuss the problem, to say nothing about coming to grips with it. Farmers feel highly dependent on commercial fertilizer; farmers are voters, and elected officials survive on votes. Both farmers and their representatives know, furthermore, that any attempt to limit the consumption of commercial fertilizers could activate a decisive constituency—the housewife with a major interest in keeping food prices down. There is no doubt that major reductions in the use of commercial fertilizer would greatly increase the price of food.

Not that an adequate food supply is dependent on a continuation of the current consumption levels of commercial fertilizer. If we were willing to consume less meat (the average American consumes twice as much protein as his body can use), we could easily feed ourselves while sharply reducing our consumption of commercial fertilizer. One acre of cropland will feed as many people as seven acres devoted to livestock. Therefore, the problem is clearly soluble if we are willing to pay the price. We aren't —not yet.

As Professor Commoner and others have recommended, the nation would be well advised to return its sewage to the soil rather than return it, treated or untreated, to rivers and oceans. The necessity for so much commercial fertilizer would be considerably reduced if the vast amounts of human and animal wastes were returned to the land. Although no fertilizer is so restorative of soil health as manure, we blithely proceed with plans for secondary sewage treatment plants, which insure that human wastes are flushed (ultimately) into the ocean. We also permit huge quantities of manure to accumulate in livestock feedlots, contaminating the soil and the water through its excessive concentration, instead of returning it to the soil as Nature intended. It is currently not profitable to pay the transportation costs of hauling and distributing such manure into farm areas, and since it is not directly and immediately profitable the job is not done. The long-run loss to the soil is ignored.

About 5 percent of our sewage is being converted into fertilizer, which is sold to the general public. Perhaps this practice will be expanded in the future. Current indications are, however, that it is usually not profitable to do so and that we are not prepared to do the job on a nationwide scale. Nothing is being done about septic tank runoff and nothing is likely to be done. Interest in the subject seems minimal.

Pesticides? Although the banning of DDT represents a solid victory for ecologists, the larger danger of our prodigious use of insecticides is unresolved, and the prospects for its resolution are not at all bright. The U.S. Department of Agriculture has been experimenting for decades with *predator control*—that is, with insects that prey upon other insects that plague the farmer. Though an occasional success is reported, knowledgeable scientists doubt that advances in predator control will do much in the near future to reduce the need for pesticides. Dr. Norman Borlaug, Pulitzer Prize–winning agronomist, estimates that the discontinuance of pesticides would slash crop production 50 percent and raise food prices 500 to 600 percent.[32] Americans' interest in ecology apparently does not extend to a willingness to pay this price. They will hope, instead, that degradable pesticides will prove to have minor adverse effects. In this hope they may prove right—or tragically wrong.

As for recycling, though a few interesting and well-reported experiments are taking place (as in Franklin, Ohio), the nation has yet to begin a major effort in this direction. Less than half of our iron, steel, and copper is recovered for further use; only about one-fifth of our paper is recycled.

Professor Commoner has calculated that trucks burn 400 to 600 percent more fuel and add 400 to 600 percent more contamination per ton-mile of traffic than do freight trains.[33] This is a sobering statistic and one that a nation deeply concerned about its resources and its environment would take to heart. Again, however, no elected public figure dares advocate that long-haul truck freight be largely turned over to a rejuvenated railroad industry. Truckers constitute a powerful and well-organized pressure group; their voting power, supplemented by their power to call a crippling nationwide strike, would give pause to any legislator seeking to put the national interest ahead of the truckers' interests. The issue, therefore, is hardly discussed.

We could, if we wished, devote much more of our transportation resources to developing mass transit facilities instead of letting our cities become more choked with pollution-rich traffic congestion. Americans have had a prolonged love affair with the automobile, however, and it is doubtful that they will trade the comfort and convenience of their car for even the most modern mass transit. (Nonpolluting engines may make mass transit less imperative, however.)

Noise pollution? Apparently we could reduce noise to satisfactory levels on most, if not all, noisy machines if we were willing to add 5 to 10 percent to their cost. The technology seems to be available. The Federal Noise Control Act of 1972 authorizes the EPA to set noise pollution standards for construction equipment and for railroads, trucks, and buses. The EPA has begun this work but how successful it will be remains to be seen.

Curiously, although Congress has banned cigarette advertising on television, it has not been willing to ban it from other media. It would be a simple matter—and eminently reasonable—for Congress to enact a statute forbidding the advertisement, in interstate commerce, of any product which as ordinarily consumed has significant carcinogenic effects. But Congress will not deign to consider such legislation. Why advertisers should be permitted to spend $200 million a year encouraging the consumption of products that may cause more damage to health than all other pollutants combined is never explained.

Perhaps the most important fact about pollution is our ignorance of what it means for our future. Among the salient questions we cannot satisfactorily answer are:

1. How serious is oceanic pollution? Is it really as ominous as some scientists believe, or is the ocean capable of coping with far more indignities than the fearful believe? No one can provide more than an educated guess.

2. What is the lavish application of commercial fertilizer doing to the quality of our soil? It may be doing no harm whatever—or it may be weakening the soil. No one really knows. (We do know it pollutes the drinking water in many areas.[34])

3. If weed killer is powerful enough to kill weeds and weed seed, what is it doing to essential soil bacteria? We can't be sure.

4. How dangerous is the prolonged use of ever more potent insecticides on Nature's carefully wrought ecological balance? No one can give us an authoritative answer.

5. What are the 500 new chemicals that enter the environment each year doing to organic life, to say nothing of the scores of thousands of chemicals that preceded them? (The World Health Organization estimates that 75 to 85 percent of all human cancer is caused by the introduction of man-made substances into our environment.) Who can say?

6. Will the billions of tons of fuel burned each year permanently alter the quality of the air and the climate on the earth? We can only speculate.

This much we know: Mankind is playing a supremely dangerous game as it goes forward with chemical and technological developments whose ultimate impact cannot possibly be known. Maybe we will be supremely lucky; we had better be.

As this chapter is written, pollution control has fallen behind economic recovery and energy development as matters commanding the nation's primary interest. Only a disaster or a credible threat of impending disaster can restore it to front-rank attention again. Unhappily, such a disaster seems almost certain to come, although the form it will take is beyond our predictive ability.

If we fail to do the job that must be done to insure our survival, the villain won't be the system, the bureaucrats, or the capitalists. It will be ourselves and our reluctance to give up things we treasure today in return for a better and safer environment tomorrow. We might give them up if the "experts" were agreed it was absolutely necessary. But these "experts" disagree to a maddening degree. There are always optimistic experts to reassure us that the pessimistic experts are unduly pessimistic. Under these circumstances, perhaps the public cannot be altogether blamed for believing what it wants to believe—that is, what least disturbs their way of life.

We can only hope that the experts will agree before it is too late, for this is one issue on which we can't afford to be wrong.

NOTES

1. Richard C. Schroeder, "Global Pollution," *Editorial Research Reports,* December 1, 1971, p. 930.

2. Jacques Cousteau, "Our Oceans Are Dying," *New York Times,* November 14, 1971, p. 13E. Also see George Taylor, "The Threat to Life in the Sea," *Saturday Review,* August 1, 1970, p. 70, and Michael Harwood, "We are Killing the Sea Around Us," *New York Times Magazine,* October 24, 1971.

3. Richard A. Frank, "The Law at Sea," *New York Times Magazine,* May 18, 1975, p. 62.

4. Frank, "The Law at Sea," p. 63.

5. Helen B. Schaffer, "Protection of the Environment," *Editorial Research Reports,* June 19, 1968, p. 449.

6. Robert Heilbroner, *Inquiry into the Human Prospect,* New York, Norton, 1974.

7. Paul Brodeur, "Annals of Chemistry," *The New Yorker,* April 7, 1975, p. 48.

8. Rachel Carson, *Silent Spring,* Boston, Houghton Mifflin, 1962.

9. René Dubos, "We Can't Buy Our Way Out," *Psychology Today,* March, 1970, p. 20.

10. Barry Commoner, *The Closing Circle,* New York, Knopf, 1971, p. 176.

11. Commoner, *The Closing Circle,* chapter 12.

12. Luther L. Carter, "The Environment, A 'Mature' Cause in Need of a Lift," *Science,* January 10, 1975, p. 46.

13. *New York Times,* August 15, 1971.

14. Lord Ritchie-Calder, "Mortgaging the Old Homestead," *Foreign Affairs.* January 1970, pp. 210–211.

15. Theodore Berland, *The Fight for Quiet,* Englewood Cliffs, N.J., Prentice-Hall, 1970, p. 37, David M. Lipscomb is unsure of rock's effects but believes it should be heard sparingly. *Noise: The Unwanted Sound,* Chicago, Nelson Hall, 1974, pp. 127–128.

16. David Dempsey, "Noise," *New York Times Magazine,* November 23, 1975, pp. 31, 66, 74, 82.

17. "The Assault of Sound," *The Washington Monthly,* November 1970, p. 42.

18. John Hamer, "Environmental Policy," *Editorial Research Reports,* December 20, 1974, p. 958.

19. Louis A. Goth, "The Great Lakes are Scarcely Great but Getting Better," *New York Times,* June 9, 1974, p. 2E; R. Tunley, "Fresh Start for the Great Lakes," *Reader's Digest,* December 1974.

20. Allen V. Kneese and Charles L. Schultze, *Pollution, Prices and Public Policy,* © 1975 by The Brookings Institution, Washington, D.C.

21. Kneese and Schultze, pp. 60–61.

22. Kneese and Schultze, p. 62.

23. Kneese and Schultze, p. 91.

24. Kneese and Schultze, pp. 7–8.

25. Kneese and Schultze, p. 76.

26. Kneese and Schultze, p. 116.

27. *Time,* March 18, 1974, p. 26. Also see Donald E. Carr, "The Lost Art of Conservation," *The Atlantic,* December, 1975, p. 70.

28. *Time,* December 2, 1974, p. 104.

29. "Dirty Water in the Bulrushes," *New Republic,* June 14, 1975, p. 18.

30. Noel Mostert, *Supership,* New York, Knopf, 1974.

31. Commoner, *The Closing Circle,* p. 152.

32. *Dayton Journal-Herald,* January 31, 1972, p. 6.

33. Barry Commoner, "Trains into Flowers," *Harper's,* December 1973, p. 80.

34. Commoner, *The Closing Circle,* chapter 5.

TWO
Energy: The Shape of the Future

When the sheiks and potentates of the Near East decided to strike it rich, they changed the shape of the world. America suddenly woke to the fact that energy was truly central, that energy resources were scarce commodities, that energy—incredibly—was very expensive. It was a rude jolt and one that, in conjunction with Vietnam, Watergate, President Nixon's resignation, and the Great Recession, left carefree and confident America shaken, bewildered, aware of its vulnerability and uncertain of its destiny. It was as if a sheltered and happy-go-lucky adolescent was suddenly forced, by family tragedy, to make his way in a bitter and seemingly friendless environment. America came of age in the mid 1970s. The fragility of its prosperity, the limits of its military power, its susceptibility to the political diseases that more mature and experienced nations had long taken for granted—these were harsh realities for a nation with a "chosen people" and a "manifest destiny" complex. America saw, really for the first time, that it was one nation among many, subject to the limitations, the pains, the fears and the sense of mortality of its fellow nations.

The energy shortage would have surfaced soon even without an Arab boycott. America had been living beyond its means for years; the days of reckoning could not have been postponed much longer in a world in which energy was becoming scarce in relation to human wants. America had acted as if boundless energy was there for the taking and as if economic development could proceed, willy-nilly, in any direction and at any pace our fancy desired. The Shah of Iran and King Faisal of Arabia, displeased with American friendship for Israel and possessed of the cupidity normal to man, opened our eyes with one fell blockade. America would never be quite the same again.

America has long used far more than its share of the world's supply of energy. With only about 6 percent of the planet's population, America has consumed about one-third of its energy. A series of post-World War II developments accelerated this demand for energy:

1. America experienced a period of unusually rapid economic expansion, with maximum growth regarded as the nation's highest goal. If America's growth rate fell behind that of western Europe, or especially Russia, the nation took alarm; economists, politicians, and editors promptly clamored for government to stimulate the economy. Making a strong showing in the "growth sweepstakes" was regarded as essential to an administration's self-respect and public esteem. No statistics were seen as more damning—as the Eisenhower administration learned—than those showing the U.S. failure to maximize its potential gross national product (GNP), thereby forfeiting potential tax dollars and an improved standard of living. The postwar "baby boom" also added to demands on U.S. energy. The combination of a fast-growing population and a generally brisk economy meant that America was doubling its energy consumption every decade.

2. The Federal Highway Act of 1956, one of the few domestic legislative "triumphs" of the Eisenhower years, planned and provided funds for 41,000 miles of interstate highways, setting the stage for a phenomenal growth of cars and trucks. The United States moved from a nation averaging one car per family to two cars per family, plus one for each adolescent male (and, in the more affluent families, one for each adolescent female, too).

3. The auto industry launched the "horsepower derby," building ever-larger and more powerful motors to satisfy the consumer's seemingly insatiable thirst for more takeoff speed, passing speed, highway speed—speed period. Equating personal status with the possession of sleek, powerful, and spacious cars, the American consumer (spurred by advertising messages skillfully exploiting this childish mania) supported a trend that led to 400-horsepower motors and cars weighing nearly half a ton more than their predecessors. Miles per gallon dropped sharply but a money-flushed people scarcely noticed. Gas was cheap—30 cents a gallon—and of course the supply was inexhaustible.

4. Railroads use far less energy per ton-mile of freight than trucks, but truck traffic was rapidly outdistancing rail traffic. Railroad passenger service dwindled to insignificance and mass transit (a major energy saver) lost half its customers from 1950 to 1970. People preferred the comfort and convenience of their cars, heedless of the energy losses in-

volved. (Cars currently take 80 percent of workers to their jobs, with mass transit serving only about 7 percent.)

5. Suburbanization was also a factor. The mass exodus from the farm had clotted the city with people; as incomes rose, the middle class fled the noise, dirt, polluted air, traffic, cramped living space, "undesirable" neighbors, and high taxes of the inner city for the attractions of suburban life. Traveling half an hour or an hour to work was preferable to life in the city—but gasoline consumption inevitably rose as "suburban sprawl" made its way.

6. An affluent society demands comfort. Since summer heat can be unpleasant, air conditioning became one of the nation's most thriving industries, not only in stores, offices, and private homes but in cars as well —even in some tractors! Today America uses as much energy for air conditioning as China does for its entire economy! The proliferation of electric appliances in homes also made increased demands on energy reserves.

7. American farmers increased their use of commercial fertilizer tenfold after World War II; nitrogen, which is a major component of farm and garden fertilizer, is usually produced from oil. The manufacture of massive quantities of synthetics and plastics also requires large amounts of energy.

8. Long-continued underpricing of natural gas led to its excessive and wasteful consumption. The Federal Power Commission (FPC) controlled the interstate price of natural gas, and, while its policies pleased consumers, natural gas was priced so cheaply in relation to other energy sources that field production was often as wasteful as commercial usage. The result was a premature depletion of a valuable energy resource, as well as occasionally severe natural gas shortages.

9. In general, Americans have been shockingly wasteful in their use of energy. Neither producers, business firms, nor homeowners have exercised much concern for the prudent usage of the energy at their disposal. It has been reliably estimated that pre-OPEC America wasted one-third of its energy, as much as highly industrialized Japan now uses. We use twice as much energy, per capita, as Sweden, even though our GNP per person is about the same.

10. Finally, the energy shortage reflected a lack of foresight and national planning by the government. Until the Arab boycott struck, no administration had attempted to formulate a national policy to conserve and rationalize the use and development of energy—to say nothing of preparing for the eventuality of a possible Arab boycott. Perhaps the government should not be judged too harshly on this score, however, since the nation's intellectuals had not alerted it to the need for such a policy. Governments can be expected to follow the lead of prominent

scientists, writers, and editors in matters like this but not to be more prescient than they.

BIG OIL AND THE GOVERNMENT

The government has always been benevolent toward the oil industry. During the Depression, when "cutthroat competition" threatened an industry hit hard by slack consumer demand and an overabundance of oil, lobbyists persuaded the oil-producing states to establish a system that prorated the desired amount of oil production within the state to individual producers. Informal arrangements among the oil-producing states kept state quotas at levels approximating the same share of production that individual states had previously enjoyed in the national market. The goal was to balance supply and demand at a reasonably profitable level for all producers. Then, to insure that the system worked, the industry convinced Washington to pass the Hot Oil Act of 1935, making it a federal offense to sell oil in interstate commerce which had been produced in excess of the state's quota for a given firm. The free market —free competition system that had prevailed in oil since the oil trust was broken by antitrust action—was thus supplanted by a "managed" oil economy.

In 1950, apparently to appease Arab countries owning vast amounts of oil and disgruntled by American support for the newly established state of Israel, the National Security Council secretly directed the treasury to permit American oil companies to deduct royalties paid to foreign nations (mostly Arab) from their federal tax obligations on a dollar-for-dollar basis.[1] This was far more profitable to the oil companies than permitting them to deduct royalties as a business expense. Although Arab royalties promptly rose, the overall effect of this policy was an intensification of foreign exploration and investment, since the higher royalties did not cancel out the tax gains then accruing to the oil companies.

In 1954, the oil industry persuaded the Eisenhower administration to discontinue a government research program designed to develop natural gas from coal.[2] Although the oil companies were naturally eager to stifle research into a competitive energy source, the decision may have been our worst postwar energy blunder.

In 1958, the government obligingly imposed import quotas to prevent cheap foreign oil from competing with domestic oil. This cost the consumer an estimated $5 billion a year in higher oil prices—and promoted the more rapid depletion of our domestic oil reserves. Earlier, Congress had given oil the much-treasured $27\frac{1}{2}$ percent depletion allowance (minerals were eligible, too, but generally at much lower rates) excusing them from any federal tax obligation on that proportion of each dollar of profit. Justified as a device for encouraging drilling and equating the depletion allowance with depreciation on manufacturing assets, this provision cost the government about $1.5 billion a year. Economists generally regarded it as an unconscionable rip-off, the product of political clout rather than economic necessity. Congress finally pared the allowance to 22 percent, then largely eliminated it in 1975—to the astonishment of many cynics. But with oil prices and profits soaring, it had become difficult to maintain the fiction that the allowance was needed to induce timid oil magnates to invest more money in new domestic wells.

The oil companies were also authorized to deduct ''intangible drilling costs'' when calculating their federal tax bill, thereby saving themselves nearly a billion dollars a year. Thus, while the federal corporation tax (for all but small corporations) is 48 percent, major multinational oil companies found themselves paying less than 7 percent of their net income to Washington.[3] (Just why Congress did not vote the oil companies an annual Christmas bonus is not altogether clear!)

What accounted for oil's privileged position? During the long years when southern Democrats (from what was then a one-party region) dominated Congressional committees through chairmanships won by seniority, senators and representatives from oil states thoughtfully obtained seats on the House Ways and Means and Senate Finance Committees. During most of the Eisenhower years, Lyndon B. Johnson (from oil-rich Texas) was Majority Leader of the Senate and Sam Rayburn (also from Texas) was Speaker of the House. Oil-wealthy Senator Robert Kerr (Oklahoma) dominated the Senate Finance Committee, followed by oil millionaire Senator Russell Long (Louisiana). Members of the House not regarded as sufficiently appreciative of oil's contribution to the general welfare somehow failed to obtain membership on the Ways and Means Committee. Of equal and perhaps of greater importance, the oil industry (or its executives) were lavish contributors to the campaigns of potentially winning candidates to Congress—including candidates from both parties and sometimes to competitors for the same office. Many influential legislators were also investors in oil stocks, a fact which doubtless conditioned their attitude toward measures affecting oil. Oil, furthermore, was able to enlist the services of some of the nation's most skilled lobbyists to represent their interests. Finally, oil men are usually wealthy men, and wealthy men are listened to more respectfully by legislators everywhere than are men of more modest means.

When the Arab oil boycott was sprung, and gas shortages and long gas lines developed throughout the nation, the oil companies were not wholly displeased. The importance of oil was now impressed upon all; the nation would presumably be willing to do what seemed necessary to assure maximum supplies of domestic oil and a minimum dependence on foreign oil. When oil profits leaped skyward, the oil industry argued that ''adequate'' profits were imperative if drillers were to be induced to invest in speculative oil ventures. After all, there were lots of dry wells, and oil drilling was an expensive operation. Unless the incentive of substantial profits was present, they warned, the exploration of new oil fields would be inhibited and the whole nation would suffer. Thus the government should permit oil and natural gas prices to rise to their "natural" levels, that is, the levels dictated by the Arab-dominated Organization of Petroleum Exporting Countries (OPEC). And government should take other measures to facilitate the development of our oil and natural gas resources.

While the talk about "adequate" profits was partly valid, it conveniently overlooked a few key points. First of all, the future demand for energy, both in the United States and in the rest of the world, was such that no industry could face a more rosy future in terms of assured demand in relation to supply. If that prospect would not encourage oil drilling speculators, it is hard to see what would. Secondly, the demand for higher profits to provide incentive could be made, whatever the existing level of profits. Were they already high? They must be higher! Why? To provide incentive! Oil was unwilling to be judged in relation to the profit level in other industries. Whatever the level, more was needed or disheartened oil drillers would go home, slump in their chairs and brood over their sad lot. Finally, the oil industry did not deign to note that there was *no* price ceiling on oil produced from *newly discovered* fields. Such oil could already sell at OPEC monopoly prices. But for some mystical reason, incentives demanded virtually unlimited profits from the old fields as well as the new. In the imperishable words of Bill Campbell, it was enough to gag a maggot.

The Arab oil boycott brought numerous welcome dividends to the oil industry. Profits promptly doubled, with still bigger profits in the offing. Several thousand independent gas dealers, whose lowered prices proved annoying to the major companies, were squeezed out of business. The oil industry received the green light on the Alaska pipeline, construction of which had been delayed by environmentalist challenges in the courts. The same was true of offshore oil drilling, which had heretofore faced heavy resistance from environmental groups but now foresaw relatively smooth sailing.

Oil suffered one major loss, however. In the past, American journalists had largely ignored the oil industry, partly because of the difficulties of mastering the intricacies of oil economics, partly because of a lack of reader interest.[4] Washington politicians also had taken little interest. From here on, however, some first-rate journalists and legislators were sure to keep a hawk eye on oil, oil statistics (sometimes doctored in the past), and oil profits. If the oil industry were to be prevented from pulling off one of the great consumer hold-ups in U.S. history, "pitiless publicity" (in Woodrow Wilson's classic phrase) would probably be the preventive instrument. The duel among skeptical journalists, consumer-conscious legislators, and the oil industry's public relations experts should be fascinating to watch.

The oil companies will doubtless raise prices gradually enough, given a free hand, and keep profits at sub-preposterous levels, to avoid the kind of public indignation that would lead to stern federal controls.

THE ARAB SHEIKS TAKE OVER

Before analyzing the energy alternatives we must choose from, a few relevant facts should be set forth.

About 50 percent of our energy comes from oil, almost 30 percent from natural gas, and 17 percent from coal. We import almost 40 percent of the 6 billion barrels of oil we use each year. And dependence on imported oil is increasing. Domestic oil production has been steadily falling since 1971 and may continue to decline until the late 1970s, since it takes many years to develop offshore oil, and the Alaska pipeline, scheduled to bring in 2 million barrels a day, won't be gushing oil until that time.

How much domestic oil remains to be discovered? Estimates vary, but a twenty to thirty year supply is the most common prediction. A 1975 report by the National Academy of Sciences estimates Mideast oil will be used up in thirty years and world oil reserves in fifty years.[5] The need to develop alternative energy sources, therefore, is clear and urgent.

In the meantime, America will have to buy an increasing share of its oil at stratospheric OPEC prices.

The OPEC countries are not apologetic about their role.[6] They insist they learned all about cartels from the West, that the industrialized countries had long exploited them through multinational corporations, paying far less for their oil than it was worth. They need, they say, to develop a strong agricultural and industrial base before their oil runs out. Why shouldn't they be as wealthy as the nations of the West? Besides, high oil prices are a blessing in disguise. They force other nations to consider their dwindling energy reserves and plan for the day when they are exhausted. If oil prices had remained low, other nations would not have been alerted to the impending energy shortage in time to develop alternative sources. So while the shock therapy was painful, it will all be for the best.

Maybe this argument is valid, but again, the same arguments could be used if OPEC were charging $25 a barrel, or $50. Increased OPEC prices are one thing; quadrupled or quintupled prices are something else again. Even a good thing (if it *is* that) can be carried too far. On the other hand, it can also be argued that very high gasoline prices may force us to take conservation steps that are long overdue and reduce a rate of industrial growth that will deplete many of our resources and add unduly to the levels of pollution. Possibly it *is* a partial blessing in disguise for the more affluent nations, although certainly not for the developing countries.[7] (If only a nation like India could have been the main beneficiary of the OPEC dollars instead of Bedouin chiefs presiding over Arabian sands and plotting the destruction of Israel!)

With oil costly and short-term prospects for improvement bleak, what do we do about it? President Nixon sought to deal with the problem by looking the nation straight in the eye and solemnly promising energy independence by 1980. President Ford sought to cut back domestic consumption by imposing a tariff of $3 a barrel on imported oil and eliminating price controls on domestically produced oil and natural gas, a policy deliberately calculated to sharply increase their prices and hence oil company profits. This, Ford argued, would tend to reduce gasoline and natural gas consumption, stimulate energy conservation measures, and provide the oil companies with the capital needed to increase oil production (Alaskan, continental, and offshore), develop alternative energy sources, and make America self-sufficient at the earliest possible date. Deeply committed to the free market and fearful of the formidable complications and difficulties attending a gas rationing program, the president flatly rejected this option.

Critics contended that the market for oil was no longer free, thanks to the OPEC cartel. They saw no reason why domestically produced oil should sell for the unholy prices OPEC demanded, prices bearing no relation to cost of production—either at home or abroad. (Saudi Arabian oil could be produced for 20 cents a barrel, while selling in the U.S. for nearly $15.00 a barrel.) Ford suggested a modest and temporary windfall tax to cope with possibly excess oil company profits—a tax the Democrats found wholly inadequate.

The overall impact of major price boosts for oil, gas, and natural gas would be a leap in the already high rate of inflation and a slowdown in the recovery from the Great Recession (since consumers would have less money to spend on nonenergy products). All of which might be condoned *if* the government had made a convincing case that the towering profits awaiting the oil and gas industries were really necessary to give them the capital needed to finance exploration for more oil and natural gas and the development of other forms of energy. This case the administration was unable to make; its argument continued to be, in effect, that since energy development required *more* capital than in the past, then whatever profit oil could wring from the energy crisis was in the public interest. One would expect the oil industry to hold that view; presidents are expected to take a more statesmanlike stance. But President Ford disliked federal controls, had a warm and cuddly attitude toward business, and was a conservative to the core.

After a prolonged deadlock between President Ford and the Democratic Congress, a compromise bill was finally enacted in 1975. Price controls would not only be continued but the controlled price of domestically produced oil would fall more than a dollar a barrel through 1976 (an election year!). This would reduce gasoline prices about 3 cents a gallon but as controls were gradually phased out over a 40-month period, gas prices were expected to rise again to 3 or 4 cents a gallon more than 1975 prices.

The statute also called for the establishment of a national oil reserve, guaranteed loans for expanding coal production, and fuel efficiency standards for cars and household appliances.

Oil from Western shale? Some "experts" thought enough oil could be wrested from that source to last the nation for a century. (That is, if the west's water supply proved adequate for large-scale shale oil production.) But industry seemed reluctant to make the huge and chancy investment involved unless the government would guarantee a profitable price for that oil when it was ready for market. Oil executives feared that the OPEC cartel might either be broken or the cartel would lower prices enough to make synthetic oil noncompetitive, leaving them with a large white elephant on their hands. As for developing synthetic oil and natural gas from coal, this was technically feasible but still financially risky.[8] Research was going forward, the task would no doubt eventually be done, but for the present the oil industry preferred to concentrate on doing what it knew best—developing offshore oil, Alaskan oil, drilling for new oil at home and abroad, and exploiting a dream-come-true price situation for newly discovered oil. Thus the Ford Administration argued for high oil profits so the industry could pour huge sums into new sources of energy, and industry refused to make that investment until government assumed all the risks! Not exactly the way Adam Smith's capitalist system was supposed to work!

THE ATOMIC ENERGY GAMBLE

A few years ago the confident prediction was that atomic energy would be producing 50 percent of our electricity by 1990. That estimate has been repeatedly scaled down; it is now producing not much more than 1 percent of our energy (and about 8 percent of our electricity). By the mid 1970s the industry was mired in a series of problems and uncertainties that were delaying the timetables. Labor problems, shortages of critical parts, environmental wrangles, and unexpectedly high capital costs were taking their toll.[9] The dispute over the issue of safety was endless. The big question was whether, if a "reactor core meltdown" occurred, the emergency cooling system assuredly would prevent the reactor from spewing lethal radioactive materials into the atmosphere. Since the emergency cooling system really had never been tested, its per-

formance remained uncertain. The *Wall Street Journal* noted that ". . . scientists have issued incredibly complex reports both defending and questioning the safety of the plants."[10] Atomic Energy Commission (AEC) experts insisted that atomic energy was one of the safest of industrial enterprises; not one serious accident had occurred in the history of the industry, the chances of an accidental explosion were said to be zero, and the likelihood of death from a major lethal leak was a thousand times less than the risk of a major hurricane or earthquake.[11] Ralph Lapp, a highly respected authority, insisted that in 1980, when over 100 reactors would be in operation, ". . . the chance of *any* nuclear accident would be 1 in 10,000 for a single year." And for a given community located near a reactor, only 1 in 1 million.[12] Lapp reminded us there are risks in plane flights, auto travel, coal mining, and cigarette smoking but Americans are undeterred by these hazards. To ask guaranteed, absolute safety is to ask too much.

Ralph Nader vehemently dissented, insisting that "If the public knew what the facts were and if they had to choose between nuclear reactors and candles, they would choose candles." An article in *Progressive* sketched the scenario accompanying a failure in the emergency systems and said that the possibility of a disaster costing several hundred thousand lives "somewhere in the United States within the next several decades is quite real."[13]

A petition signed by 2300 scientists (including nine Nobel Prize winners) took an opposite stand. Defenders insisted that rapid development of nuclear energy would help stretch out our supply of fossil fuel, provide cheaper electricity over the long run (despite very heavy initial costs), give us our most pollution-free form of energy, and best meet our immense energy needs during the decades ahead.[14]

Part of their confidence stems from the Atomic Energy Commission's superprecautionary posture. The AEC is acutely aware of the fact that just one major leakage, killing large numbers of people, could jeopardize and perhaps wreck the entire program and the huge investment of money (an estimated $1 trillion by the year 2000), time, and energy that has gone into it. Having given the public so many assurances of safety, a serious accident could undermine public faith so much that the entire program might have to be abandoned. Some of the many delays and unanticipated costs, therefore, have been occasioned by the AEC's determination to do whatever it feels must be done to insure that the dangers involved are kept to an absolute minimum.

On several other counts there was less dispute. After decades of wrestling with the problem, the AEC still didn't know how to handle radioactive atomic wastes. As we discussed in Chapter 1, these wastes are dangerous for centuries (plutonium 239 does not fully decay for 250,000 years), have a tendency to eat through their containers, and pose a constant leakage threat to the environment. Until that problem is clearly solved, the nation will not feel very comfortable with atomic energy.

Although uranium 235, used in most current atomic plants, is becoming scarce, the fast-breeder reactor is relied upon to solve that problem. This remarkable process bombards U-238 (which is plentiful) with U-235, producing plutonium 239. In effect, the fast-breeder reactor produces its own fuel, but that fuel is so deadly that one writer declared that "plutonium is so cancer-producing that a concentration the size of a meatball could destroy life on earth."[15] Many people are understandably uneasy about investing too much of our energy future into a substance like that. In any case, the breeder reactor will probably not produce much energy before the second or third decade of the twenty-first century.

Finally, there is the danger that misanthropes will be able to steal enough atomic materials to build a bomb and use it to terrorize a government into paying whatever outrageous price they may have in mind. It is acknowledged that an A-bomb can be built by a physics major from information readily obtainable in a public library if the fissionable material is on hand. Unhappily, the development of such a bomb no longer can be regarded as a bit of science fiction fantasy. It could happen—and that possibility is one more reason why many observers think the atomic basket is too precarious to put many eggs into it.[16]

The future cost of the atomic energy industry, then, remains in considerable doubt. Rising costs are a major factor. For example, a nuclear reactor planned for Midland, Michigan, in 1968 was expected to cost $260 million, but the ultimate cost is now expected to be at least 500 percent higher. Nor is this an isolated instance. Overall, the projected cost of nuclear energy per kilowatt is now expected to be almost four times as much in 1985 as was estimated in 1972. Frequent shutdowns of operating reactors (for inspection and repairs) have reduced their anticipated margin of efficiency. Uranium prices have soared and a shortage of that essential substance is feared within twenty-five years. Growing doubts about the safety of the breeder reactor has caused the Federal Energy Administration to reject a crash program to speed up its development until more research can put serious fears to rest. In sum, while the nuclear power program will continue, it is wholly unclear how far the harnessed atom will go to meet our energy needs.

COAL, SOLAR POWER, FUSION

Indications are that America will turn to coal as its major substitute for declining domestic oil production. There is an abundance of coal in this country, enough to meet our energy needs for hundreds of years. It is a sure and dependable source of energy, providing the most energy per investment dollar[17] and lacking the hazards of atomic energy and the uncertainties attending other energy sources. Before the oil embargo and the precipitous rise in oil prices, antipollution pressures were bringing about a shift from coal to natural gas in the generation of electricity, but that trend has now been reversed.

Not that coal is without problems. For the immediate future there appears to be a lack of trained manpower for expanding coal production. The number of engineers from mining schools has been steadily decreasing, and this will take time to change. Half of our coal is deep-mined, and although the Coal Safety Act of 1969 produced such stringent safety requirements that it almost doubled production costs (and refuted those who believe business always dominates where its vital interests are concerned), there may be difficulty persuading enough young people to enter a dirty, still dangerous, and generally unattractive line of work. The west has far more strip-mine coal than the east but the west also has a shortage of water, and getting the water it needs may be an expensive operation. (The water shortage may also severely limit the commercial prospects of producing synthetic oil and natural gas from the coal and shale resources of the West.)[18] Transportation costs for moving western coal to the east are also high unless coal mixed with water is moved by pipeline (Here again the western water shortage problem intrudes.) Because strip-mined coal can be produced more cheaply than deep-mined coal, and because western coal is low in sulfur—coal's principal pollutant—major efforts will be made to solve these problems. It is possible to remove sulfur from Eastern coal but the process is currently costly. Some promising techniques for dealing with this problem are being developed, but their commercial feasibility has not been clearly established at this writing.

One of the principal objections to strip mining lies in its devastating effects on the land, since it leaves the terrain barren, scarred and unproductive. This is not unavoidable, however. In many strip-mined areas, the topsoil can be returned, reseeding and reforestation can take place, and the land be restored to its pristine condition. The process is not prohibitively expensive—running from $3,000 to $7,000 an acre—but it cannot be successfully applied to steep Appalachian slopes. Whether it will seriously disrupt the underground watercourse flow and impair the quality of precious underground water supplies in the west is unclear, although many mining engineers are optimistic. One thing seems sure—we are going to find out!

Edmund Faltermayer has written in *Fortune* magazine (September, 1975) about "The Clean Synthetic Fuel That's Already There." That fuel is methanol, or wood alcohol. It can be produced from waste wood products, garbage, manure, or coal. It can be manufactured at a cost no greater than synthetic natural gas and almost all of our energy-using devices can burn methanol. That includes cars, which can run well on it, with a minimum of pollution besides. In West Germany, incidentally, about one-fourth of the population uses electricity derived in part from garbage.

Geothermal steam involves tapping hot water deep in the earth for its steam potential. In a few areas this may prove an important source of energy (nonpolluting, too), but the scarcity of sites will confine it to a comparatively minor role. Some believe that holes can be bored down to hot rock miles below the earth's surface. Water could then be poured down and steam produced and released through a second hole nearby. An intriguing possibility, now being tested, but it seems improbable as a major source of energy. Similarly, there is a possibility of harnessing wind power, tidal power, and the heat from warm ocean currents, but hopes are not high on any of these fronts.

Solar power is much more promising. The sun annually lavishes 18,000 times as much energy on the earth as mankind uses. If solar heat is effectively concentrated, stored, and used, it would have many advantages: It would be cheap and nonpolluting; it would involve an inexhaustible supply; and the Arabs could not corner the market! Australia, Japan, and Israel use solar water heaters rather widely. The water flows through glass-covered panels, is heated by the sun, and is piped to storage tanks. The hot water can then be used for bathing, dishes, radiant heating, and (to a limited extent) for air conditioning.[19]

In the United States, solar heating might not be feasible for the colder third of the nation, but experimentation by governmental and nongovernmental groups is going forward rapidly in the warmer zones as well as abroad. Currently "solar power is mainly for the rich," says the *Wall Street Journal*,[20] because the equipment is expensive and its durability is uncertain. It is necessary to use it as a supplement, rather than a replacement, for conventional heating systems. Solar equipment technology is not sufficiently well-developed to produce electricity on a competitive basis, but by 1985 it seems likely that we will be able to heat and cool buildings economically. By century's end, we may be getting 25 percent of our electricity from solar power—if all goes better than it probably will![21]

There has been considerable talk of installing massive solar heat collectors in the Arizona, New Mexico, and California deserts but this appears somewhat dubious, at least for most of this century. The National Science Foundation expects less than 1 percent of our electricity to be generated in this manner by the year 2000,[22] although some scientists are more hopeful than that.

In the long run, our hopes rest heavily on the development of atomic fusion, which has been likened to "burning water." One gallon of sea water, subjected to the fantastic energy-releasing process of fusion, could yield the energy equivalent of 300 gallons of gasoline. The process would be almost completely nonpolluting. It would end, once and for all, the danger of exhausting our energy reserves. Apparently there is no danger of either an uncontrolled explosion or of poisonous leakages, since an automatic fail-safe process is inherent in fusion. For technical reasons that need not be described here (as if a political scientist could!), if fusion begins to get out of control it automatically shuts itself down.

Fusion can only take place at temperatures of 100 million degrees. This has heretofore posed an insuperable difficulty, since no substance known to man can contain heat of that magnitude without dissolving. It is believed, however, that it is possible to contain this heat by a magnetic field that keeps the energy "plasma" in a state of harmless suspension.

Many scientists believe fusion will be developed into a successful energy source within twenty years; at least one knowledgeable student believes a crash program akin to that which landed men on the moon could give us fusion power in a shorter time.[23] Whenever it arrives, its potential value will be almost unlimited. For example, a *fusion torch* system could be used to convert any material into its basic form—atoms. This could solve the solid waste disposal problem (especially plastics) by reducing them to a manageable form. Of perhaps greater importance, it could be used to reduce the life span of lethal radioactive wastes to only a few years; deadly plutonium 239, by a process of *transmutation,* would remain dangerous for $21\frac{1}{2}$ years instead of 250,000 years and strontium 90 for $6\frac{1}{2}$ years instead of 439 years.[24] Since we now know of no safe method of storing radioactive wastes, this coup would be of incalculable importance.

The long term prospects, then, look good for energy *if* everything works out as fusion enthusiasts hope. But almost certainly there will be hitches along the way, unsuspected problems will emerge and things will not go that smoothly. We cannot even be certain that we will be able to tame the 100 million degree genie at all. But in a world with so many seemingly insoluble problems, it is nice to have a few possibilities in sight that *could* work to man's advantage in a dramatic way.

If there should be a major and early breakthrough on fusion which jeopardized huge investments in other forms of energy, that would touch off a titanic struggle. We could be sure that the oil, natural gas, and coal interests would put up the fiercest possible resistance to development at a pace that would be seriously detrimental to their holdings. In our political system, they would doubtless succeed in delaying that development—in the name of the public rather than of their private interests, of course—until they had established a firm foothold in the new industry and could profit from its growth. When in doubt, always bet on oil.

The United States has begun to do something and could do more to relieve the energy shortage by rigorous conservation measures. Air conditioning could be set at higher temperatures in the summer and houses could be heated less warmly in the winter. Industry could cut its energy usage more than 10 percent by turning off unused lights and machinery. Recycling more of our metal products could save considerable energy. (We recycle a smaller percentage of our products than we did a generation ago.) Eliminating throwaway soft drink and beer cans would also help. Better insulation in new homes could save one-third on fuel costs. Use of car pools could save more than most people realize. So could the improvement and greater use of mass transit facilities.

MASS TRANSIT, RAILROADS, CARS, AND TRUCKS

From 1880 to 1920, mass transit was the key feature of the urban transportation system of America. After Henry Ford developed the historic Model-T and Americans flocked to buy it, mass transit went into eclipse, only to make a comeback during World War II. Then another long period of decline set in. Despite the population boom, mass transit steadily lost customers, and despite fat fare increases it recently has been losing $300 million a year or more. (Even the highly praised mass transit systems of Europe and Japan lose money.[25]) Two hundred fifty bus and subway companies have bit the dust since 1954; the cities usually took them over by a process often referred to as *bankruptcy socialism*. The cities continued to provide the transit service that many people needed, but the systems remained solidly in the red despite persistent experiments with this and that method of attracting more customers or cutting costs.

Many factors have contributed to the withering of mass transit. Foremost is the public's pronounced preference for private cars, which are more convenient, more comfortable, and often faster. With neither cars nor trucks paying for highways or expressways by adequate taxes (on city expressways, e.g., only about 1/7 of the cost is met by tolls and gas taxes), this traffic was in effect heavily subsidized from general revenues. As customers deserted mass transit, the latter failed to generate the revenues needed to maintain good service. Deterioration manifested itself in dirty, noisy, ugly, and antiquated facilities which proved crowded and uncomfortable in rush hours. Poorly heated, lacking air conditioning, increasingly crime-ridden, operated by personnel who were often impersonal if not rude, unable to meet their time schedules—all of this added to riders' frustrations. Nothing succeeds like success or fails like failure, as the sinking spiral of mass transit so sadly demonstrated.

In spite of these woes, recent events have conspired to bring about a modest renaissance of mass transit. Auto congestion in downtown areas has often reached ludicrous dimensions. Bumper-to-bumper traffic moving at tortoise speed emits far more pollution than more rapidly moving traffic, creating downtown pollution levels that worry many citizens.

Parking fees have risen again and again, discouraging less affluent drivers. As the OPEC cartel jacked up gasoline prices, city dwellers began considering alternative modes of transportation. Government officials and concerned citizens remembered that individual cars use up to ten times as much energy per passenger mile as subways and rail transit; bus transportation is also far more energy conserving. Others noted the need for more and better mass transit for a society in which an ever-larger proportion of the population is over sixty-five and for low-income, inner-city job seekers faced with the flight of industry to the suburbs. Finally, business persons with heavy downtown investments who apprehensively observed the growth of suburban shopping centers and the decay of the central city have learned that big city downtown areas can rarely flourish these days without an adequate mass transit system.

All in all, the time seemed ripe for a revival of mass transit. Congress began appropriating substantial sums ($10 billion over a 12-year period) to subsidize its development, and cities took renewed interest in modernizing, improving, and extending their transit facilities. For awhile, planners were bemused with visions of ''space-age, Buck Rogers'' transit facilities,[26] the kind that titillate readers of the Sunday rotogravure newspaper section. With more experience, however, and the failure of various experimental systems, planners are coming back to earth and recognizing that some mixture of relatively conventional rail, bus, and subway systems is probably our wisest bet—with heavy emphasis on buses. Subways need at least 40,000 riders daily if they are to be a practical investment, and apparently only cities of a million or more can use rail transit effectively. Even then, rails serve only high-population density areas of a city successfully. The more strung out and decentralized a city is, the less likelihood that rail transit will be feasible.[27] The initial investment in rail transit and subways is necessarily very heavy; a fraction of that money spent on buses usually brings far better results in relation to cost, especially if accompanied by traffic lanes reserved for buses only. (*Consumer Reports* thinks massive investments in Washington, D.C. and Atlanta rail transit systems may prove to be massive blunders.[28])

The public's continued attachment to their beloved automobiles thus far has meant that the increase in mass transit riders is usually disappointing. Even if fares are experimentally reduced to very low levels or even to zero, potential passengers cling grimly (rather, they cling contentedly) to their fifth appendage, the car. Nor does improved quality service necessarily wean them from cars as much as has been predicted. People complain bitterly about service when it is poor but respond indifferently when it is improved. In San Francisco, officials of the highly touted and then rather disappointing BART (Bay Area Rapid Transit) system—incorporating all the latest wrinkles in streamlined, comfortable, speedy, automated (but not trouble-free) service—discovered, to their dismay, that when traffic congestion in San Francisco declined because more people were using BART, that very decline prompted people to resume using their cars again. Dollar-a-gallon gas may turn the trick; nothing else seems to work very well. Or perhaps imposing heavy taxes on cars entering downtown areas or banning private cars altogether in those areas should be considered. But would that simply send people in larger droves to suburban shopping centers? If only people loved their spouses as they love their cars, divorce courts would go bankrupt and domestic tranquility would descend upon our land!

A hopeful development for cars clouds the future of mass transit. If current indications are borne out and relatively low-pollution, energy-economical cars become commonplace, the necessity for mass transit will be greatly reduced. Congestion will remain a problem, but the major liabilities of the auto will have been largely overcome. If so, people can have their cake and eat it, too!

What about regular railroads? Since they use only about one-fifth as much energy for long-haul freight as trucks and pollute about one-fifth as much, they would seem to be excellent candidates for major growth in an energy-conscious, pollution-conscious age. Logically, the case is airtight, but that does not guarantee their future.

First, a bit of history. Railroads have fallen upon evil days since the emergence of the truck. The latter, railroad men complain, must pay only a small part of its share of highway construction and maintenance costs, whereas railroads must maintain their roadbeds entirely at private expense. (Truckers retort that the railroads received huge land subsidies when they were in their infancy and still own land the size of Pennsylvania.) Union *featherbedding* (requiring railroad workers to be kept on the payroll after their services were rendered superfluous by technological advances) has hampered railroad efficiency. So did a stifling array of cobwebbed Interstate Commerce Commission (ICC) rules, which came to govern almost every conceivable railroad activity and decision. Most academic students of the railroads also believe that the industry, for the last few decades, has been plagued by poor management and has failed to be alert to the technical innovations which could have done much to cut costs and improve operations. Too, railroads inherently lack economic adaptability; lines are laid to serve a given industry (like anthracite coal) or a region (like New England), and if that industry fades or if manufacturing moves elsewhere (as when New England textiles and other industries moved South after World War II), the railroads cannot adapt to the changing geographical configurations of industry as easily as the more flexible trucking industry. The tracks are there, they represent a large investment, and they cannot be packed up readily and moved when business moves out.

Perhaps most important, the ICC has forbidden the railroads to discontinue unprofitable rail lines serving small communities. About one-fourth of all the rail lines in America carry so little freight that the railroads regularly lose money on them. But the ICC, responding to clamorous local protests that in turn are reflected in protective Congressional attitudes, usually will not permit the railroads to abandon the obsolete lines.[29]

As the railroads sank deeper into the red, they were unable to modernize passenger trains (in what might have been a vain effort to hold onto passenger travel); passenger miles dropped 80 percent from 1947 to 1973. They were also financially unable to keep their roadbeds in a state of good repair. As maintenance declined and roadbeds deteriorated, freight runs were forced to slow down. Many freight trains in the East travel an average of only 10 miles per hour; nationally boxcars average only 18 miles per hour.[30] Accidents (although mostly minor) have risen to about 10,000 a year. Thus, the downward spiral phenomenon, with low profits or losses leading to deterioration of trains and tracks, leading in turn to less business, producing still more losses, leaving less money for modernization, etc., nearly wrecked an invaluable national asset. The Penn Central went bankrupt (along with seven other Eastern rail lines) after record losses, and Penn Central promptly set another record for a bankrupt business by losing $1.3 billion from 1970 to 1974.[31] The government has been making heroic efforts to save the major Eastern lines by consolidation (Conrail), by subsidizing the purchase of new engines, freight cars, and road repairs and by permitting—finally—about one-third of their unprofitable lines to be dropped. How it will all turn out remains to be seen.

But whatever the difficulties of the railroads up to this point, the case for maximizing their use hereafter is formidable. Railroads use far less fuel than trucks, spew far less pollution, are far less noisy, are far safer. They can use our abundant supplies of coal when our oil is gone. By piggybacking, they can carry trucks long-haul and drop them off for the short-haul operations at which trucks excel. Railroad passenger traffic, except for shorter runs between major metropolitan centers, may never make a full recovery but freight traffic is the railroad's natural meat. As indicated in Chapter 1, however, the government dares not offend the powerful trucking interests by a deliberate national transportation policy designed to replace most long-haul trucking with rail traffic. The Teamsters are powerful enough, disciplined enough, tough enough, and determined enough to force the nation to put their private interests ahead of the public interest.

ENERGY: AN OVERVIEW

So where do we stand on energy and where do we go from here? America is much better off than most industrialized countries, since we are less dependent on foreign oil than they. We also have an abundance of coal and a 10–20-year supply of natural gas; and we are farther along in the development of atomic energy than any other country. The crucial questions ahead seem to be these: Will we be fortunate enough to avoid a major atomic reactor accident? Can the water supply problem in the West (and the possible contamination of underground water) be solved so that strip mining and synthetic oil and gas production can go forward? How long before synthetic fuel becomes commercially competitive? Can we remove sulfur from coal without incurring prohibitive costs? How much offshore oil is really there? Can we learn how to recover the large amounts of oil which remain in abandoned oil fields (said to be up to ⅔ of what was originally present)?[32] Can the OPEC cartel be broken?

The vast amounts of research—drawing on both public and private funds, going into the discovery of new sources of energy and the fuller exploitation of existing sources—will take time to bring to fruition. On obtaining oil and gas from coal, a writer for *Fortune* observed that "no matter how promising a process may be in the laboratory, it cannot really be tested until it is built into a large pilot plant, costing from $15 million to $30 million and cannot be fully proved out until it gets into a larger demonstration plant . . . costing up to $200 million."[33] This is the principal reason we may not reap large dividends from new energy sources until about 1985.

Dubious about the wisdom of giving the oil industry too free a hand in guiding the nation's energy development, Senator Adlai Stevenson, Jr. has proposed that the federal government develop the substantial oil and natural gas resources in the public lands (such as naval oil reserves). The government corporation's cost of production would become a kind of yardstick by which to measure the validity of private oil and natural gas company claims that their prices were fair and reasonable. In the New Deal period, the Tennessee Valley Authority (TVA) served as such a yardstick for private utilities and managed to bring their rates down one-third without pauperizing them. If the Stevenson proposal were enacted, however, there would be interminable arguments over the comparability of its statistics with those of private firms, just as there were with TVA. But will an "oil TVA" be established? Americans may mistrust "big oil" but they don't trust big Government much more. Nor do they have much faith in big government's ability to manage economic enterprise more efficiently than private enterprise.

One thing is clear. The nation badly needs to formulate a coherent long-range energy plan but doesn't know how until technical developments point the way. In other words, economic developments will shape our political decisions more than the other way around. (Just like Karl Marx said!)

NOTES

1. *New York Times,* February 11, 1974, p. 42.
2. *New York Times,* February 11, 1974, p. 42.
3. For studies of oil profits and oil politics, see Ronald Dugger, "Oil and Politics," *Atlantic,* December 1969; Britt Hume, "The Case Against Big Oil," *New York Times Magazine,* December 9, 1973; Fred Harris, "Oil: Capitalism Betrayed in its Own Camp," *Progressive,* April 1973; Sam Love, "Energy: The Crisis Behind the Crisis," *Progressive,* January 1974; Philip Stern, "Oil Profits: Where the Loot Goes," *New Republic,* March 2, 1974; Les Aspin, "A Solution to the Energy Crisis: The Case for Increased Competition," *Annals,* November 1973; John Hamer, "Oil Taxation," *Editorial Research Reports,* March 15, 1974; Linda Charlton, "Decades of Inaction Brought Energy Gap," *New York Times,* February 10, 1974.
4. Robert L. Samuelson, "The Oil Companies and the Press," *Columbia Journalism Review,* January–February 1974, pp. 13–14.
5. Tom Wicker, *New York Times,* July 27, 1975, p. E17.
6. A good description of OPEC and its effects is in "Faisal and Oil," *Time,* January 6, 1975.
7. "Faisal and Oil," *Time,* January 6, 1975, p. 12.
8. *Wall Street Journal,* November 14, 1974, p. 1. Also *Business Week,* January 27, 1975, pp. 108–113, and *New York Times,* January 26, 1975, p. 4E.
9. *Time,* April 14, 1975, p. 73.
10. *Wall Street Journal,* July 9, 1975, p. 1.
11. *Wall Street Journal,* July 9, 1975, p. 1.
12. Ralph Lapp, "Nuclear Salvation or Nuclear Folly," *New York Times Magazine,* February 10, 1974, p. 72.
13. Richard H. Sandler and Peter Greenstein, "Power From Fission: Potential for Catastrophe," *Progressive,* November 1973 pp. 36–37.
14. John Hamer, "Nuclear Safety," *Editorial Research Reports,* August 22, 1975. For a brief but informative review of the status of the nuclear power industry, see "The Great Nuclear Debate," *Time,* December 8, 1975, pp. 36, 41.
15. Richard A. Frank, "The Law at Sea," *New York Times Magazine,* May 18, 1975, p. 63.
16. Robert Heilbroner thinks it not improbable that the less-developed countries will construct A-bombs and use them for blackmail to coerce the wealthier nations into sharing their wealth. Heilbroner, *An Inquiry into the Human Prospect,* pp. 42–46. Also see John McPhee, *The Curve of Binding Energy,* New York, Farrar, Straus, & Giroux, 1975.
17. Sidney Rolfe, "Whatever Happened to Project Independence?," *Saturday*

Review World, January 25, 1975, p. 27. Also see "Gas from Coal Comes a Small Step Closer," *Business Week,* November 24, 1975, p. 28.

18. *Business Week,* January 27, 1975 and *Wall Street Journal,* December 16, 1974, p. 1.

19. On the development of solar energy, see Peter Barnes, "Solar Derby," *New Republic,* February 1, 1975, and Michael Harwood, "But Not Soon," *New York Times Magazine,* March 16, 1975.

20. *Wall Street Journal,* March 18, 1975, p. 1.

21. Michael Harwood, "But Not Soon," *New York Times Magazine,* p. 47.

22. Harwood, "But Not Soon," p. 47.

23. Stephen K. Greer, "Fusion," *Cleveland Plain Dealer Sunday Magazine,* May 11, 1975, p. 32.

24. Greer, "Fusion," p. 22.

25. *New York Times,* March 2, 1975, p. 2E; Barry Commoner, "Trains into Flowers," *Harper's,* December 1973, p. 85.

26. See "Trouble in Mass Transit," *Consumer Reports,* March 1975.

27. "Para-Transit," *Consumer Reports,* April 1975, p. 264.

28. "Para-Transit," *Consumer Reports,* p. 264.

29. For good brief analyses of the plight of the railroads, see Ralph C. Deans, "Railroad Nationalization," *Editorial Research Reports,* June 20, 1973, and Rush Loving, Jr., "Getting the Eastern Railroads Back on the Tracks," *Fortune,* December 1972. For pleas on behalf of railroads, see Barry Commoner, "Trains into Flowers," *Harper's,* December 1973, and Lewis Mumford, "In Praise of Trains," *Harper's,* August 1972.

30. Brock Adams, "The Shameful State of Transport," *Reader's Digest,* February 1975, p. 65.

31. David Boorstin, "Railroad Reorganization," *Editorial Research Reports,* March 7, 1975, p. 166.

32. "Exploiting Our Resources," *New Republic,* February 15, 1975, p. 6.

33. Lawrence Lessing, "Capturing Clean Gas and Oil from Coal," *Fortune,* November 1973, p. 131.

THREE

Inflation and Unemployment: The Perennial See-Saw

Ask the president (next time you're visiting him) what his major domestic responsibility is and he will probably say, "Keeping the economy healthy." If he says that, most Americans would approve (except for a minority who would place protection of the Bill of Rights at the top of their lists).

Keeping the economy healthy used to mean keeping employment at a high level. Today it means keeping employment high and inflation fairly low. And that has become a job worthy of Solomon. How well that job is done affects almost everything in the public domain. It helps determine: the demand for energy; the priority given to pollution control; the capacity of government to generate tax funds for new (and old) programs; the capacity of private enterprise to generate investment capital and its willingness to invest; the state of the stock market; the level of taxes; the pressures for tax reform and income distribution; the temperature of black unrest; the strength of the dollar; our balance of payments; the political fate of a president and his party; and what Walter Cronkite talks about.

For years the U.S. government has been preoccupied, at any given time, with either recession or inflation. One or the other was either with us or knocking on the door. In 1957–1958 the nation was bewildered by the simultaneous appearance of rather high inflation and relatively high unemployment. That phenomenon was short-lived and was attributed to a special set of circumstances. Now, however, it appears that high inflation *and* unemployment may co-exist for long periods, with governments unable to eliminate either but hoping to keep both at politically tolerable levels. Too much of either can topple any administration.

The nation had an excellent record of price stability from 1954 to 1968. Prices rose an average of less than 2 percent a year during that period, a rate far lower than that experienced by most industrialized countries and one which is hardly regarded as inflation. (Inflation can be defined as a *substantial,* sustained increase in prices.) At the same time the jobless figure was kept rather low—at least in light of today's standards. Then inflation jumped to 5 percent a year, rising again to over 10 percent and producing cries of alarm throughout the land.

Inflation, the textbooks used to say, occurs when the volume of money in circulation increases faster than the volume of goods and services being produced. Under these conditions, sellers can raise prices and still sell their goods or services, so raise them they do.

There is still much truth in the textbook explanation. But inflation in the complex economy of today (which includes the even more complex world economy) also has complex causes. The inflationary burst which began in 1968 and has been with us ever since can be attributed to at least eleven ''parents'' and several ''grandparents.''

1. President Lyndon B. Johnson can be properly blamed for putting inflation in higher gear. When he decided to make the Vietnam war our war (or should we say ''his'' war?), the huge military expenditures involved called for higher taxes if inflation were to be kept in bounds. But eager for Congress to continue funding his prized Great Society programs (education, housing, poverty, etc.) and anticipating that if it were asked for higher taxes it would grant him enough to wage the war but not enough to finance his domestic programs, Johnson adopted a policy of duplicity. He deliberately falsified the figures on the projected cost of the war, leading Congress to believe higher taxes were not necessary. But they were needed, and needed urgently; Johnson's deceit (which *New York Times* economist Edwin L. Dale, Jr. called the most irresponsible act by an American president in his fifteen years of Washington reporting[1]) boomeranged in the form of a strong inflationary kick.

2. Wars always bring inflation, even if LBJ's aren't in charge. Two factors account for this. First of all, governments are reluctant to impose the heavy taxes, which would prevent inflationary pressures from rising, because voters are reluctant to have them do it. Secondly, since many persons withdraw from the civilian working force to enter the military and many citizens produce military goods instead of consumer goods, the volume of consumer goods declines in relation to the demands

for them. That automatically brings their prices up. When governments spend more than they receive in taxes, they must borrow from private banks or other investing institutions (like insurance companies and pension funds) by selling them government bonds bearing an attractive rate of interest. This is called *deficit financing*.

Deficit financing may or may not be inflationary. If there is a considerable amount of unemployment and industry is running well below capacity, deficit financing increases the amount of money in circulation and hence the demand for goods and services, which in turn prompts business to hire more workers to produce the goods needed to meet this demand. The increased volume of money in circulation, then, is accompanied by increased production of goods and services; this is noninflationary. But if deficit financing occurs when unemployment is already low, the increased flow of money cannot be balanced off by more production; inflation will follow. And that is what happened during the Vietnam war years. The U.S. deficit, despite low unemployment, was $25 billion in fiscal '68, and $23 billion, $23 billion, and $14 billion, respectively, in fiscal '71, '72, and '73.

During 1964–1973, deficit financing (supplemented by an above-average amount of business borrowing from banks and by a consumer credit binge) helped increase the U.S. money supply by 120 percent while goods increased only 50 percent.[2] That in itself tells much of the tale about inflation.

The United States was not alone in inflating its currency during those years. The major industrialized countries doubled their money supply from 1965 to 1970 without coming close to an equivalent increase in the production of goods and services. These countries were not at war, but their inflation was largely caused by the next factor to be discussed, a factor which also applied to the United States.

3. Since World War II, the industrialized countries have deliberately pursued full employment policies even if they knew these would be inflationary. Economists do not know how to obtain full employment without stimulating the economy—through deficit spending, tax reductions or monetary inflation—to a point that unavoidably triggers inflation. Since economists don't know how, governments don't either.

Governments prefer an uncomfortably high rate of inflation to a high rate of unemployment because the public fears recession more than it fears inflation (unless inflation becomes *very* high, that is). The reasons are:

a. Recession hits the poor and unskilled (and the blacks) hardest; political liberals oppose any policies which have this effect.

b. Although only 6 to 9 percent may be unemployed in a typical recession, many other persons fear layoffs and welcome policies which allay that fear.

c. The memory of the Great Depression is still vivid in the minds of millions; they and others fear a recession might slide into another depression unless vigorous measures are taken to combat it.

d. Profits fall sharply during a recession, while wages remain stable or even rise. Businessmen, therefore, also tend to prefer inflation to recession.

e. Government fears recession more than inflation, partly because tax revenues fall at a time when demands for government aid are likely to be greatest, partly because it can pay its debts more easily during inflationary periods, and mostly because recessions are more politically dangerous to incumbent administrations than is inflation.

It must be emphasized, however, that we are talking about inflation which runs no higher than 8–10 percent per year. Peacetime inflation of over 5 percent a year is a new phenomenon in America, and we don't yet know how to fully assess its political impact at various rungs on the inflation ladder.

The detrimental effects of inflation are not as uniform as might be supposed. Pure inflation, in which all wages and prices rise equally, would only hurt creditors. But inflation isn't that way; it always affects some commodities and groups more than others, thereby helping some and injuring others. One major study indicates that the poor were not hurt by the very moderate inflation from 1952 to 1967.[3] And, while we tend to think that the aged on fixed incomes are victims of inflation, this is much less true now that social security payments are tied to the cost of living. The real losers in the inflation from 1968 to 1975 were the blue- and white-collar workers, whose real purchasing power dropped during a number of those years. Taxpayers who were nudged into a higher tax bracket through inflation were also losers. The winners in the 1973–1975 inflation were those who bought bonds at high interest rates, owners of oil stocks and wells, debtors, some speculators, and some farmers.

Distinguished economist Robert Solow believes the public's greater fear of recession than of inflation is rational, considering the total economic impact of the two evils on the economy.[4] And he rightly reminds us that—in terms of current national economic well-being—we should keep our eye on the (real) gross national product. If that is growing, the national pie from which we all feed is growing; if it is falling, we are in trouble. Money is paper with various interesting marks on it, but the GNP represents actual goods and services that go to make up our standard of living. It is the key statistic.

Because businessmen know that modern governments are ideologically and pragmatically committed to full employment and hence to strangling recessions in their infancy, their own decisions reflect this appraisal.

They do not cut prices as they might if they expected recessions to be of considerable depth and/or duration, nor do they resist inflationary demands of labor unions as resolutely as they might otherwise do. So the government's determination to halt recessions creates an economic climate conducive to continued inflation.

4. The unprecedented rate of industrial growth, and the growing affluence of Japan and Western Europe from 1960 to 1972 as well as of some other countries, tended to bring a shortage of certain metals and industrial raw materials, thus driving up their prices. Since U.S. prices are shaped considerably by world prices, inflation received an important stimulus from this quarter.

5. Devaluation of the dollar also boosted U.S. inflation. Heavy government spending in support of the Vietnam war, combined with exceptionally large U.S. business investments abroad in the late 1960s, caused American dollars to pile up abroad and demand for the dollar to weaken. Noting that the dollar was overvalued in relation to other currencies, and anticipating devaluation, businessmen and speculators transferred about $30 billion abroad in 1971 alone, converting it into foreign currency. When devaluation did occur—twice—they were able to buy more American goods and services with their converted money than if they had kept it at home. Since devaluation of the dollar means that foreign currencies exchange for more dollars, this stimulates foreign demand for American goods, which in turn tends to drive U.S. prices up. And since Americans cannot buy as many imported goods with their devalued dollars, that raises the prices of those goods.[5]

6. Medical costs figure substantially in the inflation of recent years. They had tended to rise by 10 percent a year long before the overall inflation rate had reached that level. Why? A more prosperous society seeks more medical care, for one thing; higher demand for medical services drives their prices up. Medicare and Medicaid also added to the demand for medical care. Our private health insurance system operates largely on a cost-plus basis, with no effective pressures within the system to hold costs down. Hospital rooms are ever more lavishly equipped (everything but a billiard table in some of them!), and hospital administrators take pride in being able to offer the latest—and most expensive—equipment and services, however limited the demand may be for those services. Admirable, perhaps, but costly and hence inflationary.

7. Unionization of public employees and white collar employees proceeded at a rapid pace in the late 1960s. This raised the scandalously low wages of people like hospital employees and retail clerks and brought the wages of garbage collectors (oops, I mean sanitation engineers!) in New York City to over $14,000 a year. In general, public employees came to make as much or more than their counterparts in private industry. Justice, perhaps, but inflationary.

8. President Nixon deliberately instituted an inflationary agricultural policy in 1972 in an effort to drive farm prices up and woo the farmers' votes that year. Acreage allotments were reduced and record subsidies were paid farmers to keep land out of production. Dairy price supports rose, too. The strategy worked; farm production fell, farmers' income rose almost 20 percent, and the farmers gratefully voted for their sterling champion. But grocery prices went up.

In another decision having still greater impact on inflation, Nixon sold hundreds of millions of bushels of wheat to the Russians at bargain-basement prices, thereby all but eliminating U.S. grain reserves and causing the price of all U.S. grains and soybeans to soar. This unsavory deal, combined with poor worldwide harvests, sent grocery prices to levels that brought cries of anger and anguish from the consumer.

9. Antipollution pressures were inflationary, too. Industry was obliged to spend billions annually to curb its pollution of the air and water; the cost was unobtrusively passed on to the consumer in higher prices. Autos would be the most conspicuous example, with federal requirements for the reduction of exhaust emissions raising auto prices several hundred dollars per car.

10. The Arab oil boycott, followed by the effectively enforced OPEC cartel, was the biggest single factor in the inflationary outburst since 1973. Oil prices quadrupled, and, since oil goes into the production of numerous other items like nitrogen fertilizer and various synthetics, it indirectly spread inflation into many areas. When the price of oil ballooned, this drove other energy prices upward too: natural gas, coal, and electricity, for example. (Overall, however, OPEC could be blamed for only about one-third of the 12 percent inflation which existed in 1974.)

11. An inflationary psychology began to take hold in America, which itself became an inflationary pressure. Anticipating continued inflation at a high level, businessmen would raise prices beyond their usual markup. They also stockpiled more heavily, considering this to be a prudent policy if the same goods were going to cost more later. This made sense for the individual businessman, but it added to the demand for goods and tended to push their prices still further upward.

These were the principal immediate causes of the unexampled peacetime inflation which struck America in the 1970s. But to understand the picture more fully, we must take account of other significant inflationary forces that had persisted in the economy for many years and would continue to be with us.

The long-established, powerful labor unions in steel, auto manufacturing, chemicals, glass, and so on, are often improperly blamed for inflation. Their wage contracts are sometimes inflationary, true, but the unions were just as powerful from 1954 to 1968, when the U.S. price level was remarkably stable, as they are today. But when inflation of the magnitude of the 1970s takes place and unions find their members' purchasing power eroded by inflation, they demand wage gains which *perpetuate* an inflation that was initially triggered by other factors. During the Great Recession, union contracts large enough to compensate workers for their recently reduced purchasing power did prevent inflation from receding as fast as it normally would during hard times.

Corporate decisions also contribute to inflation from time to time. During the Great Depression, economists pointed out that prices in concentrated industries (the so-called oligopolies, where a handful of firms dominated the field) fell much less rapidly than did those in decentralized industries. Analysts of the 1957–1958 recession, in which rising unemployment was curiously mingled with rising prices, observed that when the steel industry saw its sales slipping it collectively raised prices in hopes that higher prices for reduced sales would keep profits at their previous levels. The same thing occurred during the Great Recession, when numerous corporations raised prices as demand fell instead of lowering them to attract more customers—as capitalist markets were supposed to behave.

Another long-term inflationary factor, although not limited to the time frame since 1968, is the shift from manufacturing to services. Because advancing technology reduces the need for manufacturing workers in relation to a given volume of production, and because technology has much less laborsaving impact on the service trades (like barbering, teaching, entertainment, motel management, government services, etc.), our economy annually requires a smaller percentage of manufacturing employees and a larger percentage of service workers. This has an inflationary effect because service wages do not lag far behind those in manufacturing, where man-hour output rises about 3 percent a year; it rises hardly at all in the service trades. Thus, while higher wages in manufacturing need not be inflationary because they are matched by higher output, corresponding wage increases in the services *are* inflationary. The more the labor force shifts to the service sector, the more inflationary the economy becomes.

The women's liberation movement, incidentally, will also have a minor inflationary effect. If women's pay is upgraded to the level of men's pay for the same work, this will tend to raise the overall level of wages and hence of prices. Eminently fair—but inflationary.

THE GOVERNMENT'S TOOL CHEST

How does government usually seek to bring inflation under control? Four major steps can be taken, singly or in combination. The Federal Reserve Board can reduce the potential money supply through its control of the lending resources available to the nation's commercial banks. By requiring member banks to carry greater reserves, by raising its rediscount rate, or by selling government bonds on the open market, the board can reduce the amount of money that banks can lend and, therefore, the amount that borrowers can spend.

Although the board's control over credit is one of our most prominent checks against inflation, this device has its limitations and disadvantages. The Federal Reserve Board has no control over the investment of internal savings by business enterprise, and big business in particular finances most of its expansion through this means. The board cannot control the lending power of insurance companies, savings and loan associations, pension fund custodians, and retail concerns (that is, installment buying). Thus, a substantial part of the nation's investment and credit machinery lies beyond its reach. The board's credit pinch bears down unevenly, also, because small business (like housing) feels the restraints far more severely than big business. When the board engaged in an unparalleled crackdown on bank lending in 1968–1969, American banks drew heavily from Europe to compensate for money shortages at home. *Tight money* therefore failed to materialize.

A second method for checking inflation is to reduce federal spending. This would also diminish inflationary pressures on goods and services, if Congress had the wisdom and will to do the job. Congress has never demonstrated any notable talent in this area, and realists discount this as an effective means of inflationary control.

A third technique would involve the imposition of higher taxes without higher federal spending. This, too, would reduce the total amount of spending in the economy. However, Congress is always exceedingly resistant to raising taxes, except when defense emergencies force its hand.

Another means of controlling inflation is the so-called *jawbone approach:* The president seeks to convince labor unions that the public welfare demands restraint in wage requests, while seeking to persuade major industries that price increases unjustified by cost increases are equally inimical to the nation. In addition to generalized appeals, the president may single out particular industries or wage contracts for concentrated attention. An effort may be made to shame the parties concerned, or an appeal to their patriotism may be made. The jawbone approach may be supplemented by the actual or threatened diversion of defense contracts from offending companies or by the actual or threatened release upon the market of government-stockpiled materials in an effort to keep prices down.

When public opinion supports the president and inflationary pressures are moderate the president can have a measure of success, but when basic inflationary forces are strong the government's efforts at persuasion cannot succeed for long.

Mandatory wage and price controls are usually seen as a last resort.

Business and labor usually violently oppose them, except in wartime, although the American people welcome them once inflation reaches a fairly severe level. But such controls lack the flexibility needed in a dynamic economy, require a sizable bureaucracy to enforce them, lead to the creation of black markets, to under-the-table payments to industrial purchasers, and to dodges such as lowering the quality of goods while holding prices firm. A writer for *Fortune* put it this way: "By garbling the vital signals usually conveyed by the free pricing system, controls misallocate resources, create shortages and deter capital investment. Delicate price relationships that have gained wide social acceptance are upset by controls; impossibly difficult moral judgments by men are substituted for the neutrality and anonymity of the marketplace. Regulations become ludicrously complex and businessmen waste energy and ingenuity devising ways to circumvent them. . . . Prayers imploring the great god Krishna to keep the dollar sound are liable to accomplish more than wage and price controls."[6] Price and wage controls may seem to work for a brief period, but the longer they last the more ineffective they become. And the heavier the inflationary pressures, the less successful such controls are found to be.

On the other hand, some prominent economic liberals, while agreeing that overall price controls may not be desirable, believe that the only way we can achieve relatively full employment without serious inflation is by imposing price controls on the major corporations and wage controls on the unions they bargain with. John Kenneth Galbraith, for example, would slap permanent price controls on the 2000 largest corporations, which account for about one-half of our gross national product.[7] This would include the corporations located in the most concentrated (or oligopolistic) industries, since these corporations are believed to have and to exercise the power to raise prices even when demand is sluggish or falling. Logically, of course, controls roughly limiting wage increases in these areas to average annual man-hour productivity gains would need to accompany the price controls.

Just how well even this more restricted program of wage-price restraints would work is highly speculative. Unless national monetary, fiscal, and government spending programs keep a rough balance between the total volume of money in circulation and the volume of goods and services being produced, *no* system of controls can work for long. The fundamental laws of economics cannot be circumvented by *any* political strategy, appealing though that strategy may seem. But given proper respect for those laws, this more limited form of wage-price controls might have some value. No one really knows.

Less drastic single-shot measures could be taken to hold prices down. Tariffs could be reduced, thereby permitting lower-priced foreign goods to reach the consumer. The Jones Act permits only ships bearing American flags to carry goods between U.S. ports—and they usually charge more than do foreign vessels. Abolishing the Interstate Commerce Commission and requiring free competition in the transportation industry would probably save the consumer $5-$10 billion a year. ICC rules often deny truckers the right to take the shortest route or bring back a full load on their return trip. Truckers travel empty 30 percent of the time, thanks mostly to the ICC. Applicants for ICC licenses may not even cite lower costs or faster service as a reason for receiving a permit. In this way, price competition largely is eliminated in the interstate trucking business. All of which is great for existing truckers and trucking firms, since they make higher wages and higher profits (about twice as large, in relation to investment, as other businesses), but is tough on the consumer who indirectly pays excessive transportation bills. The regulated truckers would fight to the death any attempt to institute free competition in the transportation industry; they know a good thing when they see it. (Next time you hear a trucker express his displeasure with government red tape and his deep yearning for free competition and a free market— don't hit him. He's probably bigger than you are.)

Prices could also come down if the government limited large businesses (say, those with 10,000 employees or sales of over $10 million a year) to writing off as a business expense (in computing their corporation taxes) an average of about one-half as much advertising as they now employ. The nation is drenched in advertising which gives no real guidance to consumers and which seeks to distinguish between substantially indistinguishable products (liquor, cigarettes, toothpaste, soap, gasoline, patent medicines, etc.). These massive advertising sums serve no valid public purpose. For those who believe they help "move the goods" and keep the economy healthy, one question should suffice: Would you (or your parents) be unable to find ways to spend your money if national advertising were cut in half? Nor is the current volume of advertising even in the private interests of the major companies; if all the big companies reduced their advertising by 50 percent, they would stand in the same comparative competitive position with one another as they do now. The proposal suggested above would not deny small business a chance to grow through advertising, just as it does now. Nor would it deny any business a chance to advertise as much as it wished. It would simply limit big business to the privilege of writing off no more than roughly half its current advertising budget against its tax bill, reducing an indirect public subsidy to more defensible levels. The billions upon billions which business would save could be used to reduce prices. (No politician dares even whisper that such a policy might be desirable because advertising, *as an object of public policy*, is one of the most sacred of all sacred American cows.)

These, to repeat, would be one-shot measures, applicable to the economy at any given time and inadequate by themselves for dealing with a serious inflation. But they could be helpful—and won't be done because the economic interests involved are too powerful for the government to handle unless an aroused public opinion backs these reforms. An active, sustained, solid majority of those who really care about a particular issue almost always prevails in a democracy. Usually, however, the majority of those who care most about an established economic privilege are those who profit from it.

THE GREAT RECESSION

The Nixon and Ford administrations sought to curb inflation by wage and price controls which followed the pattern described above, by reducing federal expenditures (impoundment, by Nixon; vetoes, by Ford) and by encouraging a Federal Reserve Board tight money policy. The "Fed" adopted a money policy which was so tight, forcing interest rates up above 10 percent, that most economists felt it was largely responsible for the depths reached by the Great Recession. But several other factors can be blamed, too. The construction industry found itself in a near-depression at least partly because building costs had reached such astronomical heights that new housing was virtually priced out of reach of the middle class. The high cost of land, heavy foreign demand for lumber, high union wages and the "breather" which naturally follows a prolonged building boom all contributed to the collapse of the construction industry.

Another major cause of the Great Recession was the oil embargo, which pushed the prices of gas and oil so high (as well as producing gas shortages that auto owners feared might recur) that the auto industry was staggered. Because that industry occupies such a central place in the economy, affecting so many supplier industries, a depression in Detroit means at least a recession in the nation. It takes years to convert from heavy, expensive cars to less expensive, economy-model cars and most of the public was only interested in buying the latter once OPEC made its move and gas prices headed toward European levels.

The *Wall Street Journal* contended that runaway inflation itself had caused the Great Recession. "Inflation swelled profits and sales figures, producing a phoney euphoria among businessmen; it distorted government economic statistics, making it hard to see that a recession was brewing; it bred a buy-and-stockpile psychology among businessmen even as it was eroding purchasing power and increasing the income tax bite on consumers, producing a save-and-retrench attitude. Inflation's impact is the key thread linking the many causes of recession, including the Federal Reserve's heavy-handed tight money policy of 1974 that sought to stop the frightening price spiral at all costs."[8]

Finally, the Ford administration was late in recognizing the need to deal with the recession. Ford continued to seek tax increases, in order to halt inflation, long after it was clear to most economists that unemployment and a declining GNP were more pressing problems than inflation control.

The Great Recession gradually brought the inflation rate down but also eroded the GNP and pushed unemployment to over 9 percent, the highest since the Depression. The economy, at its nadir, was operating only at 75 percent of capacity and producing $200 billion less than it would have at full employment. Government revenues fell off sharply, leaving the nation with almost a $50 billion budget deficit—even before the tax cut. At one point the nation did some serious worrying lest the recession slide into a full-fledged depression. Economists reassured the public that 1929 and 1975 were not comparable in significant economic respects and that the so-called built-in stabilizers would prevent the recession from plummeting all the way to rock bottom.

The Great Depression is generally believed to have been caused by these factors:

1. American agriculture had plowed under millions of acres of land during World War I to help feed our allies. The land was kept in production after the war, but when World War I belligerents got their agricultural economy back to normal a worldwide food surplus developed. A farm depression preceded the national depression, therefore, and helped set the stage for a more general collapse.

2. A decline in residential construction followed an extended housing boom. The market for new housing became temporarily glutted.

3. Auto production, after a steep climb in the early and mid 1920s, leveled off because most people who could afford a car had bought one, and the yearly trade-in habit had not been widely established.

4. There is fairly good evidence that the American economic system had not been distributing the income widely enough to enable workers to buy the products of industry.[9] Maldistribution of wealth was considerably greater before 1929 than it is today, and the lack of adequate consumer purchasing power (the *underconsumption* theory) may have been an important factor.

5. The Federal Reserve Board had pursued an excessively *easy money* policy, leading to unrealistic amounts of business borrowing and to extravagant stock market speculation that pushed stocks to absurd levels. When the days of reckoning came, stocks dropped 80 percent in a little over four months, creating a general sense of dismay and uncertainty that was destructive to the economy.

6. The infamous Smoot-Hawley tariff of 1929 raised U.S. tariffs so high that it was difficult for other countries to sell to us. In retaliation, they raised their own tariffs so high we could not sell to them. The mutual

curtailment of foreign trade, as well as the international character of the Depression, diminished U.S. exports and led to layoffs in export industries.

Few economists, if any, thought the Great Recession would tumble to depression depths. (Economist Paul Samuelson would call an economic downturn a depression if unemployment reached 10 percent of the working force.) There *was* worry that the total volume of debt had left the nation in singularly precarious shape unless speedy governmental action were taken to arrest the decline. Corporate debt had reached $1.25 trillion; consumer debt, $200 billion; housing mortgage debt, $400 billion; state and local government debt, $200 billion; and federal government debt, $500 billion. The grand total of $1.4 trillion provided the raw material for a super smashup if the recession had gone unchecked and defaults touched off a chain reaction of financial disaster.

But economists were more aware than the general public that many New Deal reforms and other changes in our political and economic system militated against the kind of catastrophe that, in the Great Depression, had given us a 25 percent unemployment level, a per family farm income of $237, a stock market in shambles, and the failure of one-third of our banks. Banks are closely regulated these days, with deposits insured up to $40,000 per depositor; social security checks keep pouring out—economic rain or shine—propping up purchasing power for the elderly; a system of unemployment compensation serves the same purpose for the jobless; the more than one-half trillion dollars of federal, state and local government spending is of a volume far exceeding, in proportion to the size of the population, that of the 1930s, and this also has a stabilizing effect; farm price supports and subsidies stand between the farmer and the kind of price collapse which brought fifteen cents a bushel for corn and twenty-five cents a bushel for wheat in the Depression; much more powerful and extensively organized labor unions insure that employers would not be tempted to cut wages, intensifying a downward economic spiral by further reducing worker wages. Above all, the federal government stands ready, unlike the 1930s, to take whatever steps are needed to invigorate the economy by tax reductions or increased federal spending.

Whenever business activity stumbles and unemployment rises, it is usually because total spending for goods and services is not rising as fast as the work force increases. Total spending consists of purchases by business (with investment playing a crucial role), by domestic consumers, by foreign buyers and by state, local and national governments. The total spending for finished goods and services is called *aggregate demand,* which in turn equals the GNP. If any of these spending components dips and is not offset by appropriate increases in spending by one or more other components, the economy worsens and unemployment rises. Furthermore, the decline tends to be of an accelerating or "snowballing" character. For example, if the auto industry cuts back investment by 10 percent, the steel industry's sales will fall. It will be obliged to lay off men or institute a shorter working week, thereby reducing the purchasing power of steel workers. They will buy fewer goods from the retailers, who in turn will buy less from wholesalers. The wholesalers will then be obliged either to lay off workers or reduce their hours, while their reduced profits will shrink their spending capaacity and discourage new investment. Wholesalers will buy less from the manufacturers, who will buy less from raw materials producers, who are obliged to lay off workers, whose reduced purchasing power further shrinks business activity. The downward spiral will pick up momentum and widen unless there are offsetting factors at work in the economy—which there often (but not always) are.

On the other hand, if one or more of the spending components increases spending, which is not canceled out by a decline in the spending of another component, an upward cycle is set in motion involving precisely the opposite characteristics.

Recessions are costly in many ways. In addition to the personal distress involved, government costs of welfare (and sometimes of extended unemployment compensation) rise steeply. Every 1 percent increase in unemployment adds over $15 billion to the federal deficit—and hence to the national debt—because jobless persons are usually a drain upon the treasury rather than tax contributors to it. Tax revenues at 8 percent joblessness, compared with 4 percent, are almost $60 billion less (at all levels of government); GNP is about $150 billion less. This is why economists believe that temporary tax cuts (to stimulate consumption and hence production and hence jobs) or increased federal spending (having the same effects but less rapidly, since it takes time for governmental programs to get into gear) soon generate enough additional federal revenue to more than pay for the initial costs. A bigger federal deficit, therefore, is often the only way to insure that that deficit is eliminated or reduced as rapidly as possible.

With all this in mind, Congress and the president resolved in 1975 to take corrective action to rejuvenate the sagging economy. There was general agreement that a major tax cut, placing more purchasing power in consumers' hands while government borrowing kept federal spending at its usual level, would give the economy a quicker stimulus than would increased government spending. (There were also fewer ideological objections.) There was some difference of opinion between the president and the Democratic Congress on how much tax stimulus was needed. No one could be sure because the economy is so complex that no one can predict with certainty precisely how much it will respond to a given tax tonic. The Democrats were primarily concerned with insuring that the tax relief would be ample enough to guarantee a rapid and full recovery. President Ford wanted enough too, but feared that the Democrats' generous interpretation of that term would bring a fresh burst of inflation along with its gift of economic recovery.

Neither Democrats nor Republicans relish inflation or unemployment. But Democrats worry more about joblessness, because (1) liberals are largely concentrated in the Democratic party, and they are solicitous of the underdog, in this case the jobless; (2) the party draws proportionately greater voter strength from low-income groups, who are most affected by spreading unemployment. Republicans, on the other hand, tend to fear inflation most because their constituency is more conservative and more affluent. Propertied people and creditors feel more threatened by inflation than do the less prosperous, whose debtor status is somewhat alleviated if they can pay their debts with inflated dollars. If it is a case of unavoidable evils, then Democrats will tilt toward policies minimizing unemployment even at the risk of feeding inflation, and Republicans will lean toward policies which undercut inflation even at the risk of increasing unemployment.

President Ford, consonant with these tendencies, wanted a somewhat smaller tax cut than the Democrats were willing to accept but compromised on a $23 billion reduction. This was compared to the $11 billion tax cut in 1964 that, following a period of economic stagnation and a 5 percent rate of unemployment, proved highly successful in restoring the economy to health. Given the much larger GNP in 1975, a comparable tax cut would have been $26 billion. So many economic elements are involved in any given economic upturn or downturn, however, that no precise parallels can be drawn. To an uncomfortable degree, Congress and the president were guessing how much tax cut was needed—and they knew it.

The $23 billion tax cut almost insured a federal deficit exceeding $70 billion, a figure which left conservative Republicans in a state of shock. But they were partly mollified by President Ford's assurances, later religiously carried out, that he would veto Democratic spending measures which were for other than humanitarian purposes or to promote energy development.

The tax measure also gave a tax stimulus to business investment (through an investment tax credit) and provided a tax credit for the purchase of new homes. Later, the administration released new mortgage money to help the housing industry; the Federal Reserve Board, acting independently but with presidential and congressional blessing, sharply reduced interest rates to encourage business borrowing for new investment and adopted a monetary policy designed to increase steadily the volume of money in circulation. The result is now history.

Among Democrats, support was growing for the Humphrey-Hawkins "Equal Opportunity and Full Employment Act," which would guarantee full or parttime work for *every* adult who wanted it. But the bill represented more of a broad political aspiration than a carefully worked-out plan to cope with the staggering difficulties involved in reaching such a goal. America was clearly a long way from reaching that utopian vision.

As indicated earlier, the nation faces a seemingly permanent dilemma in choosing between inflation and unemployment. Whatever fiscal and monetary policies bring about a full recovery from recession simultaneously stoke the fires of inflation, and whatever measures effectively squelch inflation simultaneously ignite an unbearably high rate of unemployment. Recalling the long list of causes of the current high rate of inflation, it is clear that many of them represent enduring tendencies that will not go away in the foreseeable future. The nation will try to keep inflation at tolerable levels, but in a crunch it will prefer a high rate of inflation to high rates of unemployment. The debate over just how much emphasis governmental policy should give to one problem or the other and the measures needed to achieve the balance favored by one side or the other promise to dominate public policy discussion for many years to come.

This much seems clear. Unemployment is primarily a problem of the unskilled and the semiskilled—that is, the blacks, teenagers, and women. Each 1 percent increase in unemployment means a 4 percent increase in joblessness for low-income groups. Currently teenage unemployment is nearly 20 percent, but among black teenagers it is closer to 40 percent. The difficulties and means of coping with this problem will be dealt with in Chapter 4.

THE POLITICS OF A LAGGING ECONOMY

It now appears that the euphoric American experience of an ever-rising standard of living seems almost over. And if this is true, America will become more of a political cauldron in the years ahead.

It's the growth rate which poses the problem. For a long time the real U.S. growth rate (that is, the rate adjusted for inflation) has been about 4 percent a year, enough to absorb new workers and enable higher manhour output to give almost everyone a regularly rising standard of living. This high growth rate has been a social solvent of enormous importance, since the increased federal, state, and local tax revenues that flowed from it provided funds for financing an endless succession of social programs without bringing comparably higher taxes. It also gave the nation a sense of buoyancy, of progress and of hope for a better tomorrow. Social conflicts were muted by a soothing economic milieu which promised and delivered more for almost everyone.

All of this, it now appears, may be drawing to a close. While a healthy growth rate accompanied the recovery from the Great Recession, that rate seems destined to fall off once we approach the 5½ to 6 percent unemployment level. Otherwise, given the inadequacies of current economic wisdom, we will resume an inflation rate which seems politically unacceptable.

There are many reasons why the accustomed growth rate of 4 percent will probably be unattainable once we have reduced unemployment to about 5 to 5.5 million.

Many economists foresee a severe capital shortage, which will hobble our efforts to achieve the "normal" rate of growth.[10] This shortage is attributable mainly to heavy demands for energy research and development (estimated to total up to $0.5 trillion by 1985); to the need to increase general business investment rates, which have lagged for years behind those of comparable industralized countries; and to massive federal deficits in the mid 1970s requiring Washington to borrow huge sums that would otherwise be available to meet the capital demands of private enterprise. The resulting capital drought is likely to have a depressing effect on our economic performance through the balance of this decade, at least. (It takes about $40,000 capital investment to create one job and $80 billion annually to create jobs for each year's new crop of potential workers).

The price of energy, of course, is very high and may go higher, since it will be 1980–1985 before offshore oil, Alaska oil, oil and natural gas derived from coal or shale, or other energy alternatives begin yielding substantial dividends. This will put a damper on economic growth.

Although pollution control has recently lost ground in terms of national priorities, we will still be spending nearly $20 billion a year for a number of years on environmental protection. These funds add immeasurably to the quality of our lives, but they do not add much to the standard of living *as Americans tend to conceive that concept*. They do not add the kind of consumer goods and services that the average citizen perceives as bettering his life. Rather, they absorb funds and resources that in earlier days would add directly to the consumer's perceived sense of economic progress.

Agriculture's growth rate, more than double that of industry since World War II, now seems to be leveling off. Manhour output will increase, no doubt, but much more slowly than in the past. Farmers are applying about as much fertilizer as the law of diminishing returns permits, and improvements in seeds, weed killers, insecticides, and tillage practices are coming along slowly. In sum, the major boost which our incredibly rapid increase in farm productivity heretofore has given the overall growth rate is now petering out.

With a declining percentage of the population engaged in manufacturing and a corresponding increase found in the service trades, this trend can only diminish growth rates.

A mounting percentage of the population is retired, living off the output of a shrinking proportion of workers. Initially, seven workers supported one person on Social Security. Today the ratio is three to one. This, too, tends to retard the rate of economic growth.[11]

There is some indication, moreover, that a variety of social factors have appreciably undermined the "work ethic"; both manhour output and the quality of work seem to be dropping.

Adding these up, if we haven't already reached a no-growth economy, we are probably coming pretty close to it. If real growth rates—especially in areas which produce conventional consumer goods and services—either stand still (once we reach full employment) or rise very slowly, the implications for the future are manifold—and troubling.

For example, the population of the poor is likely to enlarge rather than diminish in the next few years. Arthur Okun, former member of the Council of Economic Advisors and a highly reputable economist, says we need a 4 percent rate of growth to keep the unemployment rate steady at any given level. For every 1 percent of additional growth, the unemployment rate will be reduced one-third of 1 percent. Thus, according to *Okun's Law*,[12] it will take a 7 percent growth rate to bring unemployment down from 9 percent to 8 percent, and a 10 percent growth rate to reduce it to 7 percent. Or, to put it differently, it would take a 7 percent growth rate from 1975 to 1979 to bring unemployment down to 5 percent.

Let us suppose that Okun's Law works, and after, say, four years of 7 percent growth we have reduced unemployment to about 5½ or 6 percent. At that point, given what economists have concluded about contemporary economic behavior, we can make inroads into the remaining unemployed only by stimulative fiscal and monetary policies which will once again push inflation to a dangerously high level. (That level may well occur even earlier.) Economists do not agree on why the economy acts this way, but an apparently substantial majority believe that, for whatever reason, it is exceedingly difficult to get unemployment below the 5½ to 6 percent level without generating a politically damaging rate of inflation. This means that the recovery from the Great Recession is likely to be incomplete, leaving us with a permanent body of unemployed numbering at least 5 to 5.5 million persons. And that is one more reason—and one of the most significant ones—why economic growth is unlikely to regain the levels we once took for granted.

Of these 5 to 5.5 million, perhaps 2 million are frictional unemployed—which need not concern us. (Frictional unemployment involves persons who have voluntarily left a given job to look for a more satisfying one.) Another million are what might be called the *psychologically unemployables*—alcoholics, dope addicts, and those whose family environments were so devastating that they lack the emotional health needed to get and keep a job. But we face the very real possibility that another 2–3 million persons, able and willing to work, may become permanent casualties of the war on inflation and our lagging growth rates.

What can be done about this? A possible answer is found in the following chapter on poverty.

As the economic growth rate sags, the entire question of income distribution will probably become more salient. Innumerable groups in America feel they are getting less than they deserve. As their economic situation freezes, their frustration and sense of outrage will become more intense. Professor Charles Lindblom of Yale University has said that "one of the great puzzles of 20th century history is that masses of voters in essentially free democratic societies do not use their votes to achieve a significantly more equal distribution of income and wealth. . . . What needs explaining is why they do not try."[13] If standards of living stabilize rather than grow, the campaign for a more equitable distribution of wealth may pick up momentum. That will surely mean more social strife.

We have already seen property crimes increase during 1974, an increase generally attributed to our economic difficulties. If the frustrations of blacks and others become more acute, considering the intractability of inner-city economic problems, we could expect this trend to continue. Nor would it be too surprising if the riots of the mid 1960s were reenacted in the great metropolitan centers if black joblessness is high and prolonged.

Thus far, the women's liberation movement has faced relatively limited overt opposition from American males, to the surprise of many observers. But that movement, in its economic aspects, provokes much less antagonism when the economy is running full speed than when it is limping along. As the struggle for jobs becomes more fierce, with women determined to win their rights and men realizing the full implications of equality, the women's movement doubtless will face greater obstacles and greater male hostility than it has met to date.

Other important results may be forthcoming. With Congress unable to finance many new programs, administrative skills and congressional administrative oversight will rise in esteem. Administrative abilities have been looked upon as among the least important criteria for judging presidential performance, but that may change. Our infatuation with big, glittery—and often untested—social programs has clearly reflected our national psyche. We love big things done on a big scale, dramatic public (and private) initiatives that capture our imagination and inject bursts of political adrenalin into the body politic. But once legislation is on the books, our interest in nursing these glossy programs into constructive, day-to-day grass roots reality has always been minimal. Good administration is not newsworthy, and good Congressional oversight produces little publicity unless it strikes a vein of corruption. The president and Congress won't salute the rising importance of administration, but circumstances may compel them to give more attention to responsibilities that have been badly neglected in the past.

Economists and businessmen will have a lot of psychic and practical adjustments to make. Both have been so attuned, viscerally and theoretically, to a high-growth economy that adapting to a no-growth or low-growth economy will be a painful process. For many corporate managers, merely holding their own will not be a very exhilarating prospect. Economists will have to invent some brand-new theories to cope with a creeping rather than a galloping economy. The stock market, after much twitching and jerking, may settle into a period of muttering doldrums.

All of this may contribute to a sense of national malaise, a deepening of the already present sense that "the best days are behind us," a fading of the spirit of dynamism and forward-lookingness which has marked most of our history. A different national ethos will appear, one conducive to a less frenetic and materialistic way of life for some but also marked by an inability on the part of many individuals and groups to accept the new reality. Their frustrations may produce a great deal of violent thrashing-about in an effort to restore the years of hope and correct the economic inequities now so keenly felt.

Whether this thrashing about will leave democracy intact is one of the major questions. William Ophuls, writing in *Harper's,* believes the energy shortage and the efforts to overcome it will so dominate our lives during the balance of the century that much tighter economic controls are inevitable. Almost equally inevitable, he believes, is "the end of political democracy and a drastic reduction of personal liberty."[14] Robert Heilbroner, taking a longer view, arrives at much the same conclusion.[15] To which one can only say, they may be wrong but there's more than a chance that they aren't.

Our principal source of optimism is to be found in the incapacity of economists to read the future with any degree of confidence. They almost uniformly failed to predict the height and duration of our current inflation. Or the depth of the Great Recession. Maybe the minority of "experts" who are superoptimists about the energy crisis will prove to be correct. Herman Kahn, the editors of the London *Economist,* Buckminster Fuller and Edward Teller,[16] all tell us everything will turn out roses in a few years. Maybe the Arab oil cartel *will* be broken one of these fine days. Maybe something will happen. . . .

Well, something had better, or we're in for a lot of trouble. The low-growth economy comes right out of Pandora's box. Its capacity for mischief is boundless, as we probably soon shall see.

NOTES

1. David Halberstam, "How the Economy Went Haywire," *Atlantic,* September 1972, p. 59.
2. Sidney Rolfe, "The Great Inflation," *Saturday Review/World,* July 27, 1974, p. 12.
3. Robert Solow, "The Intelligent Citizen's Guide to Inflation," *The Public Interest,* Winter 1975, pp. 46–47.
4. Solow, "The Intelligent Citizen's Guide to Inflation, pp. 65–66.
5. A good analysis of the international aspects of inflation is found in Leonard Silk, "How the World Economy Got into this Mess," *New York Times Magazine,* July 28, 1974.
6. Walter Guzzardi, Jr., "What We Should Have Learned about Controls," *Fortune,* March 1975, p. 103.
7. "The Economic Mess and What To Do About It," Interview with John K. Galbraith, *U.S. News,* November 3, 1975, p. 42. Also see Robert Lekachman, "Managing Inflation in a Full Employment Society," *Annals,* March 1975; and Wilfred Lewis, Jr., "The Economics of Restraint," *Social Policy,* November–December, 1974, p. 9.
8. *Wall Street Journal,* April 25, 1975, p. 1.
9. John Hicks, *A Short History of American Democracy,* Boston, Houghton Mifflin, 1973, p. 776.
10. An excellent brief for this view is contained in Tilford Gaines, "An Economic Catch-22," *Manufacturers Hanover Trust,* June 1975.
11. Many of the facts cited in the preceding paragraphs were drawn from Edmund K. Faltermayer, "Ever-Increasing Affluence in Less of a Sure Thing," *Fortune,* April 1975.
12. *Wall Street Journal,* January 27, 1975, p. 1.
13. Daniel Bell, "The Revolution of Rising Entitlements," *Fortune,* April 1975, p. 100.
14. William Ophuls, "The Scarcity Society," *Harper's,* April 1974, p. 47.
15. Robert Heilbroner, *An Inquiry into the Human Prospect,* New York, W. W. Norton, 1974, p. 110.
16. Herman Kahn, Interview, *The Humanist,* November–December 1973, pp. 46, 48, 50; *Minneapolis Tribune,* January 13, 1974, p. 14a; Hugh Kenner, "Bucky Fuller and the Final Exam," *New York Times Magazine,* July 6, 1975, p. 10; Edward Teller, "The Energy Disease," *Harper's,* February 1975.

FOUR
Poverty: A Crusade Stalls

1. The History and Sociology of Poverty

Samuel Johnson once wrote that "a decent provision for the poor is the best test of civilization." His comment builds on a long line of exhortations by prophets and liberal reformers who have associated social justice with alleviating the lot of the poor. In Old Testament times, the prophet Isaiah cried out, "Is not this the fast [the Lord] has chosen . . . to deal thy bread to the hungry and that thou bring the poor that are cast out to thy house."[1] The Psalmist declared, "Blessed is he that considereth the poor," and "He that hath pity upon the poor lendeth unto the Lord." In our day Nathan Glazer writes that "social policy," at bottom, is "the relief of the condition of the poor."[2]

Find a political liberal and you will find someone concerned with improving the lot of the poor; find a political conservative and you will find someone who worries lest too much public benevolence fosters indolence and moral flabbiness. Modern society is in a state of constant tension between the two, with first one and then the other school of thought temporarily controlling public policy. On the whole, however, as standards of living have risen, the forces seeking to relieve poverty have gained ground.

American attitudes toward the poor have been formed against the background of British experience, an experience worth a brief description. The first British statute dealing with the problem of the poor was enacted in 1349 in the presence of a severe labor shortage occasioned by the Black Death. To prevent vagrancy and to insure the maximum supply of labor, the British made it a crime, punishable by branding or mutilation, for any physically fit worker to decline employment when it was offered. In 1531 the British licensed the aged and impotent poor to beg within the confines of their neighborhoods, only to prohibit all begging five years later. In its place the government established an organized system for soliciting and distributing alms to the poor. The law distinguished between those poor who were able and willing to work on public works projects and those who were not, and called for the punishment of those unwilling to work. Poor children were to be apprenticed at an early age so that they would be a minimum burden on society. The law proved inadequate because it relied on voluntary contributions to provide the necessary poor-relief funds. In 1572, therefore, a tax was levied for the poor, with the proceeds to be distributed first to the sick, aged, and disabled paupers and their families; any surplus funds were to be used to provide work for able-bodied paupers.

The famous Elizabethan Poor Law, passed in 1601, carved out the principal outlines of the relief system that was to endure in both England and America for nearly three centuries. Three categories of assistance were provided by this law: (1) able-bodied adults were to be put to work within each parish on projects of a public character; (2) when possible, paupers' children were to be sent to foster homes until they were eight years old, at which time they were to become indentured servants of their masters for the next sixteen years (girls were to perform domestic labor until they either married or reached the age of 21); and (3) others were to be placed in almshouses or workhouses (sometimes the two were combined). In some instances, however, *outdoor relief* was provided for persons or families living in their own homes if the need were temporary or the workhouses were full.

To be eligible for aid, applicants were required to take a pauper's oath, and their names were listed in publicly displayed notices. Inasmuch as foster parents were sometimes in short supply, many children were raised amidst the aged, the disabled, the chronically ill, those with minor criminal records, the mentally defective, and the insane. Some workhouses were let on contract, with the managers granted a meager monetary allowance for each inmate. Even this pittance often shrank before reaching the poor because workhouse operators sometimes lined their own pockets first, leaving the poor to exist as best they could on what remained. Not surprisingly, the latter often were so weakened from malnutrition that they fell easy prey to sickness and disease.

In 1697 paupers were required by law to wear a conspicuous blue or red "P" on their outer garments, a measure designed not only to punish them for their destitution but to discourage those who might be disposed to indolence.

The famous *Speenhamland system* was introduced in 1795. All workers whose wages fell below a minimum level were declared eligible for a supplementary allowance from the parish, with the allowance adjusted in accordance with the fluctuating price of bread and varying with the number of children in a worker's family. This system led to a variety of abuses: Employers naturally were tempted to reduce the level of wages, the number of persons eligible for aid grew spectacularly, and the costs to the parishes reached prohibitive levels.

Dissatisfaction with the Speenhamland system was heightened by Thomas Malthus, who contended that state efforts to aid the poor were inevitably self-defeating. Malthus thought he had discovered a natural law dictating that population would normally grow more rapidly than the means of subsistence. Tragic though they might appear, famines, pestilence, and wars played a salutary role in restoring a temporary balance between food supplies and population. If the poor were aided by public grants, Malthus warned, they would only remain alive longer and reproduce more rapidly than food supplies expanded, setting the stage for even greater famine at a later date. The poor must be instructed, he said, that no one had a responsibility for their condition. They were to blame for their own hard lot, did not deserve public aid, and the sooner they faced this fact, the better.

This bleak doctrine (later reinforced by the survival-of-the-fittest theories of social Darwinism) proved quite palatable to the more secure classes and to the economic masters of the Industrial Revolution. The latter were eager to shed responsibility for those who might be injured on the job, who were unable to save for their retirement, or who were unemployed. Malthus offered them a clear conscience.

In 1834 the British abolished all outdoor relief, confining public assistance to those in almshouses or workhouses. Also firmly established was the principle that no one receiving *indoor relief* was to receive as much as the most poorly paid independent worker. In the words of the government, ". . . every penny bestowed that tends to render the condition of the pauper [better] than that of the independent laborer is a bounty on indolence and vice." Long considered a disgrace, poverty now became virtually a crime.

The growing spirit of humanitarianism in the nineteenth century, spurred by official investigations and literary exposés of the plight of the poor, produced a reaction against the severity of the poor laws. In 1891 toys and books were permitted for the first time in workhouses; female inmates were permitted to have a cup of afternoon tea in 1894; trained nurses were permitted to care for the sick in 1897.

More basic reforms followed: School lunches were authorized for needy British children in 1906 and old-age pensions were introduced in 1908. In connection with his proposals for health insurance and unemployment compensation in 1909, Lloyd George proclaimed that his famous budget was "a war budget . . . to wage implacable war against poverty and squalidness. . . . Before this generation has passed away, we shall have advanced a great step towards that good time when poverty . . . will be as remote to the people of this country as the wolves which once infested its forests." The movement from poultices to the prevention of poverty was now launched in earnest. Several decades later the United States followed suit.

America had its poor houses and county welfare agencies throughout much of the nineteenth century. But no systematic public effort was made to eliminate the roots of poverty or to reduce its dimensions until recent years.

Sociologist Herbert Gans believes, wryly, that poverty serves a number of functions useful to the nonpoor, functions which tend to perpetuate poverty because the presence of the poor helps other groups achieve certain goals and satisfactions. They provide "a low-wage labor pool that is willing—or unable to be unwilling—to perform dirty work at low cost." Their low wages enable the more affluent to save more money for investment purposes; their domestic labor frees well-to-do women to carry on more professional, cultural and community activities. They create jobs and professions for those administering programs serving the poor or providing services peculiarly attractive to them (such as the numbers game, cheap wine, heroin, pawnshops, etc.). They prolong the economic usefulness of such goods as day-old bread, second-hand clothes, deteriorated cars and houses. They enable their economic superiors to deplore their allegedly inferior personal habits, thus legitimating desired social norms. They "evoke compassion, pity and charity, thus allowing those who help them to feel that they are altruistic, moral and practicing the Judeo-Christian ethic." They offer those with higher status the vicarious pleasures of deploring (while secretly relishing) the "uninhibited sexual, alcoholic and narcotic behavior in which many poor are alleged to indulge." Their culture is often adopted by the middle and upper classes (jazz, blues, spirituals and country music first originated with the poor). They provide leftists and liberals with a psychologically satisfying cause, since the amelioration of poverty gives purpose and morality to their politics. Their homes can be razed when city expressways are planned, thereby protecting the homes of the better-off from this fate. They are assigned to the infantry, enabling others to serve in more agreeable military roles. Their political passivity helps the American political system stay nearer the middle of the road, since a population of politically clamorous poor would force politicians to the left.[3]

Before proceeding further, we should explain what is meant by poverty. In 1883 William Graham Sumner contended that it is impossible to define a "poor man," that the term can mean whatever we wish it to mean. Certainly the term is highly elastic, depending upon the nation and the age to which it applies. Those stressing its relativity might note that the average family income in the United States (in terms of comparative purchasing power) is roughly five or six times higher than the world's average—perhaps double that of Western Europe and about ten times higher than that of Asia. Certainly America's poor are wealthy beyond the dreams of the poor in most countries and eras; they usually have a television set, a radio, warm clothes, fairly decent shelter, all the food they can eat (if not of the best quality), a bath, hot running water, and (sometimes) an automobile. Even the average black family lives better than the average citizen of France and Great Britain.

When serious discussion of antipoverty measures began in 1962, "experts" settled on $3,000 as the dividing line between the poor and nonpoor. Robert Lampman says, "The rationale for that mark was that at levels of income below $3,000 a majority of families did not consume an adequate and nutritious diet. $3,000 was noted as three times the minimum food budget for a family of four."[4] When the Office of Economic Opportunity (OEO) was established in 1964, it set the poverty level at $3,400 for a family of four, a figure which inflation gradually raised to over $5,000 in 1975. Economist Victor Fuchs and Christopher Jencks have suggested that the poor should be defined as those who make less than half the *median* family income (now about $13,500).

From one viewpoint, poverty statistics are highly encouraging. Assuming appropriate variations for changes in the cost of living (measured against the OEO standard), 67 percent of the population was poor in 1896, 63 percent in 1918, 51 percent in 1935, 30 percent in 1950, 20 percent in 1960, and 12 percent in 1970.[5] These figures might suggest that the passage of time would soon erase poverty in America, but that hope would be premature. The smaller the percentage of the poor, the larger the proportions of poverty that reflect social and personal pathology rather than merely economic circumstances. The reductions in the number of the poor which have occurred, it should be noted, have largely been the result of general economic growth rather than public policies designed specifically for the poor.

What are the demographic characteristics of those the government considers "poor"? About two-thirds are white. One-half live in families where the breadwinner has an eighth grade education or less. Almost half are children. In about 43 percent of the families, the father has died, divorced, or deserted. Only about one-third live in the inner cities; 40 percent live in nonmetropolitan, nonfarm areas; 18 percent live in suburbs. About one-half live in the South. Forty percent of poor families are headed by a full-time worker.

A number of factors are commonly cited as causes of poverty. Nature has dealt some persons a poor genetic hand, bequeathing them a low level of intelligence, which virtually precludes their doing other than the most menial and hence low-paying labor. Sometimes this low intelligence may be the product of protein deficiency during the prenatal period or of nutritional deficiencies during their earliest years. Often, no doubt, it reflects the normal spread of genetic differences which apply to every aspect of *homo sapiens*. If Nature supplies geniuses, it will also supply morons.

Similarly, some persons are born with (or acquire through unhealthy living practices) poor health. They lack the vital energy which contributes so much to people's success in life, or they are so handicapped by frequent illness or disability that their income is low.

To these may be added the psychological unemployables, persons with emotional difficulties reflecting either genetic flaw or crippling family environments. There may be several million persons within this category; precise figures are impossible to obtain. These persons do not have the emotional qualities needed to hold a steady job or to gain advancement in their work. (Some of our 9 million alcoholics probably belong in this category.)

Many fatherless families find it difficult to escape from poverty, since mothers of small children are often unwilling to leave the home; among those who are willing, the paucity of day-care facilities is a major obstacle. Nonetheless, 15 percent of female heads of poor families work full-time, and another 25 percent work part-time.

Millions of jobs do not pay enough to enable the wage earner to rise above poverty. Unemployment is another factor, though it accounts for only a small part of American poverty.

Racial discrimination leads to poverty in an undetermined number of cases. In a large sense, the high level of poverty in the black population is the outgrowth of centuries of economic, cultural, psychological, and political oppression that left the blacks with a heritage of poor education, an abnormal family environment, and work skills of an inferior nature. Whatever economic opportunities may exist, it will probably take several generations to overcome the handicaps imposed by centuries of black servitude.

The deeper psychological (and possibly genetic) factors which contribute to poverty are far from being well understood. Those with facile theories should be sobered by the experience of Professor Robert Coles, the distinguished Harvard psychiatrist, who spent a decade probing the attitudes and life of the poor. Joseph Epstein writes, "If such a good and decent man—and a psychiatrist at that—could spend ten years trying to 'understand' his subject and confess himself at the end no less bewildered . . . at the complexity of it all than he was at the beginning, can the rest of us . . . do any better?''[6]

In reciting the factors that cause poverty, we are reminded of how difficult it will be to *abolish* poverty, the goal of many reformers. Poverty technically can be abolished by income distribution plans, but the forces which predispose many persons to low incomes are manifold and not easily remedied. Reducing to a minimum the low income brought about by a defective social environment is not a job for a decade but for generations —if not for all time.

Our current social welfare budget (defined by the Social Security Administration as federal, state, and local expenditures for health, education, welfare, and various forms of income maintenance) now runs to well over $200 billion, compared with about $50 billion in 1960. Approximately one-third of that budget goes to the poor, or to persons who would be classified as poor if this money were not being spent. Slightly over one-half of this assistance is in the form of cash payments to the pre-transfer poor, and slightly less than half is in noncash, service benefits.[7] Robert J. Lampman observes that ''The American system of transfers . . . redistributes almost twenty percent of the GNP; in the process, the pretransfer poor—those with primary incomes below the official poverty lines— who have three percent of primary income, end up with nine percent of the secondary distribution.''[8] In the absence of these programs, the American poor would number about 45 million instead of about 25 million.[9] If this is not a spectacular achievement, neither is it a trivial one.

THE WAR ON POVERTY

One of the most noteworthy aspects of Lyndon Johnson's administration was his celebrated *War on Poverty*. Thomas Halper has written that in the 1950s, Galbraith's *Affluent Society* was peopled by Whyte's *Organization Man* and Riesman's *Lonely Crowd* but not yet by Michael Harrington's *The Other America*.[10] Harrington's classic, published in 1962 and bringing the literate public's attention to the dimensions and flavor of poverty in America, made a vivid impression on Walter Heller, chairman of the Council of Economic Advisors, who passed it on to President John F. Kennedy. Kennedy, whose image of poverty had been sharpened and accentuated by his tour of West Virginia in the primary campaign of 1960, was equally impressed and endorsed the idea of a major attack on poverty shortly before he was gunned down in Dallas. Within a week after Kennedy's death, President Johnson said, ''That's my kind of program.''[11] In an eloquent message to Congress in early 1964, he declared, ''We are citizens of the richest and most fortunate nation in the history of the world'' but one-fifth of our people ''have not shared in the abundance which has been granted to most of us, and on whom the gates of opportunity have been closed . . . we must strike down all the barriers which keep many from using those which exist. . . . We do this . . . because it is right, because it is wise and because, for the first time in history, it is possible.''

After the program was underway, a goal was set to eliminate poverty in America by 1976—a fitting event to commemorate our bicentennial celebration.

Johnson launched the Organization of Economic Opportunity, with a budget of about $2 billion a year, to coordinate federal, state and local antipoverty activities, evaluate their results, and experiment with new approaches to deal more effectively with the problem. Much of its focus was upon disadvantaged youth (the Jobs Corps, Neighborhood Youth Corps, Operation Headstart, for example), but considerable attention was also given to helping the hard-core unemployed and giving a variety of other forms of assistance to the inner-city poor.

About half of OEO's money went to support Community Action Programs (CAP), which are municipal catch-alls for the preexisting federal, state, and local poverty programs as well as for some newer programs and those of private agencies willing to cooperate with CAP. Although each city was invited to plan, organize, and coordinate its own CAP, which was then to be subsidized by OEO, many cities failed to generate their own plans, relying instead on OEO suggestions.

Initially, programs could be brought under the jurisdiction of either the existing city government *or* relatively autonomous local groups. This led to a great deal of friction; some of the autonomous groups were hostile to the city power structure and sought to mobilize the poor and their allies to ''fight City Hall'' by rent strikes, marches on City Hall, legal suits against welfare restrictions believed illegal or unconstitutional and by pressures for more municipal jobs for ethnic minorities.[12] The mayors bitterly resented these efforts and eventually managed to seize control, much to the dismay of liberal-radical civil rights leaders who felt the established bureaucracy was incapable of the fresh approaches, the enthusiasm, and the energy that a successful program required. The administration tended to support the mayors, since the presence of parallel and overlapping private groups would insure continual infighting and endless confusion. Reliance on the local administrative apparatus, rather than on a new federal administrative structure, meant that local corruption and bumbling would bring unmerited censure on OEO's national officers. This was an inevitable hazard, but preferable to centralized administration of essentially local programs.

The CAPs were to be governed by boards consisting of one-third public officials, one-third private citizens, and one-third from ''the poor or their representatives.'' The latter provision was an OEO interpretation of a statutory provision calling for the ''maximum feasible participation'' of those living in a poverty area.

How were the ''poor or their representatives'' to be selected? This was a puzzle. The OEO attempted to encourage the poor to select their own representatives by organizing elections in poor urban areas. Despite earnest efforts to publicize these elections (at least in some cities), they were abysmal failures. Less than 5 percent of the eligible voters turned out at the polls. Mayors were often obliged to make their own selections; in many cases, local black political activists sought a major voice in their selection. Sar Levitan believes the CAPs made an important contribution in drawing blacks into the ''power structure'' and giving them valuable political experience.[13]

Incidentally, it is always difficult for the poor significantly to affect policymaking at any level. They are generally poorly educated, not very articulate, politically inexperienced, and unsophisticated, and they lack a general ''overview'' of various problems. Levitan believes, however, that the poor have had more influence in the CAPs than elsewhere in government.[14]

Over 1,000 cities established CAPs. Their programs helped the unemployed find jobs or upgrade their job skills, promoted adult literary classes, provided free legal services, assisted the poor in finding better housing or obtaining necessary home repairs, offered consumer counseling and advice on obtaining small loans at reasonable terms, established health centers, and furnished birth control information (hesitantly at first, but more freely as time went on). ''Little City Halls'' were often created at convenient points within the city to help and advise needy persons who felt apprehensive about approaching City Hall itself.

One of the more popular OEO programs was Operation Headstart, designed to help preschool-age children from culturally disadvantaged homes to obtain preschool experiences (under the direction of skilled personnel) which would enable them to enter the first grade on a more even basis with middle-class children.

A Neighborhood Youth Corps was created to finance community jobs for potential or actual high-school dropouts. These were mostly summer jobs, but in some cases part-time jobs were provided during the regular school year so that students tempted to quit school and get a job would have enough spending money to remain in school.

The Job Corps was also a major part of the poverty program. It will be discussed later.

Evaluation of the overall work of the Poverty Program proved exceptionally difficult, since the quality of the CAPs varied from city to city and results were hard to measure. Most observers, however, do not think the program was very successful. One critic called it ''the most successful social welfare program that ever failed.'' There were limited gains here and there, but Operation Headstart proved a disappointment, the Job Corps failed to measure up to expectations, and life for the poor went on much as usual.

Why was the program less than successful? Many reasons have been advanced:

1. The program was drafted in a ''crash'' atmosphere, with numerous ideas hastily amalgamated, rather than carefully winnowed and integrated into a well-thought-out program. The Democrats handed it to the Republicans on a ''take-it-or-leave-it'' basis, creating partisan rancor that persisted for years. Although its first director, Sargent Shriver, was a man of great energy, enthusiasm, and ability, he was probably overanxious to achieve ''measurable'' results which would impress Congress and the voters. The program's potential was oversold to the public; when the results proved more modest than people had been led to expect, disillusion followed.

2. Some believe the OEO was financed too niggardly, since only $1.5 to $2 billion a year was appropriated for it. Others argued, more convincingly, that Congress was ill-advised to pour more money into a program which was yielding such meager results.

3. The quality of CAP administration was often mediocre or worse. The administrative structure in 1,000 cities ranged from excellent to appalling and the performance of the local CAP tended to reflect the level of administrative competence which existed before OEO was created. Some agencies seemed more interested in fighting competitive groups for control of the program than in serving the poor. Richard M. Pious observes that the CAPs ''were little more than a number of separate 'component programs' put together in one binder. It was the rare program that developed those linkages among programs that community action was supposed to facilitate.'' The CAPs, he adds, could have ''become coordinators or social planners if the President had moved vigorously to support such a role. In practice CAP was starved for funds, given more territory to serve than it could handle, and then deserted by politicians who sent it into battle.''[15]

4. The problem is a brutally tough one. The OEO sought to deal with the roots of poverty, rather than with only the symptoms. But as Amitai Etzioni writes:

. . . the pace of achievement in domestic programs ranges chiefly from the slow to the crab-like . . . maybe something even more basic than the lack of funds or will is at stake. . . . We are now confronting the uncomfortable possibility that human beings are not very easily changed after all.[16]

Those who dissent from Etzioni's pessimism are almost invariably those with the least experience in coping with long-standing social problems.

The first Nixon administration had little enthusiasm for the OEO and the poverty program. Greater emphasis was placed on funding various experiments to see what might work. The Job Corps was cut back and other components of the program were administered with a marked lack of enthusiasm.

Eventually Nixon sought to abolish the OEO entirely, while transferring some of its programs to other agencies. The Democrats resisted vociferously; when the Great Recession arrived, however, the War on Poverty was neither discontinued nor fervently supported. Many of its functions had become embedded in the status quo, with bureaucratic maneuvers and pork-barrel appeals playing an increasing role in its survival. (It has now become the Community Services Administration.) The initial excitement and crusading spirit had faded and much of the organization's vitality had ebbed away. The crusade against poverty had stalled, partly because of the immense difficulties involved, partly because of unsympathetic Republican administrations, partly because of Watergate, the energy shortage and the Great Recession, partly because the public was weary of the whole business.

But weary or no, there was no way to avoid continuing concern with certain aspects of the problem. Four prongs of antipoverty strategy deserve special attention: (1) obtaining jobs or better jobs for the unskilled and semiskilled (which most of America's jobless are); (2) obtaining adequate housing for the poor; (3) improving the welfare system; and (4) improving educational opportunities for children of the poor. Although these needs apply to all of the poor, they have special relevance to the black poor in the inner cities. Black families currently earn less than 60 percent as much as white families; while part of this is due to continuing discrimination, most of it exists because blacks are more poorly educated and have fewer labor skills than whites. The problems of black America, in brief, are mostly those of inadequate jobs, inadequate housing, a faulty welfare system, and inadequate education.

NOTES

1. Isaiah 58:7.
2. Nathan Glazer, "The Limits of Social Policy," *Commentary,* September 1971, p. 51.
3. Herbert Gans, *More Equality,* New York, Pantheon Books, 1973, pp. 106–114.
4. Robert J. Lampman, *Ends and Means of Reducing Income Poverty,* Chicago, Markham, 1971, p. 54.
5. James Tobin, "It Can be Done," *New Republic,* June 3, 1967, p. 16.

6. Joseph Epstein, "Dr. Coles Among the Poor," *Commentary,* August 1972, p. 63. Reprinted from *Commentary,* by permission; Copyright © 1972 by the American Jewish Committee.

7. Robert J. Lampman, "What Does it do for the Poor?—A New Test for National Policy," *The Public Interest,* Winter 1974, p. 70.

8. Robert J. Lampman, "Measured Inequality of Income: What Does it Mean and What Can it Tell Us?" *Annals,* September 1973, p. 85.

9. Lampman, *Ends and Means of Reducing Income Poverty,* p. 119.

10. Thomas Halper, "The Poor as Pawns: The New 'Deserving Poor' and the Old," *Polity,* Fall 1973, p. 85.

11. Mark R. Arnold, "The Good War that Might Have Been," *New York Times Magazine,* September 29, 1974, p. 56.

12. Arnold, "The Good War that Might Have Been," p. 61.

13. Sar Levitan, *The Great Society's Poor Law,* Baltimore, Johns Hopkins Press, 1969, p. 114.

14. Levitan, *The Great Society's Poor Law,* p. 116.

15. Richard M. Pious, "The Phony War on Poverty in the Great Society," *Current History,* November 1971, p. 272. Reprinted by permission of the author.

16. Amitai Etzioni, "Human Beings Are Not Very Easy to Change After All," *Saturday Review,* June 3, 1972, p. 45.

2. Jobs for the Unskilled: A New WPA?

For many years, the rate of unemployment has been much higher for the unskilled and the semiskilled than for others. This, combined with the low wages usually paid these workers, has contributed substantially to the volume of poverty in America. The problem may worsen if prophecies prove correct that our recovery from the Great Recession will be incomplete, leaving perhaps 5 to 7 percent of our working force unemployed, compared with the 3 or 4 percent regarded as "normal" by earlier standards. If this rate of joblessness persists, our previously stabilized poverty population of 24 million seems sure to rise. Robert J. Lampman estimates that a 1 percent increase in unemployment increases the number of poor persons by about 1.5 million.[1] With a jobless rate of more than 5 percent, however, a larger proportion of heads of households may become involved, leading to a higher figure than Lampman had calculated.

The demographic facts about the jobless are both interesting and significant. In 1972, studies showed that about one-fourth of the unemployed were teenagers, many seeking only part-time employment. (Teenage unemployment, incidentally, has been steadily increasing. In 1930, it was 150 percent higher than the general level of unemployment; in 1950, it was 250 percent higher; and in 1972, it was 300 percent higher. Among teenage minority members, joblessness is twice as frequent as among white teenagers.) One-third of the jobless were adult women, many of whom were seeking a particular kind of job rather than just any job. All of this points up another important trend: In an affluent society with a tolerably acceptable welfare system, even the unemployed become somewhat choosy about the jobs they take. Many Help Wanted advertisements fail to attract applicants even for relatively unskilled positions, partly because the unskilled often lack job information, partly because of transportation difficulties, but partly because many unskilled workers will not take a job if it pays poorly, offers little opportunity for advancement, or does not represent steady employment.[2] An undetermined number of potential job applicants will not accept jobs paying less than welfare checks. This is a serious aspect of our unemployment problem for which there is no easy solution.

First, a brief review of what has been done for the jobless, then a discussion of proposed alternatives.

During the Depression, the New Deal established the Works Progress Administration (WPA), under which Washington financed local public projects for the unemployed. The WPA built thousands of schools, bridges, and federal buildings throughout the nation. Roads were improved, sidewalks were built or repaired, and numerous other projects were carried out. Because unemployment was so widespread, skilled as well as unskilled labor profited from the programs. Although ridiculed by its critics for boondoggling during the 1930s, the WPA, in retrospect, is believed to have been far preferable to the dole and to have left a substantial legacy of permanent improvement.

When the Poverty Program was launched in 1964, one of its principal features was the Job Corps, which recruited young males (and a few females) between the ages of fourteen and twenty-one, sending them to over 100 urban and rural camps for remedial education, job training, and medical help. The camps were run primarily by private corporations under contract with the federal government. A typical staff consisted of company officials, teachers, retired military men, psychologists, and VISTA volunteers—with an average of one staff member for every three corpsmen.

The youth were given thorough physical examinations; most of them had never been to a doctor or dentist before. Those with remedial defects were then given the necessary medical treatment.

About three hours of each day were devoted to vocational education. The Department of Labor identified jobs with future promise but still within the ability range of these youth: welding, cooking, printing, carpentry, machine repair, operating heavy equipment, and so on. Another three hours were devoted to improving basic educational skills; the educational approach was as closely related to the acquisition of job skills as possible so that maximum interest would be developed.

Recruits were also taught such elementary things as how to introduce themselves, shake hands, dress presentably, apply for a job, and fill out simple forms. The importance of toning down their language during interviews and on the job was explained.

Corpsmen were given modest monthly allowances and a lump-sum terminal pay of $50 for each month of service. Although persons entering the Job Corps probably tended to be better-than-average risks (compared to other poor youngsters), many of them were high-school dropouts. The Job Corps was also plagued with dropout fever; about one-fourth of the recruits stayed less than a month. Less than half stayed for six months, though strongly encouraged to stay for nine months to a year.

As previously indicated, the program was not very successful. The General Accounting Office released a well-researched study early in 1969, which concluded that the cost of the program was about $8,300 per recruit per year and that "it also appeared that the Job Corps terminees had not done materially better than other eligible youths who had applied to enter the program and then chose not to participate."[3] The Nixon administration, though disenchanted with the Job Corps, cut back its operation without terminating it.

The national government has operated a host of manpower training programs, some of which directly aim at the unskilled and the underemployed. In addition to the Job Corps, there was the Manpower Development Program (created during the late 1950s to retrain persons in high unemployment areas and those with obsolete skills) a half-billion dollar vocational rehabilitation program, Operation Mainstream (for chronic jobless rural adults), New Careers (for jobless urban youth), the Work Incentive Program (for jobless welfare mothers), the highly touted JOBS program (Job Opportunities in the Business Sector), and special programs for blacks, Chicanos, Puerto Ricans, Appalachian whites, and Vietnam veterans. Another half-billion dollar program supported vocational education in the high schools. Overall, Washington has been training about a million persons a year at a cost of nearly $2 billion annually.

The JOBS project and vocational education (vo-ed) warrant special attention. After the black riots in 1966 and 1967, the government took a greater interest in the so-called hard-core unemployed—a term which applies to those who have been jobless for a prolonged period. The bulk of these were blacks, and black activists were vigorously demanding more consideration for their needs.

The National Alliance of Business was organized in 1968 when Lyndon Johnson asked Henry Ford II to persuade leading businessmen to organize a recruiting and a training program for the hard-core unemployed in conjunction with a supporting federal agency. Considerable expert opinion held that on-the-job training was more fruitful than governmental programs resembling high school vo-ed for adults. The JOBS program was ultimately intended to put 500,000 of the hard-core unemployed to work (no one knew just how many persons belonged to this category).

Businessmen were told that many jobless do not apply for jobs or do not persist in the search because they (1) lack information about job openings; (2) cannot fill out detailed application forms; (3) cannot pass mathematics and comprehension tests; (4) fail the physical exams; (5) are rejected because of a crime record; or (6) feel the situation is hopeless and have gotten out of the job habit. Companies were urged to go into the slums, to actively seek out the unemployed, and to waive the entrance requirements, except for the most obviously unfit. Once they were on the job, extraordinary efforts would have to be made to keep them there.

Many of the hard-core unemployed who are unaccustomed to regular work seem to have great difficulty getting to work at 8:00 A.M., five days a week. This demands a certain amount of self-discipline, a quality ill-developed by their life experiences. Since America has an estimated 10 million adults who are functional illiterates, many hard-core unemployed cannot read signs well enough to find the plant location, or even such signs as Men's Room, to say nothing of filling out complicated application forms. They may not have alarm clocks or be accustomed to using them. There is a tendency to celebrate the first check with a weekend "blowout," miss work Monday morning, and then decide that there is no use going back because they will probably be fired anyway. If they are sick or have car trouble, they may not think to call and explain; once again, they may not report back, thinking their jobs are gone. Men who have "knocked about" for years tend to do a lot of fighting on the job; gambling in the plant is a constant temptation; female employees are openly propositioned. Thievery rates are high among these employees, and traffic in drugs may become a problem.[4]

Most of the cooperating businessmen have been warned about these problems, and various arrangements have been made for dealing with them. Sometimes a *buddy system* is established; a permanent employee is given responsibility for keeping track of his buddy. Personnel offices and foremen are urged to find out what is wrong if an employee fails to show. The absentee might be called by phone, or after several days a plant official might go to his home and talk things over with him. As with the Job Corps, only about 50 percent of those recruited stayed on the job for six months or more. Over two-thirds of the companies said they believed those who stayed were as productive as their other employees and did not produce more disciplinary problems. But the program shifted from an initial concern with older hard-core jobless to concern with younger workers; the bulk of those hired in the early 1970s were age sixteen to twenty-two.

The economic slowdown during much of the Nixon and Ford administrations seriously hampered the program, since business firms are unable to hire the hard-core unemployed when their own work force is either stabilized or layoffs are taking place.

When James Bryant Conant suggested in 1959 that greater emphasis should be placed on vocational education for disadvantaged slum children,[5] he was greeted with a storm of abuse. Was he trying to relegate black youth to a lifetime of menial labor? Shunting them into vocational education while other children were headed for college and a full share of America's abundance seemed to many a defeatist, if not racist, view.

Dr. Conant seems now to have been closer to the mark than his critics, and not just for slum children (black or white) but for many other youngsters as well. Although we are not "over-educating" our youth in humanistic terms, it is increasingly clear that we are sending more of them to college (including many who have no real taste for the typical academic menu) than we have "prestige" jobs for them to fill. By 1980, the Department of Labor estimates, 80 percent of the jobs will not require a college degree,[6] but well over 40 percent of our young people are going to college. For students who see college as an opportunity to get a liberal education, higher education serves their needs. For those who see college as the key to a well-paying and prestigious job, we may be creating expectations leading to bitter disillusionment. By the early 1970s large numbers of erstwhile college-bound youth, in fact, decided college was not for them after all.

But if college education may not be desirable for as large a percentage of our population as we once thought (since the percentage of students who love learning for its own sake is not phenomenal), a first-rate high school and post-high school vocational education program has become a prime desideratum. We are, however, a long way from that goal. Vocational education has long been the "depressed area" of secondary education, attracting less competent teaching personnel than other fields. Many programs continue obsolete training practices, are sadly underequipped in terms of needed training facilities, and are plagued by an academic snobbery which persists in relegating vo-ed to the bottom of the prestige ladder. Since 1963 Washington has been pouring funds into vo-ed and some schools have established excellent programs, but in general, the improvements seem to be modest. The U.S. Commissioner of Education believes 80 percent of high school students should be getting some vo-ed training—as against 25 percent who are.[7] (The percentage may now be somewhat higher than 25).

Many observers believe work-study programs are preferable to conventional high school vo-ed. They are doubtless correct, but, especially in the larger cities, finding a sufficient number of employers willing to cooperate with this program and to train apprentices in permanently useful skills, arrange the necessary transportation, and administer the program is a truly formidable undertaking.

Most economists believe that the general health of the economy is of greater importance to the unskilled and semiskilled than all the governmental and educational programs combined. An economy which is moving along at a brisk clip automatically stimulates demands for all forms of labor; employers do not need to be urged to hire the less skilled and arrange training programs for them, since it is in their self-interest to do so. But indispensable as this seems, many economists no longer believe it will suffice. An economy which is sufficiently active to absorb the unskilled also makes such demands on skilled and managerial labor and on industrial supplies and consumer goods that inflation surges forward at intolerable levels. Are we trapped, then, in a Scylla and Charybdis dilemma from which there is no escape?

Not necessarily, some writers believe. Economist Melville Ulmer agrees that the national fiscal and monetary policies which could bring full employment (that is, 4 percent unemployment) would also yield an inflation level no administration could tolerate. But rather than accept several million able-bodied persons as permanent casualties of the war on inflation, he has repeatedly proposed a federally financed public service corps to utilize their services.[8] The funds required for this corps would be mildly inflationary but much less so than the overall fiscal stimulus needed to absorb these jobless workers into the private sector of the economy.

Certainly there is ample useful work to be done. The nation has an appalling backlog of railroad bed maintenance work. Environmental work, roadside beautification, street repairs, assistance in hospitals, mental hospitals, nursing homes for the aged, security forces for violence-ridden schools—the list of needed services can be endlessly lengthened.

To keep costs as low as possible, wages might have to be kept (except for supervisory personnel) to about $1000 a year more than a Northern urban family of four on welfare receives. Those who did unsatisfactory work could, of course, be fired. To prevent counties and municipalities from laying off certain employees and rehiring them via this program (at Washington's expense), it might be necessary to stipulate that no one would be eligible for the corps unless he or she had been jobless for, say, four months.

The corps' work would be locally planned and administered. This means that the work programs would be as good and as bad as the quality of local governments tends to be. Undoubtedly there would be waste, mismanagement, poor planning and poor execution of many local projects. Undoubtedly the program would cost more than welfare handouts—a great deal more, in fact. But we now look back upon the WPA of depression days as an agency which built many useful schools, roads, bridges, and public buildings which have served us well for decades; it administered a program which, despite its warts and blemishes, we recognize as infinitely preferable to the dole. If enforced idleness on a major scale becomes a byproduct of inflation control, Ulmer's public service corps will some day be seen as a humane, sensible, and productive alternative to letting people rust and rot in idleness, with all the searing effects that has on people's psyche, identity and family.

What about raising the minimum wage to insure a fair return to the unskilled who find a job? Some writers argue that it is absurd to limit workmen, whether in public or private employment, to wage levels which consign them to poverty despite a year-round work experience. If people are doing work which is socially useful, they deserve a "living wage," it is said. Raising the minimum wage, moreover, would not cost Congress a dime, although the consumer might have to pay somewhat higher prices in some instances.

The editors of *Fortune* commented, "It is hard to think of a single economic-policy issue on which professional opinion is so united as on the minimum wage. Economists all across the political spectrum agree that raising the minimum wage leads to higher unemployment totals."[9]

They cite Paul Samuelson, "What good does it do for a black youth to know that an employer must pay him a minimum wage if the fact that he must be paid that amount is what keeps him from getting a job?" The effort to find mechanized replacements for unskilled labor may be accelerated by raising the minimum wage. It also could lead to a readjustment of the entire wage scale in America. Unions strive to keep an appropriate margin between the income returns of skilled and unskilled labor. When the price of unskilled labor rises, unions seek to raise their members' wages accordingly. So, raising the minimum wage can have an inflationary impact which eventually leaves the lower-income worker at the same proportionate position in the wage hierarchy as he was before.

Edward S. Banfield has proposed that minimum wages be lowered to provide more employment opportunities for teenagers, who presumably suffer most from existing minimum wage levels. Professor Banfield is aware that his proposal is politically unrealistic but believes it to be a valid position nonetheless.[10] In its excellent brochure *Training and Jobs for the Urban Poor,* the Committee for Economic Development suggested ". . . that some differentiation in minimum wage rates be made for the below-20 age group, the aged, and the partially disabled to avoid the real danger that employers will refuse to hire inexperienced or otherwise less productive workers at wages as high as those required for the more experienced and able.[11]

An alternative has been suggested by the highly esteemed economist, Arthur Okun. To encourage the unemployed to take jobs that now offer unattractive wages, he suggests that Washington add a supplementary wage payment to those holding or accepting jobs that presently pay only the legal minimum wage. He would raise the total compensation to a point halfway between the minimum wage and the *median* wage of the American worker.[12] This would add more than a dollar an hour to millions of jobs at a cost of a little over $2 billion per million jobs involved. This would also be a means of reducing poverty by an arrangement that might be politically acceptable to the American people.

The proposal is not without drawbacks, of course. There would be no wage notches between the minimum wage and the median national wage, since no employer would upgrade his workers' wages in that area so long as the government's offer stood. And it would not do much for the inner-city jobless, since the steady exodus of business firms to the suburbs is depleting the inner city of even low-paying jobs. But it is worth a very close look. Whatever encourages the choosy jobless to work, is administratively feasible, alleviates poverty, and is politically appealing as well is a rare jewel indeed.

A few final recommendations for helping the jobless might be noted. The Committee for Economic Development believes too many employers demand high school diplomas for jobs which really do not require this academic achievement. The Civil Service Commission, it is said, also sets educational standards which are largely irrelevant to the performance requirements of many jobs. A more flexible attitude by both private employers and by Washington might prove helpful to the jobless without exacting a price in inefficiency.

Some way might also be found to provide more information to inner-city residents about job opportunities in the suburbs; mass transit facilities should be improved to give inner-city job seekers more adequate access to those jobs.

Some experts believe the Labor Department could develop a computerized *job bank* listing employment opportunities throughout the United States. Citing the example of Sweden, they further suggest that Washington pay the moving expenses of jobless workers wishing to move to areas where jobs are available.

Finally, it is believed that many technical and professional jobs can be subdivided in such a way that the truly professional aspect is isolated from those portions that require less technical training.

Unfortunately, there apparently will be a great deal of "dirty work" to be done in the foreseeable future—jobs that are physically dirty and unpleasant or that historically are regarded as having low prestige and that pay accordingly. When the immigrants were pouring into America, there was so much dirty work to be done that those who did it had lots of company, as well as an expectation that this might well be their fate. But today, as Herbert Gans puts it: "Affluence has created rising standards for job equality and working conditions, and improved communications have made sure that every American, rich or poor, has learned about these standards and applies them to himself. When he must take a dirty job, social and emotional problems are likely to follow."[13]

Everyone wants a good job with a future. Some jobs are unpleasant, have no future, yet they must be done. Considering the extension of the welfare state and the reluctance of unskilled workers to take low-paying jobs without "dignity" in an affluent society, how will the dirty work get done in the years ahead?

NOTES

1. Robert J. Lampman, *Ends and Means of Reducing Income Poverty,* Chicago, Markham, 1971, p. 154.
2. Elliott Liebow, *Tally's Corner,* Boston, Little, Brown, 1967, Chapter 11.
3. New York Times, March 23, 1969, p. 8E. Also see "Controversy over the Federal Job Corps," *Congressional Digest,* January 1968, pp. 13, 27.
4. See Gertrude Samuels, "Help Wanted: The Hard Core Unemployed," *New York Times Magazine,* January 28, 1968; also *New York Times,* January 19, 1969, p. 5E; and "On Hiring the Hard Core Jobless," *U.S. News and World Report,* October 14, 1968.

5. James Bryant Conant, *Slums and Suburbs,* New York, McGraw-Hill, 1961, pp. 44–53.
6. Mary Costello, "Education for Jobs," *Editorial Research Reports,* November 3, 1971, p. 845. Martin Mayer lowers this figure to 13–14 percent in "Growing Up Crowded," *Commentary,* September, 1975, p. 44.
7. Costello, "Education for Jobs," p. 858.
8. Melville Ulmer, "A Workable Program for Economic Stability," *New Republic,* February 22, 1975; "How to Fight Inflation," *Atlantic,* October 1974; "The Pitfalls and Promises of Public Employment," *Challenge,* January–February 1975. For a dissenting view, see Robert I. Lerman, "The Public Employment Bandwagon Takes the Wrong Road," *Challenge,* January–February 1975.
9. "Let's not Raise the Minimum Wage," *Fortune,* July 1972, p. 36. The editors of *New Republic* say, "Most economists concede increases result in some job cutbacks and a few business failures. But in every instance there has been less economic disruption than critics expected." (January 29, 1972, p. 7.)
10. Edward S. Banfield, *The Unheavenly City,* Boston, Little, Brown, 1968, p. 245.
11. Committee for Economic Development, *Training and Jobs for the Urban Poor,* July 1970, p. 17.
12. *Wall Street Journal,* August 8, 1975, p. 29.
13. Herbert Gans, "Income Grants and 'Dirty Work,'" *The Public Interest,* Winter 1967, p. 111.

3. The Black Ghettos: Experiments, Illusions, Hopelessness

About 20 million people, living in 6 million households, occupy shelter that falls below the standards of decency in our society. Some have no indoor toilets or share them with other families; some have no running water in the house; some live in buildings or shacks beyond repair.

The percentage of substandard homes has been declining steadily since 1940, when the census found almost half of American homes in this category. A prolonged housing boom after World War II met the needs of the American middle class reasonably well but left the nation's poor more ill-housed than our resources justify.

Anthony Downs sees the problem in this light:

Most Americans have no conception of the filth, degradation, squalor, over-crowding, and personal danger and insecurity which millions of inadequate housing units are causing in both our cities and rural areas. Thousands of infants are attacked by rats each year; hundreds die or become mentally retarded from eating lead paint that falls off cracked walls; thousands more are ill because of unsanitary conditions resulting from jamming large families into a single room, continuing failure of landlords to repair plumbing or provide proper heat, and pitifully inadequate storage space. Until you have actually stumbled through the ill-lit and decaying rooms of a slum dwelling, smelled the stench of sewage and garbage and dead rats behind the walls, seen the roaches and crumbling plaster and incredibly filthy bathrooms, and recoiled from exposed wiring and rotting floorboards and staircases, you have no idea of what bad housing is like. These miserable conditions are not true of all inadequate housing units, but enough Americans are trapped in the hopeless desolation of such surroundings to constitute both a scandal and a serious economic and social drag in our affluent society.[1]

Many factors account for our poor record in meeting the housing needs of low-income families:

1. Especially in recent years, the price of land has soared, partly because of the population boom and partly because property tax practices encourage land speculation. This makes building an expensive operation for everyone.

2. Construction costs are also high. The average hourly wage for *all* construction workers in 1975 was about $11 an hour, with the figure running higher in larger cities.

3. There are over 5,000 separate building codes in America, often requiring outmoded construction practices and restricting the use of new

technology and new materials. How do you mass-produce housing for low-income families if it must meet the requirements of over 5,000 highly detailed building codes?

4. American inventiveness has not been applied to housing construction as fully as to other industrial areas. We spend about $15–$20 million a year on housing research, compared, for example, to $250 million for agricultural research. Only in mobile home construction has fabled American know-how been given free rein.

The decentralized character of the housing industry acts as a deterrent to major investment in research. "Large scale" in this industry refers to companies which produce more than 100 housing units annually; the largest conventional-type builder in the nation turns out only one-third of 1 percent of total national production. Small producers can not afford to invest heavily in research.

5. Mortgage credit money has not been available in steady and ample amounts for the housing industry in general and for low-income buyers in particular. During periods of special concern about inflation, Washington tends to crack down on such credit as a means of promptly reducing inflationary spending pressures. Turning the mortgage credit spigot off and on from time to time does not prevent the more affluent from building, but it does adversely affect the building and buying plans of lower-income groups.

6. Almost two-thirds of our inadequate housing is in rural and semi-rural areas. These dwellings, being scattered, attract little attention. If they were concentrated, as in urban slums, greater public efforts would doubtlessly be made to deal with them. ". . . Rural poor live cheaply in substandard housing and urban poor pay dearly for standard housing."[2]

7. In recent years slum owners often have let their property deteriorate because that property is not very profitable. Contrary to popular belief, "slumlords" usually do not make much money. Their returns on investment are lower than those of most other investments: Operating costs are high; repairs are costly; insurance is expensive; vandalism is often appalling; and property taxes have risen sharply. Rehabilitation costs being as expensive as they are, they must be followed by higher rents, which the poor often cannot afford to pay. As a result, mass deterioration of our poorer housing stock is occurring. Worse yet, thousands of slum dwellings that could be rehabilitated are instead being abandoned annually.

8. Better housing is a fairly low priority item for most low-income people. Even though housing construction credit terms are liberal, the poor often prefer other comforts, conveniences, or pleasure to expending their limited income on improved housing. Not that they *like* poor housing, but apparently they tolerate it more readily than they do other aspects of poverty.

Better housing for low-income families is not a high priority item for Congress either. Although it has been chipping away at the problem for decades, it does not give it the sustained attention and support that other problems often receive. Schussheim writes, "Time and again, what the Congress has given, the Congress has taken away by cutting appropriations for programs such as rent supplements, Model Cities, and administration of the fair housing law. No ground swell of reaction rose from the country to protest these cuts. Americans, it would appear, are not at all convinced about the priority of such programs."[3]

One of the first major national efforts to provide low-income housing came in 1949. One of the principal authors of that effort, Senator Robert A. Taft, Sr., was a conservative who would move left if the facts were sufficiently compelling. After a long and careful study of the subject, he concluded reluctantly that the private enterprise system could not supply satisfactory housing for low-income families. Joining with Senator Robert Wagner, Sr., (of the famous Wagner Labor Act) and Senator Allen Ellender of Louisiana, he helped shape and push through the Housing Act of 1949, designed to produce 810,000 low-income housing units within six years.

Twenty years later the nation was still considerably short of meeting the goal. Why? A conservative coalition of Southern Democrats and Republicans controlled Congress from 1946 to 1964, and it had little stomach for public housing. With machine-like regularity, it limited public housing to 35,000 units per year. During his years in the presidency, Eisenhower seldom prodded Congress very vigorously, and low-income housing was far down on his list of priorities. Public housing gradually became a dirty word as stories circulated about the abuses committed in, and on, it by semibarbaric inhabitants. When a renewed interest in low-income housing reappeared in the Johnson years, the Vietnam war blocked serious action.

URBAN RENEWAL, PUBLIC HOUSING, ET AL.

The story of low-income housing from 1954 to 1962 was largely the story of urban renewal. The Housing Act of 1949 was amended in 1954 to incorporate the concepts of rehabilitation and *blight prevention*. Instead of replying exclusively on slum clearance, public housing, or both, the Republican administration sought to rehabilitate as many salvageable neighborhoods as possible and to prevent declining areas from deteriorating further into slums. The latter was to be accomplished in part by granting federally guaranteed loans at low-interest rates to home owners who might otherwise be unable to obtain such loans from private banks. Urban redevelopment, however, was to be the major thrust of the revised housing policy. Under the urban renewal program, cities drew up de-

tailed programs for renovating their slums, programs that included rehabilitation of slum housing where this seemed feasible, low-interest
loans to encourage home repairs, demolition of houses which had deteriorated irreparably, public housing projects to provide shelter for those
displaced by slum clearance (unless adequate housing could be found for
them elsewhere in the city). Community improvements such as better
streets, storm sewers, better lighting systems, parks, new schools, and so
forth were authorized for redeveloped areas so that they would not rapidly revert to slums again. Washington would supply most of the money
—once local plans met federal requirements—and the municipalities
would foot the rest of the bill.

The urban renewal program was not limited to meeting the needs of
low-income groups. It could be used to spruce up decaying downtown
shopping areas or to build on the site of a former slum a new shopping
center, an industrial park to attract new industry and jobs, parks and
playgrounds, or luxury apartments to attract high-income groups back
into the cities from the suburbs. As things developed, urban renewal
provided relatively minor help for low-income people and a great deal of
help for commercial interests within the cities.

Urban renewal came under sharp attack from both the left and the
right. One of the most potent assaults came from Martin Anderson. In
The Federal Bulldozer, Anderson drew together and documented virtually all of the attacks on the program.[4] He accused it of engaging in
"Negro removal," that is, of being used by middle-class people as a respectable way of getting poor, unwanted Negroes out of sight. Washington, he charged, had a "bulldozer mentality" that preferred to raze large
areas rather than rehabilitate as many homes as possible. The program
ruthlessly uprooted neighborhoods against the wishes of their residents
and callously ignored the rich network of human relationships that had
made the area a true community despite external appearances. For many
inhabitants, urban renewal was a traumatic experience, forcing them to
leave old friends and cherished scenes and start life anew among strang-
ers. Displaced persons received little help, whatever the government's
claims. Often they were forced out of one slum only to enter or create
another. Their new rents were usually higher than those they had been
paying, though they preferred their previous homes. The cities concerned
suffered heavy losses of tax revenue because so much taxable property
was destroyed; it took ten to twelve years, moreover, to complete a project. The public housing projects that were sometimes built on the site of
the previous slums were drab, depressing, box-like affairs. Worst of all,
urban renewal had destroyed more low-cost housing than it built.

Anderson wrote a polemic rather than a balanced study. Because it
was a carefully researched work, however, it seems to have had a considerable impact on urban renewal.

Public housing, which rents to low-income families at subsidized rates, accommodates about 2.5 million persons. It is generally viewed with distaste these days, partly because of the bleak and cheerless appearance of the old high-rise apartment complexes, the institutional atmosphere that tends to prevail, the dismal vicinity in which public housing projects are forced by public pressure to be located, and the high development costs. Mostly, however, public housing has fallen into disrepute because it has attracted a large number of broken families on welfare. As Roger Starr, former executive director of New York's Citizen Housing and Planning Council put it, "It is the fatherless households that cause the most vandalism, are responsible for the greatest amount of crime, both on the streets and inside the housing projects."[5]

Starr says that as long as public housing catered to the working poor, projects were reasonably successful. But when project directors began taking in broken families on welfare (unless careful prior investigation showed them to be good risks), the conditions popularly associated with public housing began to multiply. Crime increased, vandalism flourished, yards were littered with debris, people urinated in the halls and on the stairs, rowdiness grew, and a generally depressing atmosphere appeared. The working-class poor, who bitterly resented the influx of welfare families, began moving out. The outstanding example of public housing disaster occurred in St. Louis, where the famous Pruitt-Igoe project was launched in 1954 as a model of public housing design, construction, and management. By the early 1970s, however, the project was such a shambles that it had to be abandoned.

Starr is of the opinion that public housing will continue to lack public support as long as a high percentage of problem families enter these projects. With 15 million people on welfare and less than a million public housing units available, obviously only a small proportion of welfare families can live in these units.

Starr remains convinced that "without federally subsidized, publicly owned low-rent housing, there is simply no way of providing widespread decent homes for the American urban poor in their own life time, a statement provoked by a hundred years' history of practical experimentation with such hybrid alternatives as nonprofit ownership, highly subsidized cooperatives, or limited-dividend sponsorship."[6] He is also convinced that unless public housing directors have and exercise the authority to select and/or retain only those low-income families who are willing to abide by standards of civilized conduct, public housing is doomed. Some families would wreck the livable qualities of *any* neighborhood, whether public housing were involved or not.

It is true, moreover, that while high-rise apartments have given public housing a bad name, about 80 percent of all such housing isn't high-rise. Public housing, it should also be noted, operates with greater respect for tenants' rights than private housing. Under existing federal law, public housing tenants have a right to a fair hearing before eviction, to rent abatement if substandard conditions should appear, and to greater privacy, since there are limits on the landlords' rights of entry.[7] (Whether the *due process* eviction process unduly curbs the prerogative of the local housing manager to dispose of trouble-making families is a critical question, however.) Of course, it will remain nearly impossible to place new projects in desirable locations, and Washington is unwilling, in an age of inflation, to finance major additions to our public housing stock.

President Johnson called the Housing and Urban Development Act of 1968 "the most farsighted, the most comprehensive, the most massive housing program in all American history." It contemplated the construction of 6 million new or rehabilitated housing units for low- and moderate-income families over a ten-year period, as well as 20 million other housing units in the 1970s. If the target were met (it won't be), the housing problem would be virtually solved. Several interesting and ingenious proposals were incorporated into the act. To stimulate home ownership by low-income families, Congress authorized a system of down payments running as low as $200, with the federal government paying all mortgage interest in excess of 1 percent. The purchaser would be required to pay at least 20 percent of his gross income on his total home payments. To be eligible for the subsidy, the applicant's income could be no more than several thousand dollars a year beyond the poverty level, or somewhat higher in high-cost areas or for persons with large families. The average beneficiary of the program was paying only slightly more from his own pocket each month than Washington was paying. The subsidy declined as a family's income rose and stopped altogether if 20 percent of its income would meet the full mortgage payment. The program (Section 235) was an imaginative and bold attempt to help people whose incomes made them ineligible for public housing but whose earnings were insufficient to enable them to find decent housing in the conventionally financed housing market.

A second provision of the act (Section 236) enabled builders agreeing to construct apartment units for low-income families to receive federal subsidies covering borrowing costs above 1 percent interest. This enabled them to offer comparatively low rental rates.

In terms of sheer volume, Sections 235 and 236 were spectacularly successful. After years of limping along on 30,000 to 35,000 new public housing starts per year, these programs produced more publicly assisted housing (over 1 million units) in three years than public housing had provided in thirty years.

But, alas, all was not well. Under Section 235, builders were finding it more profitable to service persons with incomes close to the maximum allowable ceilings; those in the lower income range were still waiting for their ship to dock.[8] Many of those served by the program found that payment of the principal, utilities, and maintenance costs was more than they could manage. Foreclosure rates were high and rising; Washington was obliged to take possession of so many foreclosed properties that its landlord (slumlord?) role was reaching sobering dimensions.[9] Nor were all the homes as well-constructed or as fairly appraised as they should have been. Unscrupulous builders, real-estate operators, appraisers, and credit-rating companies often took advantage of inexperienced buyers in a scandalous fashion. *Business Week* said the Federal Housing Administration had "become entangled in shocking scandals, sickening waste of public funds, widespread ineptness, dishonesty, and greed."[10] Householders with incomes just above the income ceiling were often bitter because *they* were receiving no housing aid even though they saw themselves as equally deserving. Disillusioned Secretary of Housing and Urban Development George Romney concluded that the problem was far more complex and intractable than he had imagined.

Dissatisfaction with these programs, as well as with public housing, caused the Republican administrations of Presidents Nixon and Ford to turn to housing allowances as a possible workable alternative. This program would seek to identify vacant but standard housing renting at low to moderately low rates and to make this housing available to low-income families living in substandard dwellings. Washington would pay the difference between a percentage of the renter's income and a fair rental price. The advantages were believed to be these:

1. Why build public housing or subsidize Section 235 or 236 housing if adequate private units are available and vacant? This would give the poor taxpayer a break!

2. Compared to public housing options, the low-income family would have a wider range of choice. It could select the private housing which best suits its income, needs and tastes rather than be limited to what a public-housing project had to offer.

3. Low income families could escape a ghetto environment by locating in an area with access to good schools and a more attractive general environment. Since their new neighbors would not know that they were the beneficiaries of subsidized rent, they would not encounter the antagonism experienced by persons from public housing or low-income housing projects. Rather than being segregated (by race or income), the poor could often blend inconspicuously into their improved environment. And their children would have the advantages of a better peer-group climate, better schools, parks, playgrounds, and so on.

4. It would be more administratively efficient. The beneficiary of the housing allowance would seek out his or her own housing and pay the rent directly to the landlord. The government's only job would be to inspect the preferred dwelling to insure it met minimum hous-standards, ascertain a fair rent and ante up the appropriate monthly subsidy.

5. The program would help the poor in small towns and rural areas now not served by local housing authorities. Almost half of the poor live in such areas.

6. It would be considerably less expensive.[11]

Problems? Of course. The biggest, say the critics, are that most cities don't have enough vacant, standard housing to meet the need. It may work reasonably well in some cities, therefore, but it is inadequate for a national program. Critics also fear that maladministration of the program will lead to tenants being charged excessive rents and to landlords failing to make necessary repairs.[12] Just how well the plan will work is unclear but in conjunction with other programs, in areas that lack vacant housing, it could be an improvement over previous policies.

Another plan, which although insufficient by itself might prove helpful, is the so-called *urban homestead* plan. In 1862 the federal Homestead Act offered 160 acres of land to anyone agreeing to cultivate it for at least five years. Today, with half of our 1 million abandoned houses suitable for rehabilitation at a feasible cost, some cities are offering these homes to anyone who agrees to bring them up to minimum standards and to live in them for three to five years.[13] Tax abatement for a period of years and assurance of rehabilitation loans for promising applicants help make the offer still more attractive. Where applicants exceed the number of available houses, a lottery is held to determine the winners.

Not every family living in substandard housing has the qualifications necessary for the program, and fatherless families would rarely be able to take advantage of it. In many instances, however, applicants will be able to take a house off the city's hands, bring it up to snuff, and markedly improve their housing at little cost to the city. At the same time they will be upgrading a neighborhood which had been marred by a deteriorated vacant dwelling.

Some writers, including Martin Anderson, frankly prefer a "trickle-down" housing policy.[14] Let private builders, perhaps aided by Federal Housing Administration (FHA) and Veterans Administration (VA) financing, build an ample supply of homes for middle- and lower-middle-class families. As these families move into new or newer homes, they will vacate dwellings that, though not of the highest quality, are quite suitable for lower-income families—and at prices they can usually afford to pay. This, proponents say, is the traditional way lower-income housing needs have been met and the most sensible way. It avoids bureaucratic entanglements and governmental intrusion into an area in which government seems incapable of functioning effectively. This method, distasteful though liberals find it, has succeeded in reducing substandard housing in the United States from 37 percent of the families in 1950 to 19 percent in 1960 to 10 percent in 1970. Partisans of this approach believe that is no mean accomplishment.

Some housing students believe that our 25,000 trailer camps will become the slums of the future. With new single family dwellings costing so much that a heavy majority of Americans are unable to afford them, more and more workers are turning to mobile homes. But the relatively rapid deterioration of these structures sets the stage for slum development on a troubling scale in the years just ahead.

BREAKING OUT OF THE GHETTO

Adequate housing for the poor is more than bricks and mortar; it means housing in a good location fit to raise a family and accessible to employment opportunities and good schools. Only thus, perhaps, can the *cycle of poverty* be broken. The problem has special pertinence to the black community, located as so many blacks are in the inner-city ghetto. Breaking out of this dismal environment is becoming a major goal for thoughtful black leaders.

Realistic observers agree that *ghetto renewal*, as a means of improving the condition of poor blacks, is not a promising approach. While modest improvements can and doubtless will be made in some inner-city areas, the ghetto cannot be substantially rehabilitated unless it has a solid economic base. That base is steadily eroding as the industrial exodus to the suburbs gains momentum.

Not only is new enterprise shunning the inner city, but corporations are leaving at an alarming rate. The reasons are easily found: Land values are high; the costs of razing slum dwellings and replacing them with factories is absolutely prohibitive; and unused land space is not available. Taxes are higher in the inner city than in the suburbs; the labor force is largely unskilled or semiskilled; vandalism abounds in the ghetto, and insurance rates reflect this fact. Suburban executives dislike commuting to the inner city when transportation arteries are so highly congested. Businessmen also prefer to place a new plant in the pleasant, green, spacious milieu of the suburb rather than in the bleak and ugly surroundings of the ghetto. As for black entrepreneurs, they lack both the capital and the experience to do the job on the necessary scale. In sum, there is little chance that enough jobs can be created within the ghetto, despite strenuous public and private efforts. Too many economic and sociological forces run in the opposite direction.

As long as blacks live primarily in the ghetto, moreover, they are likely to be poorly informed about suburban job opportunities. In any case, transportation costs to the suburbs are high. Also, a ghetto renewal strategy might worsen race relations in America by freezing residential housing patterns in de facto segregated fashion. The only solution for many of the most serious black problems, then, appears to be an escape from the ghetto.

For middle-income blacks, the exodus goes steadily forward; about 800,000 blacks moved to suburban America between 1960 and 1970. Although discrimination still hampers black entry into many suburbs, suburbanites' resistance to middle-class blacks seems to be declining. But their hostility to the entrance of lower-class blacks (and whites) remains unabated. The bitter opposition of Forest Hills, New York, a largely Jewish middle-class community (and hence presumably liberal), to the construction of three 24-story apartments for 840 low-income families disabused many idealists of any illusions that middle-class America was prepared to welcome the poor into its midst. Similar developments elsewhere reinforced the point. Utilizing zoning laws that regulate the size of lots or specify acceptable levels of population density and building codes that require fairly costly materials, suburbs all over the nation dug in to repel an "invasion" by "undesirable" elements.[15] The middle-class "territorial imperative" overrides all other considerations.

It is easy to dismiss this opposition as just another manifestation of how deeply racist our society is, but this would be a simplistic and largely inaccurate interpretation. When considerable numbers of poor enter a community, the cost of providing them with municipal services (water mains, sewage lines, streets, police, and fire protection) is much larger than the taxes they will pay. (These costs run from $5000 to $7000 per housing unit.) There is also the not-groundless fear that the poor (especially poor blacks, whose rate of criminality is undeniably high) will bring more crime and hard drugs into the community. The impact on property values is also viewed with apprehension; whereas the entry of middle-class blacks into a middle-class white community will not necessarily reduce property values, the presence of low-income subdivisions or public housing projects inhabited by either whites or blacks can have that effect. At bottom, it seems, the antagonism to lower-income neighbors rests upon that most ubiquitous of social phenomena—class consciousness. Each social class wants to live among "its own kind of people." It is eager to maintain some social distance between it and the class just beneath it. "Success," for most Americans, means living in a community with nice homes, well-kept lawns and shrubbery, good and physically attractive schools, pleasant parks, and clean streets. In part, middle-class consciousness is snobbery, pure and simple—the desire for status symbols that denote success and for ego satisfaction deriving from associating with other successful people. But in part, it also represents a perfectly normal desire to live in pleasant and attractive surroundings with people whose social customs, mores, and values are roughly similar to one's own.

That middle-class resentment of lower-class penetration is not just disguised racial prejudice is proved beyond reasonable doubt by the fact that a middle-class black community is as repelled by the prospect of a lower-class black "invasion" as are middle-class whites.[16] Blacks are by no means indifferent to the behavioral characteristics and status implications of class.

Ideally, no doubt, middle-class residents should regard incoming lower-class people as innocent until proved guilty, as eager to better themselves and to take full advantage of the superior opportunities which a middle-class community provides. If some lower-class people behave differently, manifesting less concern for appearances than middle-class people do, doubtless the latter should be tolerant, understanding, and willing to induct them into their own folkways by gradual stages.

In utopia, this picture surely would be found. In reality, however, it is normal for people to behave like people. Politicians and social planners cannot expect citizens to be more altruistic than they are, to forego normal aspirations, tastes, and prejudices because of their commitment to abstract principles of moral excellence.

Having conceded this, it remains true that it is society's obligation to persuade its more fortunate members to give the less fortunate better opportunities to improve the conditions under which their children are raised. This bring us back again to life in the ghetto—an environment which must be heartbreaking, indeed, for responsible parents. In the ghetto, family discipline breaks down at an appallingly early age. The congested conditions are conducive to the formation of street gangs that prepare young men for the life of a drifter, hustler, or criminal. Aggressive and violent behavior by young blacks is the customary life-style. Petty theft often begins at an early age. Drug addiction is widespread, often acquired in the early teens. The high cost of drugs accelerates the drift toward crime. Gambling is omnipresent. Sexual practices are conditioned by life in the street; venereal disease begins early and illegitimacy is the norm. Learning to live by one's wits is an art highly prized, but living by one's wits involves skills and behavior patterns radically different from those essential to success in the plant or office. Finally, health services are inadequate, and ghetto schools are markedly inferior to suburban schools.

Getting black children out of this cruel environment should be the highest priority of those who seek black progress. The training ghetto children receive in a life-style that is crippling to their economic, social, and moral prospects is the most formidable obstacle the black race now faces in America.

The task may be insoluble; certainly it will be unless we squarely face and firmly reject the view, cherished by so many liberals, that all of the poor are equally interested in social betterment and equally capable of taking advantage of better opportunities.

Edward S. Banfield effectively attacks this view. He believes that many members of the lower class are unlikely to respond favorably to an improved environment. To Banfield, ''class'' does not have the characteristics commonly associated with it—in terms of education, income, and status. A person's class, rather, is determined by one's '' (1) ability to imagine a future, and (2) ability to discipline one's self to sacrifice present for future satisfaction. The more distant the future the individual can imagine and can discipline himself to make sacrifices for, the 'higher' is his class.''[17]

Banfield's description of the lower class is as follows:

The lower-class individual lives from moment to moment. If he has any awareness of a future, it is of something fixed, fated, beyond his control: things happen to him, he does not make them happen. Impulse governs his behavior, either because he cannot discipline himself to sacrifice a present for a future satisfaction or because he has no sense of the future. He is therefore radically improvident: Whatever he cannot consume immediately he considers valueless. His bodily needs (especially for sex) and his taste for "action"[18] take precedence over everything else, and certainly over any work routine. He works only as he must to stay alive and drifts from one unskilled job to another, taking no interest in the work.

The lower-class individual has a feeble, attenuated sense of self; he suffers from feelings of self-contempt and inadequacy and is often apathetic or defected. (In her discussion of "very low-lower class" families, Eleanor Pavenstadt notes that "the saddest, and to us the outstanding characteristic of this group, with adults and children alike, was the self-devaluation."[19] In his relations with others he is suspicious and hostile, aggressive yet dependent. He is unable to maintain a stable relationship with a mate; commonly he does not marry. He feels no attachment to community, neighbors, or friends (he has companions, not friends), resents all authority (for example, that of policemen, social workers, teachers, landlords, and employers), and is apt to think that he has been "railroaded" and to want to "get even." He is a nonparticipant: he belongs to no voluntary organizations, has no political interests, and does not vote unless paid to do so.

The lower-class household is usually female-based. The woman who heads it is likely to have a succession of mates who contribute intermittently to its support but take little or no part in rearing the children. In managing the children, the mother (or aunt, or grandmother) is characteristically impulsive: once they have passed babyhood they are likely to be neglected or abused, and at best they never know what to expect next. A boy raised in a female-based household is likely at an early age to join a corner gang of other such boys and to learn from the gang the "tough" style of the lower-class man.[20]

The stress on "action," risk-taking, conquest, fighting, and "smartness" makes lower-class life extraordinarily violent. However, much of the violence is probably more an expression of mental illness than of class culture. The incidence of mental illness is greater in the lower class than in any of the others. Moreover, the nature of lower-class culture is such that much behavior that in another class could be considered bizarre seems routine.[21]

In its emphasis on "action" and its utter instability, lower-class culture seems to be more attractive to men than to women. Gans writes:

The woman tries to develop a stable routine in the midst of poverty and deprivation; the action-seeking man upsets it. In order to have any male relationships, however, the woman must participate to some extent in his episodic life style. On rare occasions, she may even pursue it herself. Even then, however, she will try to encourage her children to seek a routine way of life. Thus the woman is much closer to working-class culture, at least in her aspirations, although she is not often successful in achieving them.[22]

The lower-class individual lives in the slum and sees little or no reason to complain. He does not care how dirty and dilapidated his housing is either inside or out, nor does he mind the inadequacy of such public facilities as schools, parks, and libraries. Indeed, where such things exist he destroys them by acts of vandalism if he can. Features that make the slum repellent to others actually please him. He finds it satisfying in several ways. First, it is a place of excitement—"where the action is." Nothing happens there by plan, and anything may happen by accident—a game, a fight, a tense confrontation with the police. Feeling that something exciting is about to happen is highly congenial to people who live for the present and for whom the present is often empty. Second, it is a place of opportunity. Just as some districts of the city are specialized as a market for, say, jewelry or antiques, so the slum is specialized as one for vice and for illicit commodities generally. Dope peddlers, prostitutes, and receivers of stolen goods are all readily available there, within easy reach of each other and of their customers and victims. Third, it is a place of concealment. A criminal is less visible to the police in the slum than elsewhere, and the lower-class individual, who in some parts of the city would attract attention, is one among many there. In the slum one can beat one's children, lie drunk in the gutter, or go to jail without attracting any special notice; these are things that most of the neighbors themselves have done and that they consider quite normal.[23]

Banfield concludes:

So long as the city contains a sizable lower class, nothing basic can be done about its most serious problems. Good jobs may be offered to all, but some will remain chronically unemployed. Slums may be demolished, but if the housing that replaces them is occupied by the lower class it will shortly be turned into new slums. Welfare payments may be doubled or tripled and a negative income tax instituted, but some persons will continue to live in squalor and misery. New schools may be built, new curricula devised, and the teacher-pupil ratio cut in half, but if the children who attend these schools come from lower-class homes, they will be turned into black-board jungles, and those who graduate or drop out from them will, in most cases, be functionally illiterate. The streets may be filled with armies of policemen, but violent crime and civil disorder will decrease very little. If, however, the lower class were to disappear—if, say its members were overnight to acquire the attitudes, motivations, and habits of the working class— the most serious and intractable problems of the city would all disappear with it.[24]

Banfield concedes that he might be wrong:

It may turn out that the lower class . . . does not exist (that whatever present orientedness exists is neither cultural in origin nor cognitive in nature) or that it exists among so few persons as to be inconsequential. Moreover, no matter what tests show, time may tell a different story. Powerful opportunities and incentives may over two or three generations produce changes that theory and observation now declare to be impossible.[25]

But he is convinced that a significant number of lower-class persons (by his definition) will be with us for a long time to come and that society should realistically take this into account.

Banfield's tentative theory has been attacked with almost unparalleled ferocity by many academics.[26] In the debate which has raged since the publication of *The Unheavenly City,* however, the writer believes Professor Banfield has held his own.

The implications for housing policy are obvious. If lower-income people are to be resettled in suburban areas, they must be chosen in such a manner that high-risk families are "selected out." If, as seems reasonable to the author, most of the poor are eager and able to make the most of better economic and social opportunities, but a minority of the poor are so mired in crippling attitudes and patterns of social behavior that they are currently unredeemable, then the latter must not be permitted to blight the prospects of the former. If all of the poor are to be treated alike, whatever their record of behavior, all will face the unyielding hostility of a middle class determined to protect its communities from unwelcome invaders.

In Rockford, Illinois, a housing plan based on somewhat similar premises has proven highly successful. Modest new homes ($16,000–$19,000) were provided for over 200 poor families (30 percent black), with the incoming poor agreeing to pay 22 percent of their monthly incomes over twenty-five years. The families were selected with care and obliged to attend classes explaining how to keep their homes in good condition. Inspections occurred from time to time to insure that the residents were adhering to normal maintenance practices. (Almost uniformly, they were.) Despite initial anger and apprehension by Rockford residents, the program has worked so well that the city is planning to add more single-family units.[27]

Whether such a program would work in larger metropolitan areas is another question. Clearly, it would be much more difficult in cities like

New York, Chicago, Philadelphia, Washington, D.C., and St. Louis. In this problem area, the nation seems to have two choices: (1) It can hope that the processes of time will slowly iron out the prodigious and seemingly irremediable problems created by inner city areas with grim economic prospects in which the street atmosphere is destructive to the young, or (2) it can institute a massive resettlement program for good-risk families—one enabling responsible parents both to improve their economic conditions and to raise their children in an environment more conducive to the development of mental, emotional, and physical health. Immense though the practical difficulties would be in identifying the families eligible for resettlement (perhaps black communities could establish their own criteria), finding appropriate places for them to go (creating New Towns, perhaps?)[28] and coping with the problems aggravated by their exodus, those difficulties seem almost insignificant compared with the incredible human havoc now being wrought by inner-city conditions that no middle-class parents would dream of tolerating if it were *their* environment. For every objection one can raise, the alternative of continuing the current disgrace is surely more objectionable. How can we condemn millions of decent people and their children to existence in the economically suffocating and morally debilitating atmosphere of the big-city, inner-city environment if there is any other way?[29]

In wartime, we learn we can do extraordinary things which would normally be dismissed as impractical or visionary. The need for a profound national commitment—one akin to that engendered by a just war —to do everything that can be done to deal effectively with this problem has to be one of our most imperative needs. And one of the sure tests of whether we are embarking on something that *might* be effective is: Does it take the breath away? If it doesn't, it probably isn't daring or imaginative enough to do the job.

We must reemphasize that there seems to be no—repeat no—feasible method of renovating either the economic or social milieu of many big-city, inner-city areas. The best minds in the nation have been baffled by the task. And the departure to the suburbs of the most promising families is proceeding at a far slower pace than we should find acceptable. Finally, if something like this is not done, the nation will pay a horrendous price in crime, riots, drug abuse, vandalism, decaying schools, welfare costs, and the moral and emotional wreckage of millions of people. Even though the proposed program would be very, very costly (Somehow we endure *any* financial burdens to fight our wars!), the true cost would be far less than the course we are following.

Of course we will do no such thing. We will not even raise it to the level of discussion. We will try to ignore the problem instead. When we can ignore it no longer we will deplore it, wring our hands, or propose superficial remedies that fit our propensity to "think small" where war or moon shots are not involved. That's the way we are. But what a magnificent thing it would be if we gave millions of people, hopelessly mired in desperately depressing conditions, a fresh start and fresh hope. *That* would be worthy of the best that is in us.

NOTES

1. Anthony Downs, "Moving Toward Realistic Housing Goals," in Kermit Gordon, ed., *Agenda for the Nation,* © 1968 by The Brookings Institution, Washington, D.C., p. 142.
2. Gurney Breckenfeld, "Housing Subsidies Are a Grand Delusion," *Fortune,* February 1972, p. 163.
3. Morton J. Schussheim, *Toward a New Housing Policy,* Committee on Economic Development Supplementary Paper #29, New York, 1969, p. 61.
4. Martin Anderson, *The Federal Bulldozer,* Cambridge, Massachusetts, MIT Press, 1964. See also Herbert Gans, *The Urban Villagers,* New York, Free Press, 1962; Jane Jacobs, *The Death and Life of Great American Cities,* New York, Random House, 1961; and Scott Greer, *Urban Renewal and American Cities,* Indianapolis, Bobbs-Merrill, 1966.
5. Roger Starr, "Which of the Poor Shall Live in Public Housing?," *The Public Interest,* Spring 1971, pp. 117–118. Reprinted by permission.
6. Roger Starr, *The Living End: The City and Its Critics,* New York, Coward, McCann & Geoghegan, 1966, pp. 88–89.
7. Chester Hartman and Dennis Keating, "The Housing Allowance Delusion," *Social Policy,* January–February 1974, pp. 36–37.
8. Irving Welfeld, "That 'Housing Problem,'" *The Public Interest,* Spring 1972, pp. 83–84, and Robert Sherrill, "The Black Humor of Housing," *Nation,* March 29, 1971. Abraham Ribicoff says the average beneficiary of the 1968 housing act had an income of $6,200. ("The Alienation of the American Worker," *Saturday Review,* April 22, 1972, p. 31.)
9. Sherrill, "The Black Humor of Housing," p. 401.
10. "The Bankruptcy of Subsidized Housing," *Business Week,* May 27, 1972, p. 42. Also see Ken Hartnett, "The U.S. as Slumlord," *New Republic,* December 11, 1971.
11. *New Republic,* March 9, 1974.
12. Hartman and Keating, "The Housing Allowance Delusion," p. 36.
13. Dee Wedemeyer, "Urban Homesteading," *Nation's Cities,* January 1975.
14. Anderson, *The Federal Bulldozer,* Chapter 14.
15. "The Battle of the Suburbs," *Newsweek,* November 15, 1971, pp. 61–70; *Congressional Quarterly,* January 8, 1972, pp. 51–55.
16. Roger Starr, "The Lesson of Forest Hills," *Commentary,* June 1972, p. 45.
17. Edward S. Banfield, *The Unheavenly City,* Boston, Little, Brown, 1968, p. 47.
18. Banfield, *The Unheavenly City,* p. 53.
19. Banfield, *The Unheavenly City,* p. 53, here cites Eleanor Pavenstedt, "A Comparison of the Child Rearing Environment of Upper Lower and Very

Low-Lower Class Families," *American Journal of Orthopsychiatry,* 1965, pp. 89–98.

20. Banfield, *The Unheavenly City,* p. 53, here cites Walter B. Miller, "Implications of Urban Lower-Class Culture for Social Work, *Social Service Review,* Vol. 33 (September 1959), and "Lower Class Culture as a Generating Milieu of Gang Dilinquency," *Journal of Social Issues,* Vol. 14 (1958).

21. Banfield, *The Unheavenly City,* p. 54, here cites Jerome K. Myers and B. H. Roberts, *Family and Class Dynamics in Mental Illness,* New York, Wiley, 1959, p. 174; A. B. Hollingshead and F. C. Redlich, *Social Class and Mental Illness,* New York, Wiley, 1958; and S. Minuchin et al., *Families of the Slums,* New York, Basic Books, 1968, p. 34.

22. Banfield, *The Unheavenly City,* p. 54, here cites Gans, *The Urban Villagers,* p. 246.

23. Banfield, *The Unheavenly City,* pp. 62–63.

24. Banfield, *The Unheavenly City,* pp. 210–211. For a critique of Banfield's views, see "The Unheavenly City: A Review Symposium," *Social Science Quarterly,* March 1971.

25. Banfield, *The Unheavenly City,* p. 223.

26. See T. R. Marmor, "Banfield's 'Heresy,' " *Commentary,* July 1972; Raymond Franklin and Solomon Resnick, *The Political Economy of Racism,* New York, Holt, Rinehart and Winston, 1973, pp. 157–172. The latter draw some blood but do not administer a fatal blow.

27. Letter from William F. Lewis, executive director of the Rockford Housing Authority, dated May 22, 1972, reaffirmed that the program had proven to be "very successful" and pointed to its proposed expansion.

28. John Fischer, "Planning for the Second America," *Harper's,* November 1969.

29. Reo M. Christenson, "On Breaking the Black Impasse," *Christian Century,* July 28, 1971, pp. 904–905.

4. Welfare: Challenge but No Decision

A mystifying thing happened in the late 1960s. Although the nation was enjoying unprecedented prosperity, with the annual economic growth equalling the total output of Canada and the unemployment rate falling to 3.5 percent, welfare rolls kept rising—rising sharply, moreover. From less than 6 million in the early 1960s the figure had leaped to almost 12 million in 1970 and had soared to 14 million in 1972. In New York City, one person in six was on welfare; in Boston and Philadelphia, one in five. Welfare costs were running to about $15 billion a year, an amount deeply disturbing to most of the general public. Indeed, no domestic phenomenon seemed to irritate so many average citizens as much as the magnitude and persistence of "the welfare problem." And no group of people, including common criminals, seemed to exasperate American taxpayers as much as welfare recipients. Any politician who failed to denounce the "welfare mess" and to pledge to help straighten it out was a curiosity indeed.

Investigators advanced a number of explanations for the swelling welfare figures. The national population was growing so rapidly that statistics tended to rise in almost every social and economic category. Most important, millions of unemployed or underemployed or poorly paid rural people—mostly from the South, mostly black, mostly victims of the agricultural revolution—were streaming into the cities at a time when the general economic demand for unskilled labor was falling. At this time, too, the inner cities were beginning to experience the straitened economic conditions created by corporation movements to the suburbs. Unable to find jobs and often with large families to feed, the disillusioned "immigrants" were forced to turn to welfare. After years on welfare, some recipients were developing a "welfare habit" and began to accept this as a more or less normal way of life.

Professors Francis Piven and Richard Cloward, who have no love for the capitalist system, make some general historical observations about welfare. The function of relief, they contend, is to "regulate labor." During periods of great economic distress, enough relief is doled out "to restore order" but when conditions improve "the relief system contracts, expelling those who are needed to populate the labor market." Those who cannot possibly work (the elderly, the crippled, the insane) are given aid, but "their treatment is so degrading and punitive as to instill in the laboring masses a fear of the fate that awaits them should they relax into beggary and pauperism." Thus the waxing and waning of relief, necessitated by the instability of capitalist economies, is used as a means of social control—to prevent disruptive degrees of public unrest and to insure a supply of docile low-paid labor when the economy recovers.[1]

Irving Kristol points out, however, that the Piven-Cloward thesis wholly fails to explain the "welfare explosion" of the 1960s, since it took place while job opportunities were improving. The black riots of the mid-1960s, which helped persuade the Establishment to further liberalize eligibility requirements for welfare and welfare benefits as well, happened at a time when people were already entering the rolls in increased numbers and receiving more generous benefits.[2] This phenomenon is better explained by Alexis de Tocqueville, who long ago noted that the poor and oppressed are more likely to become unruly when prospects are brightening than when conditions are at their worst.

Actually, Professors Piven and Cloward played a conscious role in expanding the relief rolls, even if in violation of their own thesis. Their analyses helped produce the National Welfare Rights Organization. This body, whose work was aided by many social workers, sought to encourage the poor to seek welfare and to educate those on welfare concerning their legal rights, to assist them in demanding those rights, and to compel agencies that systematically were skimping the poor to give them the full benefit of existing statutes. In many cases this involved considerably larger payments than welfare agencies, under heavy political pressure to keep costs down, had been willing to pay. At any rate, pressure from both black militants and anti-Establishment social workers added substantial (if undeterminable) numbers of poor to the welfare rosters and enlarged the benefits welfare recipients were receiving.[3]

(To the National Welfare Rights Organization, Piven and Cloward and many liberals and radicals in the late 1960s and early 1970s, the poor had moved from *being* a disgrace, as in Elizabethan England, to being a standing condemnation of a society which permitted poverty.[4] To the critics, the "deserving poor" were those who most vociferously attacked the System as unfair, unjust, and scandalous—preferably by demonstrations, protest meetings, rent strikes, etc.)

Finally, the high and increasing percentage of black fatherless families made a contribution. In 1960, 22.4 percent of black families were without a father in the home; in 1970 this figure had risen to 29 percent. It is now 35 percent. The causes of this increase, which is far in excess of that occurring in white families, is not altogether clear. It was already a factor in the major increase in persons on Aid for Families of Dependent Children (AFDC), which accounted for about 10 million of those on welfare.

In 1971 *U.S. News and World Report* shed some illuminating light on the statistical aspects of welfare. It reported that 55 percent of those on welfare were children, 20 percent were mothers, 16 percent were aged, 9 percent were blind or disabled, and only 1 percent were able-bodied males.[5] (The latter represented a far smaller percent of the welfare population than most Americans would have expected.) Although constituting only 11 percent of the population, about half of those on welfare were black.

Approximately one-third of the children receiving Aid for Families with Dependent Children were illegitimate. Payment levels for the average AFDC family of four ran to less than $200 per month, not quite enough to provide the Lincoln Continentals and mink coats which mythically abound among those on welfare. Also contrary to popular belief, most studies showed that only 1–4 percent of those on welfare were receiving money illegally.[6] A far larger percentage of the poor were eligible for benefits but were not receiving them either because they did not know they were eligible or because administrative interpretations had illegally disqualified them.

Dissatisfaction with the welfare program was well-nigh universal. Liberals were indignant because poor families were being denied minimum living standards. Most Americans, on the other hand, seemed to believe that most welfarees should be working, assailed the bumper crop of illegitimate children produced by welfare mothers, deplored the spending of welfare dollars on booze and nonessentials, and felt that payments were scandalously high in most states. Municipalities found their relief burdens so great that only Washington, they said, could save them from bankruptcy. Social workers resented all the prying and paperwork associated with their jobs, insisting that their expertise should be used to help clients with their basic problems. Many welfarees resented probes into their private affairs as demeaning and humiliating—a view fully shared by liberals. Administrative costs of the existing program were heavy, running from 10–20 percent of total expenditures. Work incentives were believed to be inadequate, since work requirements were often absent from municipal welfare programs and many families could make more on welfare than at the low-paying jobs that were usually their only alternative. The working poor, some observers thought, should not be denied all benefits from the state; instead of penalizing them for being willing to work, the state should extend cash encouragement. Finally, the wide variations in welfare payments from state to state (ranging from less than $1,000 a year in Mississippi for a family of four to $4,300 in New Jersey) struck many observers as indefensible; although some regional variation might be necessary because of living cost differentials, the differences were too great to be rationalized.

Although there was no agreement on just what should be done, it was clear to all by the late 1960s that the welfare system was ripe for a thoroughgoing overhaul.

NEGATIVE INCOME TAX AND FAMILY ASSISTANCE PLAN

A great deal of attention has been given to the so-called negative income tax (NIT) in recent years. NIT has won an impressive array of supporters, ranging from conservative economist Milton Friedman and the *Readers' Digest*[7] to such prominent liberals as Robert Lampman, John Kenneth Galbraith, and Senator Edward Brooke. Martin Luther King. Jr. endorsed NIT; so did the National Advisory Commission on Civil Disorders and 1200 economists. Paul Samuelson, the nation's most prestigious economist, called it an "idea whose time has come."

Most versions of NIT call for the federal government to assure families a guaranteed minimum income while permitting them to retain a portion of their earnings, without reducing their benefits, up to a point. Above that point, benefits would fall as earnings rose, until an income level was reached at which all aid would cease. Milton Friedman, who first proposed NIT in lectures at Wabash College in 1956,[8] later suggested a guaranteed minimum income of $1500 a year for an unemployed family of four; if the family earned $500 a year, it would receive a cash grant of one-half the difference between $500 and the income ceiling of $3,000 —or $1250. If the family earned $1500, it would get one-half the difference between $1500 and $3000—or $750. If the family earned $2800, it would receive $100. There are, of course, innumerable variations to the Friedman plan; his $3000 maximum ceilings, for example, could be raised to $4000 or $5000. But the heart of NIT is the assumption that although most citizens *pay* taxes to the government, low-income or non-income citizens would *receive* tax money.

As its proponents argue their case, NIT would take care of the most serious poverty problems in one swoop. A national income minimum would automatically be established. The millions who work regularly at the lowest-paid jobs would get a welcome helping hand. Incentive to work would be greater than under the present system, since those on welfare would be able to keep more than 30 percent of their earnings. (The law currently permits welfarees to earn only $30 a month plus 30 percent of their additional earnings without reduction of welfare benefits.) A person on welfare could take a job without fearing that, if he lost it, it might take him months to get back on the relief rolls. Needy individuals and childless couples would be helped, thus correcting a deficiency of family allowances.

"Snooping" by welfare workers would be eliminated, since payments would be based on income tax returns, perhaps submitted quarterly, with payments made quarterly or monthly, as Congress decreed. Nor would low-income people be subjected to the indignities of having welfare workers prescribe their spending pattern, as is sometimes done when welfare departments think welfarees are misspending their welfare checks. Both their self-respect and their freedom would be enhanced. Professional social workers could devote their full attention to counseling and rehabilitation of disorganized low-income families instead of slaving over endless mounds of dreary paperwork. Administrative costs would be low. Admittedly, payments levels would be lower than the poor receive in some states, but each state could supplement NIT as much as it wished. Since NIT would replace the existing welfare system, its costs would be politically practicable if payments were set at reasonable levels.

NIT has many advantages, but its disadvantages are not insignificant. First, what is a minimally satisfactory income for jobless northern urban families is clearly excessive for jobless rural southern families. Second, a tolerably satisfactory income support for most families of four on welfare would have to be over $4500 a year. But welfare fathers or mothers would not find it worthwhile to take a job at the minimum wage level, considering the transportation costs, child care costs, and possible loss of other public benefits, if they took a job paying $2.30 an hour. Realistically, there needs to be about $1000 a year after-tax differential between welfare income and working income if work is to be attractive to those on welfare." That differential would not exist, primarily because NIT (like our current welfare program) has a built-in children's allowance while low-income workers receive none.

Every writer who has made a serious analysis of NIT also admits it invites the shrewd to find ways to outwit the government, legally or illegally. The existing tendency to underreport income would be intensified. Owners of small farms, small businesses, and other income-producing property might deed their properties to relatives in order to qualify for NIT payments. Despite these and other problems, NIT continues to command a substantial amount of support from thoughtful students of public welfare.

WELFARE: A FRESH LOOK

The negative income tax, per se, never reached the floor of Congress. It was displaced by President Nixon's Family Assistance Plan (FAP). To the surprise of almost everyone, Nixon endorsed a welfare reform plan in 1969 that was at least a "kissing cousin" of NIT. His FAP would guarantee $1600 per year to a family of four (or $2400 if food stamps were included) with rates adjusted to the number of children but in no case to exceed $3920. Families would be eligible only if their assets did not exceed $1500. Eligibility was conditional, based on a willingness to accept jobs or job training (mothers of preschool age children were excepted). If an eligible father or mother rejected a job or job training, family income would be reduced by $500 a year. If job training were accepted, an additional allowance of $30 per month would be paid. To assist the job-training program, the administration proposed to finance day-care centers for working mothers; it also offered to subsidize 200,000 public service jobs for welfarees unable to find private employment. If work paid less than 75 percent of minimum wage levels, however, a worker could decline a job without suffering a loss of benefits. Overall, the administration hoped that about 2.5 million persons on welfare (obviously welfare mothers, for the most part) would go to work. (The hope was clearly unrealistic.)

Under the administration plan, the first $720 per year earned by a beneficiary would not reduce the payment level. Benefits would decline (based on a rather complex formula) for earnings above that level. Once a family's earnings reached the poverty level (then about $4000), all benefits would cease. The program thus would aid about 11 million members of the "working poor" families as well as increase benefits for some 7 million persons already on welfare.

Total program costs were estimated at about $5 billion above those which Washington was already contributing to local welfare programs. Since FAP applied only to families and involved a work requirement, it deviated from the plan conceived by Friedman and by most proponents of NIT.

Although President Nixon called FAP "the most important social legislation in 30 years," it ran into heavy weather in Congress. It passed the House, but encountered stubborn resistance in the Senate. Both liberals and conservatives expressed dissatisfaction with the administration plan, but for quite different reasons. Conservatives pointed out that FAP would almost double the number of persons on the welfare rolls, adding over 10 million persons to those rolls. In some southern states, it was estimated that about one-third of the population would be eligible for checks. What would this do to the wage level in the South? Since work and job-training programs are often farcical in practice, what would FAP do to the work incentive of southern families who were suddenly receiving two or three times as much money as they had ever known? A Republican administration should advocate something like this! Conservatives warned, also, that federal programs almost always become more costly than originally anticipated; there is a persistent tendency to liberalize benefits once they are established under any program. The eventual costs might prove both astronomical and a body blow to the work ethic of the American people.

Liberals opoposed the bill, or aspects of it, for other reasons. Some wanted to exempt mothers of school-age children, not just those of preschoolers. Others would permit beneficiaries to reject jobs paying less than the minimum wage level. (Opponents retorted: "Why should welfare recipients be permitted to reject jobs which millions of Americans must accept, since minimum wages do not apply to many types of employment?'') Others wanted payments adjusted to regional differences in cost of living; still others thought childless couples and single individuals who were poor should also be eligible for benefits. (This would make an additional 800,000 persons eligible for FAP.[11]) Many critics rejected the entire concept of work requirements, arguing not only that these programs are usually badly administered and subject to excessive administrative discretion, but also that the poor *will* work if given an opportunity.[12] President Nixon placed great stress on the work requirement, however, because he correctly judged public opinion to be strongly supportive of it. Without this emphasis, the program stood no chance of passage.

Many Democratic liberals wanted a more generous bill and were unwilling to settle for half a loaf when the salesman was Richard Nixon, their longtime enemy. President Nixon's initial enthusiasm for the bill waned when its full import was impressed on him and the public's hostility toward more welfare spending became apparent. The departure of Daniel Moynihan at the end of 1970 left the White House staff without a single believer in the program.

During the campaign of 1972, George McGovern's $1000-per-person welfare plan placed him on the defensive; the president was not interested in distracting attention from McGovern's blunder by pressing FAP—a program which would blur the difference between his and McGovern's views. President Nixon also refused to accept a compromise worked out by the secretaries of the Departments of Health, Education and Welfare, Labor, and by Senator Abraham Ribicoff; the compromise was very close to the President's own proposal but contained some features more attractive to liberals. Nixon adamantly insisted on his own bill, knowing it would not pass.[13] Finally, the poor southerners who stood to gain most from the bill were voiceless and leaderless. The only organization that might have represented them was the National Welfare Rights Organization; the latter, however, had a northern constituency, stood to gain nothing from the bill, and fought it tooth and nail. (Proving that the poor can be as selfish as the rich!)

With the death of FAP, welfare reform faded from the scene as an object of active Congressional concern. Welfare rolls even began to fall, a trend reversed by the impact of the Great Recession, which stimulated fresh interest in creating a more rational system.

How much has changed since NIT and FAP were on the front pages in 1969–1970? The total cost of public assistance at all levels was about $45 billion in 1975, with 25 million persons benefiting from it. Washington paid slightly over half the bill; 250,000 persons administered the program. The average cash monthly payment per person ranged from $15 a month in Mississippi to over $200 a month in Hawaii.

Almost all of those eligible for AFDC were now receiving aid. The food stamp program had swollen to phenomenal proportions; 19 million persons were receiving stamps (with 20 million more eligible for them) at a federal cost of $6 billion a year. A jobless family of four received almost $2000 worth of stamps; stamps were also available to the working poor, although eligible persons paid an increasing amount for their stamps as their income rose. A family earning $3000 a year would receive a food assistance worth about $1000. Eligibility technically ceased for families earning over $6450, but a complicated system of deductions (for establishing family income) meant that 13 percent of families receiving stamps were earning over $7000—and some were earning several thousand dollars a year more than that. A public clamor over "abuses" in the system (such as the eligibility of students, strikers and the voluntarily unemployed) led to Congressional efforts to tighten up the program. Liberals, however, seeing food stamps as a means of helping the working poor who were still above the poverty line, were opposing attempts to limit eligibility too narrowly. If Congress wouldn't enact FAP, with its helping hand for the working poor, let food stamps take its place! Added to the liberalizing of welfare payments in most Southern states, stamps have reduced the gap between the most generous and the least generous states from about five to one to about two to one.[14]

Surveys are now showing that more than 10 percent of those on welfare do not belong there, and various forms of welfare chiseling have become more widespread than had formerly been known to be true. With states and cities squeezed hard by declining tax receipts, campaigns to rid the rolls of "welfare cheats" are gaining momentum throughout the country. No government activity has met with such fervent public approval as have these campaigns.

There is growing concern with the number of *income-conditioned* grants for low-income persons. By income-conditioned we mean that the higher the income received, the less the grant, for low-income persons. While the principle is clearly sound as applied to a single program, it raises complications when attached to a number of related programs. Robert J. Lampman, for one, observes that ". . . a family headed by a non-worker might have combined benefits of Medicaid with an insurance value of $1000, a housing allowance worth $1000, a food stamp bonus worth $1300, a college scholarship for one youngster worth $1400 and a cash income of $2400 [from welfare payments]. This means a combined guarantee of $7100."[15] A family receiving all of these benefits would have to earn considerably more than $7100 before it would be worthwhile for the breadwinner to go to work.

Nathan Glazer observes that, considering the free health care, food stamps, housing subsidies, absence of taxes and other fringe benefits of welfare recipients, "it is a rare job in the real world that gives anything like the benefits of welfare to most mothers on welfare."[16]

The work "disincentive" problem involved in a multiplicity of overlapping income-conditioned welfare-type programs has become, therefore, a major concern for those seeking welfare reform. Glazer proposes a program to make low-paying jobs more attractive, perhaps by attaching children's allowances (which now provide benefits *only* for those on welfare), by national health insurance (since workers now lose health insurance coverage when they lose a job) and unemployment compensation covering all jobs.[17] (Arthur Okun's proposal to subsidize low-wage jobs directly is another step in this direction. See Section 2.)

Interest remains strong, in certain quarters, in establishing a simplified plan that would guarantee every family enough income to obtain the food, clothing, shelter and medical care essential to health and decency.

Indicative of the direction in which even conservative thought has moved was the plan offered by indubitably conservative former secretary of Health, Education and Welfare Caspar Weinberger in 1975. He proposed a form of negative income tax that would insure that every family earning less than $3600 per year would receive a federal check to bring its income up to that level. Those earning over $3600 would be able to keep half of their earnings up to $7200 a year, at which point all aid would cease. His program would have eliminated AFDC, food stamps and the Supplementary Security Income program.[18]

A more generous plan was put forward by Thomas Redburn. He would have guaranteed a family of four $4800 a year at an additional national cost of only $1 billion! It sounded like fiscal Houdini until Redburn began spelling out the programs his would replace: AFDC; Supplementary Security Income; food stamps and other nutrition programs; the Work Incentive program (to train people on welfare for jobs, which has never been regarded as much of a success); compensation for disabled miners; veterans pensions ($6.5 billion); state welfare costs; additional social services now provided by states with federal aid that people could obtain for themselves if their income were $4800 per family of four.[19]

Both the Weinberger and the Redburn proposals would clarify and simplify a ramshackle and confusing welfare picture which is long overdue for reform.

Because the cost of living and wage rates are so much lower in the south and in rural areas than in many northern cities, a uniform national minimum income guarantee encounters a formidable obstacle. What is high enough for New York, Boston, and Newark is much too high for many other areas. One alternative might be for Washington to establish a guaranteed minimum income which is adjusted to family size and tailored to the legitimate needs of families in low-income, low-wage areas, with Washington paying half of whatever additonal welfare costs the individual states believe desirable. Administrative costs might be reduced, furthermore, by requiring welfare applicants to fill out no more than a simple eligibility form while concentrating administrative efforts on the investigation of suspicious cases and on spot checks. If this were combined with children's allowances for low-income working families (perhaps phasing out when family incomes reached about $8000 a year), this combination might be the best welfare reform and poverty program the nation and the Congress would currently accept. Or would they accept even this?

Although predictions about future social trends and attitudes are normally high-risk enterprises, one forecast can be made with perfect confidence: Whatever reform is made in the welfare system, the public will be almost as dissatisfied as it is now. This is one area where policy planners may as well reconcile themselves to perpetual public discontent. Even the Soviet Union, which has no welfare program at all, experiences periodic press campaigns against "loafers and slackers" who fail to pull their share of the load and deviously live off the work of others. People who work dislike those who don't, as naturally as dogs chase cats. 'Twas ever thus and 'twill ever be.[20]

NOTES

1. Richard Cloward, *Regulating the Poor: The Function of Public Welfare,* New York, Pantheon Books, 1971, pp. 3–4. A brief summary of this book's major points is set forth in Frances Piven and Richard Cloward, "The Relief of Welfare," *Transaction,* May 1971.
2. Irving Kristol, "Welfare: The Best of Intentions, the Worst of Results," *Atlantic,* August 1971, p. 46.
3. Bruce Porter reports that the Piven-Cloward technique "backfired." Instead of the expected large influx of welfarees "breaking the system" and forcing constructive reforms, it led to widespread state and municipal efforts to cut back on welfare benefits. Porter says, "The left had created such shambles of welfare that it became no longer politically defensible and hence it was vulnerable to forays from the antiwelfare politicians of the right." Porter, "Welfare Won't Work But What Will?," *Saturday Review,* June 3, 1972, p. 50.
4. Thomas Halper, "The Poor as Pawns: The New 'Deserving Poor' and the Old," *Polity,* Fall 1973, pp. 71–86.
5. "Welfare Myths Versus Facts," *U.S. News and World Report,* December 20, 1971, p. 55; also "Can Affluent America End Poverty?," *U.S. News and World Report,* August 14, 1972, p. 25.
6. *U.S. News and World Report* stated that "suspected incidents of fraud or misrepresentation among welfare recipients occur in less than four-tenths of 1 percent of the total welfare case load in the nation, according to all available evidence." ("Welfare Myths Versus Facts," p. 55.) The *New York*

Times cited officials as believing that about 1.6 percent of New York's huge welfare population were chiselers. (*New York Times,* April 16, 1972, p. 5E.) Earlier, the *Times* reported that HEW investigators found that 3–4 percent of those on welfare were ineligible for such benefits. (*New York Times,* August 8, 1971, p. 3E.)

7. James Daniel, "Negative Income Tax—Better than Welfare?," *Reader's Digest,* May 1969, pp. 60–64. When the *Reader's Digest* and John Kenneth Galbraith endorse the same welfare reform, anything can happen.

8. Friedman followed up his lectures with *Capitalism and Freedom,* Chicago, University of Chicago Press, 1962, wherein he developed his belief in NIT.

9. Kristol quotes Alexis de Tocqueville: "There are two incentives to work: the need to live and the desire to improve the conditions of life. Experience has proven that the majority of men can be sufficiently motivated to work only by the first of these incentives." Kristol, "Welfare: The Best of Intentions, the Worst of Results," p. 45.

10. Half of all black families in the Deep South make less than $2,400 a year. Three-fourths of black families in that area would be eligible for FAP payments under the provision permitting aid to the working poor. For an excellent account of the legislative struggle over FAP, see James Welsh, "Welfare Reform: Born August 8, 1969, Died October 4, 1972," *New York Times Magazine,* January 7, 1973.

11. *Improving the Public Welfare System,* A Statement by the Research and Policy Committee, April 1970, p. 75.

12. Leonard Goodwin, "Environment and the Poor," *Current History,* November 1971, p. 293.

13. Abraham Ribicoff, "He Left at Half-Time," *New Republic,* February 17, 1973.

14. Robert J. Lampman, "Scaling Welfare Benefits to Income: An Idea that is Being Overworked," *Policy Analysis,* Winter 1975, pp. 3–4.

15. Robert J. Lampman, "What Does it do for the Poor?—A New Test for National Policy," *Public Interest,* Winter 1974, p. 78.

16. Nathan Glazer, "Reform Work, not Welfare," *The Public Interest,* Summer, 1975, p. 6. For corroborating evidence, see TRB, *The New Republic,* October 4, 1975, p. 2.

17. Glazer, "Reform Work, not Welfare," pp. 8–10.

18. *New York Times,* January 12, 1975, p. E5.

19. Thomas Redburn, "A Platform for the Seventies," *Washington Monthly,* October 1974.

20. Grandma told me this many years ago.

5. Education, Busing, and Poverty

One phenomenon that continues to mire a disproportionately high percentage of blacks in poverty is the educational gap between white and black children. At the end of their twelfth year of school, black youths typically are performing at about the ninth grade level. This disparity, which obviously leads to jobs of lesser skills and responsibility, largely explains why black per capita income has fluctuated around 60 percent of white per capita income.

Usually this gap is attributed to the prolonged black experience with slavery, followed by wretched educational opportunities and a century of total discrimination that prevented normal economic, political, and cultural development. These factors, together with the culture shock of massive migrations to major northern cities, combined to produce the broken families and preoccupation with bare survival that has given lower-class black children a poor background for academic achievement. They enter school with less "learning readiness" and their slower start is followed by subsequent educational, home, and street experiences that widen the gap.[1]

Efforts to cope with this stubborn and serious problem have thus far proved discouraging. Operation Headstart, designed to "enrich" the preschool years of lower-income black and white children, showed considerable promise at first, but it lessened as experience with it grew. "Compensatory education"—stressing remedial reading, lower teacher-pupil ratios, more attention to health and nutritional needs, field trips, and more parental involvement in their children's education—has also yielded modest results at best. Especially gifted teachers sometimes obtained good results from their educational experiments, but when their techniques were imitated by average teachers the results were disappointing.

It had been hoped that integrated education would upgrade the performance of black students. A massive study of the United States elementary and secondary educational system in 1966 by Professor James Coleman found that black schools were about as well financed as other schools but stressed that student performance was more dependent on family background and peer attitudes toward education than by per capita spending on education.[2] Family background is, of course, hard to alter but if lower-class blacks could be integrated into predominantly middle-class schools (black *or* white), it was believed that the more positive middle-class student attitudes toward education would "rub off" on the incoming students. Those who believed that the quality of teaching was especially important also stressed the tendency of the better teachers to gravitate toward the middle-class schools in the more pleasant suburban surroundings.

But most black students lived in the inner city. How could de facto housing segregation be overcome so that black students could enter the supposedly superior middle-class schools? Only busing, it seemed to many, could do the job. Since white middle-class parents were stoutly opposed to having their schools "invaded" by lower-class black children and violently averse to having their children bused to inner-city schools in any racially balanced school program, reformers turned to the courts. In a number of cities, federal judges concluded that subtle attempts had been made by school boards to maintain segregation. They ruled that mandatory busing was required to end this practice and bring about truly equal educational opportunity. Liberals argued that if ours was ever to become an integrated society, integration would have to start in the schools. Only busing, they said, could provide black students with the educational experiences that equal protection of the laws logically guarantees. Many whites might find this painful but the Constitution was designed to insure equality before the law and equal access to public services, not to insure minimal discomfort to a privileged majority.

Intense public opposition to busing, however, soon found growing support from many scholars. The latter reluctantly concluded that the educational impact of integrated education (including voluntary busing experiments) upon black students was not encouraging.[3] Whereas many persons believed that a well-planned race-class mix "would heighten aspirations, improve motivation, raise self-esteem and improve the academic performance of low achieving black children . . . there is little support in the professional literature for this dubious set of propositions," wrote Eleanor Wolf. ("Social Science and the Courts," *The Public Interest*, Winter, 1976, p. 107). There were some indications, moreover, that racial attitudes worsened when lower-class blacks entered middle-class white schools in substantial numbers. The self-esteem of these black students, finding themselves scholastically outclassed by the middle-class white students, was apparently injured at a time when the development of black pride was thought particularly important. Violence in the schools increased, disciplinary problems rose, and parental fears were heightened. Professor Coleman retreated from his earlier stance and warned that busing was precipitating a major migration of white families away from the newly integrated schools; the end result was even more de facto school segregation.[4] Other critics noted that middle-class black parents were almost as strongly opposed to sending their children to school with lower-class black students as were white parents[5] and that a majority of black as well as an overwhelming majority of whites opposed forced busing. How could a realist expect a major busing program to succeed in the face of the (often fervent) opposition of 83 percent of the white citizens and 54 percent of nonwhites? (Reported by a Gallup poll in 1974).

Others asked if it is unconstitutional to deprive black children of the privilege of attending the closest school, is it not equally unconstitutional to deprive white children of the same privilege? Were the champions of busing, they added, really prepared to send *their* children to inferior schools some distance from home—or was it just *other* parents' kids they had in mind?

Liberal Democratic candidates for president in 1976, confronted by adamant resistance to busing, continued to argue that court-ordered busing, where the courts found this necessary to overcome governmentally supported segregation, must be enforced. Their enthusiasm for busing, however, had declined to nearly zero.

How important to financial success is access to the "best" schools? Not very, according to Harvard's Christopher Jencks, in *Inequality: A Reassessment of the Effects of Family and School in America.*[6] The product of a $500,000 research project, Jencks' volume did not demean the importance of education per se. But it did charge that the differential impact of the "best" schools as contrasted with the "worst" schools was relatively minor. On the elementary school level, it probably amounted to no more than 5 points on a 100-point scale measuring cognitive achievements. On the high school level, the differential was "almost nothing." Black students, he wrote, who attend desegregated schools achieve only 2 to 3 points higher than those attending de facto segregated schools. (It seems difficult to believe that students would not learn appreciably more in the best suburban schools, compared to inner city schools in which most of the teachers' time is spent enforcing discipline and from which most of the better teachers have fled. The author lacks empirical evidence with which to refute Jencks, however.)

If quality schooling makes less difference than one might hope, are we back to family background once more? Much less than might be thought, Jencks declares, so far as postschool financial achievement goes. The average income difference between purely random pairs of men was $6200 in 1968; between brothers, it was $5700. Siblings with the same IQ and years of schooling have a status variation of 21 points (on a 96-point Duncan status measurement scale) compared to a status variation of 28 points for individuals selected purely at random.[7]

Jencks concludes that education, IQ, and home background combined accounted for only about 25 percent of income variations. The rest, he believes, is apparently attributable to luck and personality.

Jencks' book generally received excellent reviews, although the educational establishment was something less than ecstatic about it. But while one distinguished analyst insisted that "the statistical quality of the book is of the very highest quality" and "nonspecialist readers can read this book with confidence that they are getting the best sociology can offer at the present time,"[8] an equally eminent reviewer dissented. He asserted, after citing various methodological "flaws," that ". . . the actual findings and interpretations are at least as much a product of the value perspectives and opinions of the researcher as they are of this methodology and data. . . . The crude state of the social science art means that at the present time objectivity is unattainable."[9] That, alas, is the usual outcome when social science evaluates public policy in critically important areas.

Several years earlier, Jencks had observed:

Teachers are probably right in feeling that what their children need first and foremost is not academic skill but such 'middle-class' virtues as self-discipline and self-respect. It is the school's failure to develop these personal characteristics, not its failure to teach history or physics or verbal skill, that lies behind the present upheavals in the schools. And it is this failure to which reformers should be addressing themselves.[10]

Is it possible that the schools should devote more attention to developing these attributes than they have been? Perhaps, while continuing to press for academic excellence, they should strive harder to develop those personal qualities and values that are so vital to the happiness and economic well-being of their pupils. Or will the family environment so outweigh the school's influence that here, too, the limitations of public institutions will face us afresh?

NOTES

1. Charles Silberman, *Crisis in Black and White,* New York, Random House, 1964, p. 2.
2. James Coleman, *Equality of Educational Opportunity,* Washington, D.C., Government Printing Office, 1966.
3. See David J. Armor, "The Evidence on Busing," *The Public Interest,* Summer 1972; David Cohen, "The Price of Community Control," *Commentary,* November 1969, p. 27; Martin Mayer, "Improving Schools," *New Republic,* April 1, 1972, p. 18; John Osborne, "There Goes the Bus," *New Republic,* April 1, 1972, p. 14; Nathan Glazer, "Is Busing Necessary?" *Commentary,* March 1972.
4. *Time,* September 15, 1975, p. 41.
5. William V. Shannon, "The Busing Dilemma," *New York Times,* September 26, 1971, p. 15E.
6. Christopher Jencks, *Inequality: A Reassessment of the Effects of Family and School in America,* New York, Basic Books, 1972.
7. Mary Jo Bane and Christopher Jencks, "The Schools and Equal Opportunity," *Saturday Review,* September 16, 1972, p. 40.

8. A. L. Stinchcombe, "The Social Determinants of Success," *Science,* November 10, 1972, p. 603.

9. Henry M. Levin, "The Social Science Objectivity Gap," *Saturday Review,* November 11, 1972, pp. 50–51.

10. Christopher Jencks, "A Reappraisal of the Most Controversial Education Document of Our Time," *New York Times Magazine,* August 10, 1969, p. 44.

FIVE
Income Distribution and Tax Reform: The Fairness Test

Thinking about poverty naturally leads to questions about income, wealth, and tax distribution in America. What is the situation? Has it changed over the past fifty years? Is it fair? By what criteria? What can we do about it, if we wish to do anything at all?

Prior to investigating the current income and wealth inequalities in the United States, the reader is invited to pause a few minutes to reflect upon and ascertain the income variation which he or she regards as roughly equitable between the most highly remunerated members of society and the unskilled laborers who work regularly at useful employment. Would a "fair" differential be three to one? Five to one? Ten to one? Twenty to one? Fifty to one? One hundred to one? Whatever people can legally make?

The ratio you select may help you evaluate the equity of our economic system as the relevant facts are disclosed.

Some of the major facts about income and wealth distribution in America are these:[1] The top fifth of households earns 42 percent of personal income while the bottom fifth receives 5 percent—a differential of over eight to one. The top 10 percent receives 28 percent of personal income while the bottom 10 percent receives 2 percent—a differential of 14 to 1. The top 1 percent of family units receives approximately twice as much income as the bottom 20 percent, creating an income inequality of about 40 to 1. Those receiving over $1 million a year receive 300 times or more than the lowest-paid full-time workers. (More than 200,000 families have an income in excess of $100,000, and almost 3000 families make $1 million a year.)

The differential in terms of privately owned wealth is even more striking. The top 1 percent of families own one-third of the privately owned wealth. One-half of 1 percent own 22 percent of that wealth. (There are 200,000 millionaires in the United States—that is, families *owning* property and assets worth $1 million or more.) On the other hand, the bottom 45 percent own only 2 percent of the wealth.[2] The wealth differential for the top 1 percent compared with the bottom 45 percent is, then, over 700 to 1. Finally, 1 percent of the families own over half of all individually held stocks.[3]

Does the nation's tax structure substantially modify this picture by taxing the rich much more heavily than the poor? Surprisingly enough, the answer is no. Considering both the regressive nature of most state and local tax systems and the various tax loopholes available to the rich, the total tax bite on a percentage of income basis is roughly proportional for those in the lower income brackets and for those in all but the top 1 percent income bracket. Respected income authority Herman Miller states that the poorest fifth pay about 21 percent of their income in taxes, the top 10 percent pay 24 percent, the top 5 percent pay 25 percent and the top 1 percent pay somewhere between 29 percent and 38 percent.[4] And, in 1972, 400 persons with incomes over $100,000 paid no federal income tax whatever! Nelson Rockefeller had a total income of $47 million from 1964 to 1974 but paid the same rate of federal taxes as a man making $18,000 a year would pay.

What has been the trend? According to *Editorial Research Reports,* inequality in the distribution of *wealth* worsened in the 1920s, improved from 1929 to the late 1940s, worsened again in the 1950s, and continued that trend, slightly, in the 1960s.[5] The *income* distribution figures, however, look a bit better. Sanford Rose draws upon research with the *Gini coefficient* to demonstrate that "one premise of much of the rhetoric—that we have not been making progress toward equality—is quite wrong."[6]

The Gini coefficient measures the income inequality that exists in a given country, with zero indicating complete equality in the distribution of income and one representing a single individual's receiving *all* of a nation's income. Rose states that from 1935 to 1947, inequality among American families moved from 0.44 to 0.38, a significant improvement. From 1947 to 1970, the figure further dropped from 0.38 to 0.35.

Herman Miller declares that income distribution is virtually unchanged since 1950.[7] The Census Bureau, the Cambridge Institute, Robert Lampman, and economists Lester Thurow and Robert Lucas of

Massachusetts Institute of Technology agree.[8] The top and bottom fifths of American families retained the same proportion of national income in 1970 as in 1947—42 percent versus 5 percent.[9]

Irving Kristol insists that the after-tax distribution of income in the United States is "roughly comparable" to that in Britain, Germany, France, and Sweden.[10] It is probable, however, that the figures from which he draws his comparisons are similar to those which compare the differences between the upper 20 percent and the lower 20 percent of U.S. families—figures that show that the upper 20 percent makes over eight times as much as the lower 20 percent. Seen thus, the income disparity may seem quite reasonable to most Americans and may well be comparable to those in other modern industrial societies. But if comparisons are made between the upper 5 percent or 1 percent or millionaires, a quite different comparative distribution of income doubtless will emerge.

Whether one regards America's distribution of wealth, income, and tax burdens as social injustice or as roughly appropriate to differences in ability and diligence (or perhaps as the inevitable outcome of a basically beneficent economic system) reflects one's most deeply rooted social philosophy. Probably few questions identify liberals and conservatives more accurately than their attitudes toward income distribution and tax burdens; liberals uniformly deplore the current American income distribution and tax systems as unfairly tilted toward the more affluent members of society, whereas conservatives are likely to defend it.

The most uncompromising advocates of income equality could contend that the qualities and circumstances that bring financial success are almost wholly a matter of good luck rather than self-developed merit. Highly successful people usually are blessed with more than their share of vital energy; but this is a genetic inheritance for which no one can take credit. A willingness to work hard is the joint product of innate physical drive and the good fortune of being raised in a family that, by example and precept, encourages that behavior. Thus, a propensity for hard work is not an occasion for self-congratulation. Personality and character have much to do with financial success, and these, again, are the product of genetic factors and—to a much greater degree—family conditioning. We don't select our genes or our family. Much success comes from sheer luck—happening to be there when the good job opens up or happening to own the land which spouts oil or to inherit a million or to have the physical coordination needed to hit home runs or to have the sense of humor which blossoms into TV stardom or the creative genius which Nature occasionally and unaccountably lavishes on a chosen few.

Since these sources of wealth are not the result of equally endowed persons taking praiseworthy advantage of equal opportunities but are basically the result of plain old good luck, why should these fortunate souls derive vast fortunes from conditions and talents they did not personally create?[11] Talented and creative persons will inevitably get more satisfaction from life, whatever their income, than less-favored persons because they will receive more approbation, have more self-confidence and a greater sense of accomplishment. Why do they merit enormous incomes in addition to the nonmaterial advantages which Nature's bounties accidentally conferred upon them?

However logical this may be, few persons are prepared to accept its implications. The arguments which follow are not intended to support a goal of income *equality*, but a goal of *greater* equality than now exists. In setting forth the opposing points of view, I will draw heavily on Robert Lampman's excellent volume, *Ends and Means of Reducing Income Poverty*.[12]

THE SPIRIT OF EGALITARIANISM

The spectrum of opinion might run something like this. It could be argued that those seeking to narrow the gap between the poorest and the most prosperous do so out of pure altruism, a spirit of sympathy for the unfortunate, reflecting a generous turn of mind and a generally humanitarian outlook. Concern for the underdog is one of the constants of liberal attitudes, and it finds natural expression in tax policy that reduces the burden on lower-income groups by raising more money from the more affluent. Or, this position can represent an application of Jeremy Bentham's *felicific calculus*—adapting public policy in specific ways to provide the greatest happiness for the greatest number. It is arguable that the contribution that additional income makes to human felicity and well-being is greatest at the lower end of the income scale and diminishes as incomes rise. That is, for a person earning $5,000, an additional $1,000 would add considerable satisfaction to his life; for a person with an income of $500,000, an additional $1,000 would mean comparatively little. It is thought logical, therefore, that the income of the latter should be subject to much higher taxation than that of the former.

The more philosophical might disparage still further the importance of great wealth. Only the naive believe that those making $200,000 a year are proportionately (if at all) happier than those making $175,000, or those earning $175,000 happier than those earning $150,000, and so on down the line. Where income affects one's capacity adequately to feed, house, and clothe his family, to provide the ordinary comforts and pleasures of American life, it is reasonable to assume it makes a significant difference to a family's sense of well-being. But is not that level of income well below the figures tax reformers have in mind?

Does it take much wisdom to recognize that our happiness, once a modest income level is reached (and to a large extent, even before that point), depends overwhelmingly on the quality of our relationships with our husbands, wives, children, and those we work with, on our health and that of our families, on our range of interests, on our self-respect, on the satisfaction we derive from our work, on our temperament, on the religious or philosophical underpinning of our lives? If these are what really count, are we doing the rich a great disfavor if we seize more of their money to meet society's needs? Perhaps a stiffer tax policy might induce them to explore more rewarding avenues of obtaining satisfaction than that of pressing toward the mirage of happiness through wealth. Whether this perspective is valid or not, others would urge that the pleasures the wealthy may receive from upper-level financial increments are less important than the social value of diverting these funds to such high priority items as pollution control, the alleviation of poverty, the renovation of our cities, and so on.

Reformers might further contend that the financial rewards at the upper end of the income scale are disproportionate to the contributions its beneficiaries make to the public wealth. Granting that the more capable and energetic members of society should receive more income than others, they perceive the current differential as going far beyond an appropriate reward and as unnecessary to the encouragement of diligence and creativity. Instead, they might assert, the highest income brackets are too often occupied by those with unusual cunning, greed, luck, or skill at exploiting a defective tax system. Many high incomes accrue not because the wealthy have displayed extraordinary social energy and creativity but because they inherited wealth or they took advantage of tax loopholes which unfairly exempt certain kinds of income from normal taxation. Those loopholes are allegedly the product of political clout adroitly applied to the legislative process, rather than being reasonably related to a legitimate economic purpose.

Critics are often skeptical, moreover, that professional athletes, television entertainers, prosperous advertising men, real estate speculators, and recipients of *unearned income* (that is, income which accrues from the ownership of tangible or intangible property rather than from one's current labors) really ''deserve'' fantastically higher incomes than competent skilled laborers. The undoubted utility of the latter to society is demeaned if the former are permitted incomes far in excess of those the textile worker, electrician, carpenter, die caster, and repairman receive.

A rationale for income inequality as related to social service is offered by John Rawls. He contends that inequalities of wealth can be justified only if they are necessary to enable the more wealthy to better serve the interests of the less well-off. If inequalities are demonstrably essential to enable these citizens to improve the health or material well-being of the poor, they are socially defensible. But they are never morally permissible as the "just deserts" of those lucky enough to be born with greater talents or greater economic or family advantages.[13]

Some writers advocate a society which avoids "extremes" of wealth and poverty on the ground that more "moderate" income differences tend to reduce social discontent, promote a more stable society, and thus strengthen the social foundations of a democratic system (where that exists).

They would also assert that democracy is less vulnerable to Marxist and other criticism if the income differential between rich and poor is kept within "reasonable" bounds. America's world-leadership role and the attraction of its political and ethical ideals are considerably dependent on America's image abroad as a nation concretely concerned with social justice. Since a "fair" distribution of wealth is a criterion of signal importance to most of the world's population, an American that desires influence abroad must not be indifferent to it.

Reducing the income margin between the rich and the poor, most liberals believe, would also deemphasize the spirit of raw acquisitiveness in our society. Regarding an overemphasis on the accumulation of private wealth as the besetting sin of capitalist America, they are eager to discourage this ethic and direct energies toward more admirable ends. Less concern for "striking it rich" might ameliorate the "dog-eat-dog" character of American business and enable the more generous, humane, and artistic qualities of the human spirit to flourish.

Scaling down the upper reaches of wealth also might reduce the unhealthy political power which the wealthy enjoy in America. The impact of wealth through campaign contributions and the hiring of expensive legal and political talent to distort legislative, administrative, and judicial policy toward the interests of the rich is a commonly recognized aspect of our political process.

How much the above factors influence, at rock bottom, the preferences of those seeking greater economic equality can only be conjectured. Alas, men are rarely moved solely by considerations of pure altruism and pure compassion. A baser element is usually present. Of course, those who favor greater equality (as the author admittedly does) are prone to place the most favorable interpretation on their motives—just as their opponents are disposed to adopt the opposite course. But professions of disinterested concern for the public welfare should always be viewed with a bit of skepticism.

Professor Lampman's discussion of the egalitarian philosophy that underlies the poverty program is not directly related to higher taxes on the affluent, but his presentation of the case against the "levelers" is pertinent and intriguing. (He does not endorse it, however.) Lampman points out that it is not uncommon for egalitarian measures to be proposed before the supporting arguments are developed.[14] This suggests that a visceral or self-interested factor is often at work, with an appropriate rationalization following. Oliver Wendell Holmes once wrote, "I have no respect for the passion for equality, which seems to me merely idealizing envy."[15] Holmes' cynical attitude would be shared by many a conservative, past and present, who is loath to attribute altruism to a spirit he regards as compounded of equal parts jealousy and vengefulness. Others are convinced that intellectuals who advocate taking from the rich and giving to the poor are trying to establish and flaunt their moral superiority over lesser mortals. Such a position gives them a smug feeling, conservatives suspect, and often represents self-righteousness more than righteousness.

Others note that egalitarian movements usually take root among social groups who feel they are denied the status which is rightfully theirs and who seek an ideological weapon for improving that status. Bertrand de Jouvenel sees the "egalitarian ideal" as an instrument employed by groups seeking new leadership and an altered class pattern.[16] Daniel P. Moynihan thinks he perceives "a proclivity for seeing in the poor and dispossessed—however weak and outnumbered they may be—an instrument for transforming the larger society."[17] (Raising the status of the poor and more heavily taxing the rich are not necessarily Siamese twins, but there is often a family relationship.)

Irving Kristol sees deeper significance in the drive by intellectuals for greater equality. What really gnaws at them, he believes, is a "religious vacuum—a lack of meaning in their own lives and the absence of a sense of larger purpose in their society." This "terrifies them and provokes them to 'alienation' and unappeasable indignation. It is not too much to say that it is the death of God, not the emergence of any new social or economic trend, that haunts bourgeois society."[18] (There may be something to what Kristol says but the author does not believe in the death of God—and he is still indignant about the nation's distribution of wealth and income!)

Will more equal incomes create greater social stability? That is highly doubtful, some conservatives say. They could quote Alexis de Tocqueville:

The hatred that men bear to privilege increases as privileges become fewer and less considerable, so that democratic passions would seem to burn most fiercely just when they have least fuel. . . . When all conditions are unequal, no inequality is so great as to offend the eye, whereas the least dissimilarity is odious in the midst of general uniformity; the more complete this uniformity is, the more insupportable the sight of such difference becomes. Hence it is natural that love of equality should constantly increase together with the equality itself and that it should grow by what it feeds on.[19]

Kristol finds confirmation in contemporary Sweden. The more egalitarian Sweden has become, he says, the more incensed its intellectual classes are with the remaining inequalities and the more alienated its college-educated youth seem to be.[20] Perhaps nothing but total equality will placate the reformer, and that would destroy virtually all initiative, diminish the desire to excel, and create a society of deadly and deadening mediocrity.

Moving on, who can say how important additional income is to the satisfactions of those already affluent? Increased income leads to increased social prestige—plus a sense of personal accomplishment—and these *are* satisfying to most people. In any case, can the critics really explore the deepest recesses of the psyche and confidently proclaim the result? Why not be honest and admit that these pontifications are pure guesswork designed to support conclusions arrived at by an essentially gut process? And how many of those who would ''soak the rich'' will be among those soaked? It is easy to advocate confiscating another man's wealth and pleasant to ascribe this desire to noble motives, but it is more convincing when the advocates themselves must feel the sting of the higher taxes they propose for others.

(As an interesting aside, a cross-national survey reveals that individual income improvement—up to $15,000 per year and over—results in an increased sense of well-being only if that improvement is proportionately greater than that of other comparable persons. ''Each person acts on the assumption that more money will bring happiness; and, indeed, if he does get more money, and others do not, or get less, his happiness increases. But when everyone acts on this assumption and incomes generally increase, no one, on the average, feels better off.''[21])

Whether tax policy would make America less vulnerable to Marxist denunciation is largely beside the point. Marxists will never run out of excuses for criticizing America; they will invent grounds for their assaults if this proves necessary or convenient. We should follow those policies which are best adapted to keeping America strong, enterprising, creative, and vigorous, whether or not the Marxists or public opinion in other countries concur. One of the major ways to accomplish this is to permit generous rewards to those who provide the jobs and furnish the greatest talent in all fields of endeavor.

True, some who receive high incomes are probably unworthy of them. But this usually involves value judgments on which men widely disagree. Perhaps entertainers *do* deserve far more than workmen, considering the satisfaction they give to millions and the intense competition they must meet. In any case, this is an imperfect world and every policy has its flaws. To receive the benefits of a system which rewards genuine talent, we necessarily risk overrewarding some whose social contributions are uninspiring. If we were to deny the ''undeserving'' we would also have to deny ample rewards for those whose abilities and energies yield the greatest benefits to society. And who would decide?

Where would the capital come from if we imposed crushing taxes on "the rich"? It takes $40,000 of capital investment to create a job today; crack down on the better paid and you dry up the investment funds on which not only private enterprise (and hence workmen's jobs) rests, but also on which public revenues depend. A sagging economy will not provide the corporate or private incomes that government must tap to finance its work. Would the government be able to impose successfully near-confiscatory taxes on high incomes? Would not corporations, for example, find indirect ways to reward their executives and thus outwit the IRS? Don't skilled and ingenious tax lawyers generally manage to stay one step ahead of the reformers?

Acquisitiveness is a pejorative term for ambition, for the desire to be a success and to enjoy the fruits of success. If acquisitiveness can become a vice, so can all the substitute means men employ to achieve recognition and power. Ask the careful student of Soviet society; he will tell you that men's desire for preeminence has taken as many disagreeable forms in Russia as in the United States. He will even remind you that acquisitiveness is often as potent a force in communist Russia as in the capitalist United States.

Finally, rather than punish the successful members of our society by imposing punitive taxes, why not reform the lobbying laws to identify and publicize more effectively those who bring political pressures to bear? And why not publicly finance part or all of Congressional election campaign costs? Would that not be preferable to an economically debilitating assault on the "rich"?

A few final points will be made—doubtless reflecting the author's bias. Just as the arguments for higher taxes on upper-income groups could continue to be made even if those taxes were imposed, so the arguments for maintaining the current tax system could be advanced, no matter what income differentials existed, even with differentials of 1,000 to 1. The argument assumes there is no sensible position between extremes that could command, not unanimity, but substantial agreement among intelligent, fair-minded, public-spirited men and women.

Aristotle said inequalities of property, power, or status are legitimate only when they are generally regarded as contributing to the common good. Currently there seems to be no widespread dissatisfaction among average Americans with the distribution of wealth and income in this country (even though polls in 1972 showed that 67 percent of Americans believed that "tax laws are written for the rich and not for the average man"). But would this situation persist if the facts, the quite appalling facts, about income and wealth inequalities were well known? They are not well known, and one of the tragedies of the McGovern campaign was its unwillingness to focus seriously on those facts. If widespread disclosure led to continuing satisfaction with the status quo, critics would be largely silenced. On matters such as these, there is no appeal—in a democracy—from an informed majority. Nor is there a better basis for forming social judgments. There is good reason to believe, however, that an informed majority's judgment would support a quite different distribution than that which currently prevails in America.

Secondly, the attack on tax reform persistently revolves around the maintenance of incentives. If taxes are too high, we allegedly stifle incentive and thereby injure everyone. The contention calls for a closer look. Suppose that the best-rewarded members of our society met, say, an 80 percent tax after their take-home pay reached about fifteen times as much as the more poorly paid full-time workers (or about $60,000 a year). Would this seriously reduce incentive? Perhaps not.

The most creative members in our society are likely to remain creative, even with this income limit, simply because creativity is in their blood. They enjoy their work, enjoy the creative process, and would be wretched if they failed to respond to their strongest impulses. One must live by the deepest springs of one's nature, and if one has the creative impulse, it will not be denied.

Let us assume, however, that this is wrong, that $60,000 a year is not a sufficient incentive in itself. Other incentives exist. The top executive and professional personnel are seldom indifferent to prestige, and that is not maintained unless one does excellent work and remains in the upper echelons of the firm. If you slack off because $60,000 a year take-home pay is inadequate, ambitious persons lower down the hierarchy are eager to get your post. Begin coasting and you may coast right out of your job.

If prestige is important, so is power. Power is won, sustained, or enhanced by doing a job well and, above all, by holding one of the more powerful jobs. To assume that money is more important to man than power and prestige is to misread his nature.

Finally, Herman Miller writes that "there is virtually no scientific evidence to support the view that the incentives of the rich to accumulate would be destroyed if they were taxed more heavily." A summary of available empirical evidence prepared by Professor George Break of the University of California suggests, he says, that "income taxes exert relatively little influence on work incentives and when they do they induce greater effort as frequently as they deter it."[22]

As for the fear that insufficient capital would be forthcoming—during a period when a serious capital shortage may occur—if high incomes were heavily taxed, several points can be made. The propensity to save seems not to be closely associated with current tax levels. The rate of savings has remained at a relatively constant 6.5 percent of GNP since the Civil War despite numerous fluctuations in tax rates.[23] Moreover, about 70 percent of corporate expansion comes from internal reserves, rather than from borrowing from banks or selling stock. If more capital proves necessary, the investment tax credit already on the books could be raised to help achieve this purpose. Or higher interest rates can generate more saving.

Herman Miller again: "There is no sound economic reason why we should not resume [income redistribution] that ended one quarter of a century ago. We can have a further reduction of inequality and a different distribution of the tax burden without necessarily hurting the economy. Economists who say otherwise are going beyond the limits of the knowledge of their profession."[24]

Do we not find income differentials of 25 to 1, 100 to 1, or 300 to 1 acceptable only because our moral judgment is dulled by familiarity with the American scene? What we are accustomed to usually seems right. But if we were raised in a society in which no one received more than ten times as much as another, and John Doe proposed that we should permit exceptionally talented or energetic or lucky people to have fifty times as much as others, the notion would be regarded with incredulity. Doe would be seen as someone abysmally lacking in ordinary, garden-variety common sense to think that such people are *worth*—really worth—fifty times as much as the ordinary workingman. Worth as much in one year as many an honest, hardworking person receives in a lifetime? Well, if they aren't really worth it, why do we let them have it? Above all, why do we let them keep it?

We think of the inherited privileges of the pre-Revolution French aristocracy as outrageous, richly meriting the abolition which befell them. Then why, in a country supposedly dedicated to equal opportunity, is not the privilege of inheriting a million dollars (or even much less than that) as morally offensive as the gross inequalities accruing through inheritance to the French nobility?

Professor Lampman concluded his treatment of egalitarianism by observing that:

The economists who have sponsored egalitarianism have been interested in both more or less than economic equality. They have been interested in less than economic equality in the sense that they do not seek the elimination of all existing economic inequalities but only those which are seen to be "arbitrary," "capricious," or "functionless." . . . It may be that interest in further economic equalization will flag only as there is widespread adoption of the view that the "something less" than equality has been accomplished and only as we come to believe that existing inequalities are necessary and functional, or at least not destructive or oppressive. Finally, that interest may diminish if people come to believe that further equalization will lead away from rather than toward the "something more" than equality, namely feelings of fraternity and mutual respect.[25]

Certainly America has not yet reached the point where interest in reducing the retained income of the most affluent has faded. For liberals in general, plugging tax loopholes for the wealthy remains high on the national agenda. It will probably continue to be until greater equity is won. This writer finds it hard to understand how any knowledgeable and reasonably public-spirited person can defend the existing national tax structure.

TAX LOOPHOLES

In all probability, if tax reform comes, it will be through the elimination or drastic revision of various loopholes rather than through an elevation of general tax rates in the upper brackets. The latter is relatively futile as long as affluent citizens can invest their money in ways which nullify the impact of high tax rates. But, if the existing 14–70 percent rate can be applied to all or most upper-level income, income distribution in the United States can be markedly changed.

The major loopholes (''truckholes,'' former Senator Paul Douglas called them) which have attracted the most attention are these:

1. Capital gains: Such gains are profits derived from the sale of stocks and bonds, real estate, or other property not exchanged in the normal course of business. That is, if the investor pays $10,000 for stocks or land, for example, retains ownership for a number of years, and then sells the property for $15,000, he is taxed only 25 percent on his $5,000 profit. (Capital gains of over $25,000 in a given year are now taxed at a rate of 35 percent.) This benefit is of major importance to those whose income ordinarily places them in a higher than 25 percent (or 35 percent) tax bracket. (About one tax payer in twelve pays a capital-gains tax each year.)

The low capital-gains tax is defended on grounds that it encourages investment and thereby helps provide the fuel needed for a growing and dynamic economy. In the absence of such a favorable tax, those with substantial incomes might either save their money in ways less useful to the economy or devote it to personal consumption.

Critics regard capital gains as a vast bonanza for the well-to-do, a handout which deprives the national government of about $7 billion a year. They believes many capital gains, resulting from real-estate speculation and investment in existing stocks (as contrasted with investment in new or expanding enterprises) contribute little to our economic welfare. And they note that about 70 percent of corporation capital expenditure derives from internal reserves or borrowing rather than the issuance of new stocks.

Richard Armstrong, in an excellent analysis of the capital-gains tax in

Fortune, notes that "an asset can increase in value, yet no tax on the increase is due until the asset is sold. Because of this deferral, which enables investors to hang on to the Internal Revenue Service's money and keep it working for them long after their gains take place, the effective tax on most capital gains is only a fraction of the stated rate."[26] The real tax on capital gains from 1921 to 1960 was only about 5 percent, he estimates, with the effective rate rising to 7.5 percent from 1954 to 1960. He further observes that "someone who inherits an asset and later sells it does not have to pay tax on the entire gain since the original purchase; his cost basis is fair market value at the time of his benefactor's death."[27] (About $20 billion of capital gains annually escape taxation in this manner.)

Armstrong cogently challenges the belief that risk capital would be seriously impaired if capital gains were fully taxed. The Joint Economic Committee of Congress also believes that a persuasive argument for preferential treatment of capital gains "has yet to be made."[28] Robert W. Dietsch agrees that "nobody has ever proved that stock buying or investment would be curtailed to any significant degree if the hole were plugged."[29] It is hard to believe that someone would forego investment in a promising enterprise simply because the profit returns would not receive preferential tax treatment. The case for reform seems convincing.

There is not much disagreement that most of the hundreds of persons in the upper-income brackets who pay no federal taxes or relatively low federal taxes do so because of the capital-gains tax and/or tax-free state or municipal bonds. It is estimated that the wealthiest pay about half as much tax as they would in the absence of these tax provisions.[30]

Peter Barnes, in an ethical-economic interpretation, says two major criteria can be used to judge whether income is earned or unearned: "(1) Does the activity which generates the income add to the supply of goods and services available to society? (2) Is the income a result of its recipient's efforts, or is he merely reaping the benefits of other's exertions?"[31]

Overall, says Barnes, unearned income amounted to roughly $200 billion in 1970. This included $34 billion in interest, $25 billion in dividends, and $23 billion in rent. Capital gains accounted for much of the rest.[32]

That any form of unearned income should be given preferential tax treatment over "sweat labor" income seems morally offensive to many critics; hypocritical, too, in a nation which claims to treasure the work ethic and regards welfare recipients (who also receive unearned income) as a lower form of life.

2. Tax-exempt state and/or municipal bonds: Designed to help fiscally hard-pressed state and local governments, these nontaxable bonds can be issued at a much lower interest rate than other bonds, saving local government sizable sums of money while providing wealthy investors with a welcome tax haven. Bonds already issued presumably cannot be taxed without violating the sanctity of contract, since investors accepted a comparatively low-interest-rate return because they were assured of tax-free earnings. Newly issued bonds could be taxed, although most reformers agree the states should be given an appropriate federal subsidy to compensate for their loss. Since Washington now loses almost two dollars in tax revenue for each dollar of interest saved by local governments, it could offer an interest subsidy to local government and still gain from this reform.

Tax-free local bonds currently cost the U.S. treasury about $4 billion a year. Perhaps as important as the fiscal loss is the public indignation over high-income individuals whose earnings either go scot-free or who pay very low federal taxes. Faith in one's government partly depends on the belief that everyone is paying his share. Since the public's reaction to the phenomenon of high-income, low-taxed individuals is one of outrage, perhaps that sentiment should be respected.

3. Tax shelters: Persons in the 50 percent or 70 percent tax brackets often escape almost all federal taxes by taking advantage of so-called tax shelters. They may invest in oil wells, real estate, the Cincinnati Bengals, Paramount Pictures, cattle ranches, or whatever, for the deliberate purpose of showing a loss on their tax records while racking up financial plusses for themselves. (The facts get complicated; curious readers are invited to read chapter 9 of Philip Stern's absorbing *The Rape of the Taxpayer*.[33])

4. Death taxes: Although the federal estate tax rates are nominally fairly steep, running up to 77 percent on estates worth over $10 million (after deductions), in practice it is rare for large estates to pay over 10 percent inheritance taxes.[34]

When Senator McGovern urged, first, the confiscation of all estates worth over $500,000 (finally retreating to a recommendation of a 77 percent tax on estates of that value), this was widely regarded as a radical, if not Marxian, proposal. To deny wealthy men the privilege of passing on most of their property to their families would be, some thought, not only grossly unfair but another grievous blow at the incentive system that has made America one of the most productive nations in the world. Should not a man be able to pass along a family business or large farm or country estate of unusually attractive character to his children, thus keeping it in the family as a part of a long-established and long-treasured family tradition? And if you concede this, how do you discriminate against some forms of inheritance as compared to others?

McGovern's supporters, however, contended that the capacity to transmit large fortunes (which often expand generation after generation, since the funds and/or assets are usually managed by financial experts) is a major element in creating the deplorably wide gulf between the rich and the poor. They are willing for sufficient property to be transmitted to insure the education and proper care of the young but are less willing to permit some young people to enjoy a vast economic advantage over others through favorable tax laws. Although recognizing that true equality of opportunity can never fully exist, they would like to come much closer to that goal. Eliminating the special privilege which current inheritance laws embody would move toward that end.

A former high-level treasury official, Professor Stanley S. Surrey of the Harvard University law school, has made a careful analysis of the character and effect of deductible income provisions in our federal tax laws.[35] (So did Philip Stern, in *The Rape of the Taxpayer*.[36]) These tax deductions, Surrey said, are really tantamount to federal subsidies (Stern calls them "tax welfare benefits"), but subsidies of a nature we would usually not tolerate if they were direct treasury appropriation subsidies. They are born and persist because of their disguised character. A tax deduction doesn't *seem* like a subsidy, so when it manages to become incorporated into a tax bill, it meets far less opposition than an outright, straightforward subsidy would face.

Surrey explains it this way. If the government were to levy taxes on *all* individual and corporate income at the current rates, it would receive $80–90 billion more than it does now.[37] (Remember that the Sixteenth Amendment declares, "Congress shall have the power to lay and collect taxes on income, *from whatever source derived . . .*")

This means Congress is subsidizing various corporations and taxpayers by $80–90 billion a year, or almost twice as much as the direct subsidies it pays. One result is that persons whose incomes exceed $100,000 usually pay tax rates little higher than those of middle-income persons, and corporations pay about 35 percent on their income instead of the 48 percent rate specified in the tax laws.

What are these tax subsidies? (Technically, they are referred to as *tax expenditures* in federal statutes.) Tax-exempt state and local bonds, for example the $1 million tax-free income which Nelson Rockefeller enjoys from that source.[38] Congress might directly subsidize state and local governments to help them pay for a portion of the interest on their debt, but would it also directly appropriate $1 billion for wealthy persons' private benefits in connection with this end?

Would Congress appropriate $7–10 billion a year to well-to-do persons on condition that they invest a portion of their money in land, stocks, speculative business enterprise, and so on? Would not this be regarded as a preposterous use of public funds? But we do it via the capital-gains tax.

Would Congress vote a direct subsidy of $1 billion to companies that engage in export trade?[39] Well, it does so by agreeing to tax only half of the income received from this source.

Would Congress appropriate a direct $10 billion subsidy to (mostly middle class) persons to help them buy their own homes? This is a far larger amount than we spend for public housing and low-income housing subsidies. We *do* subsidize millions of Americans (and the housing industry) by this sum when we allow taxpayers to deduct from their income tax the interest they pay on their home mortgages.

Would Congress directly appropriate billions to private business concerns to encourage them to invest more in new plant and equipment—as it now, in effect, does almost invisibly through the investment tax credit?

Surrey and Stern do not assume that in every case in which the treasury pays concealed subsidies the public loses, but they are certain that Congress would be far more reluctant to subsidize various individuals and interests if those subsidies came under direct and critical scrutiny instead of being hidden from public view. And in many instances (including some not cited here) the subsidies would never survive open public examination.

Chances for survival would presumably be still less if the public and Congress were aware, as Surrey points out, that when Congress votes a $1000 tax subsidy, it typically provides $700 for an upper-income person, $140 to a low-wage employee and nothing for the poor.[40] This is because the more well-to-do are able to make the kinds of investments that enable them to take advantage of the more succulent tax subsidies.

How much money could Congress raise by eliminating all loopholes and other erosions of personal and corporation taxes? Theoretically, over $80 billion (assuming no adverse effects on the economy). Practically speaking, however, many deductible items are politically untouchable (such as interest on life-insurance savings, interest on home mortgages, contributions to charity, unusual medical expenses, and the $20 billion tax loss Washington sustains by permitting taxpayers to file joint tax returns). Considering the political realities, a reform-minded Congress and president might not raise over $5–6 billion.[41] A Brookings Institution study in early 1972 suggested a top figure of about $13 billion. While some Democratic presidential candidates in 1972 thought Congress might plug loopholes to the tune of around $25 billion, they were suffering the kind of psychedelic political delusion which sometimes afflict such candidates before national nominating conventions.

THE PROSPECTS FOR REFORM

What are the chances that major tax reform will actually come, a reform with real bite on the rich and the near-rich? It is safe to predict that reform of this nature is about the toughest political task any president or legislative body can tackle. Higher federal taxes on all brackets is rarely possible; sharply increased taxes on upper-income groups alone is monumentally difficult—as difficult, probably, as Senator McGovern's attempt to remove $30 billion from the Pentagon's platter. These lively dragons —the rich and the military—seem able to tromp any St. George underfoot, barring something approaching the miraculous. Raising $5 billion of additional funds by tightening loopholes would be a solid achievement; $10 billion would be downright remarkable; substantially more, the work of sheer political genius.

As indicated earlier, if the rate of national economic growth falls considerably below the historic average and prospects for improvement in the standard of living for most Americans look bleak, frustrated and disgruntled voters may become interested in more equitable income distribution through tax reform. Antagonism to high gas, oil, natural gas, and other energy costs could also fuel the spirit of reform. If black political leaders placed income-tax reform high on their lists of priorities, that could make a difference. So could a reform-minded president.

But the forces of resistance—and of inertia—currently occupying the commanding heights of the political system are better armed, better supplied and reinforced by popular attitudes that support the status quo more strongly than they do the impulse to reform. Hereafter, opponents of tax reform can cite (probably successfully) the need for more capital accumulation as an argument against tax bills which bear heavily on those upper-income groups who are most prone to save and invest. Congress, after a brief era of liberal resurgence, is likely to revert to its normally conservative mood. (Conservatives have dominated Congress in all but a few years since 1938.) Not only do many Congressmen and Senators personally profit—some heavily—from a number of these loopholes, but the Congressional committees that deal with tax reform are usually stacked with conservatives. The House Ways and Means Committee has long been a stronghold of conservatism; its right-wing bent is matched by that of the Senate Finance Committee, which is chaired by oil-rich Senator Russell Long. (More than 20 members of the House and as many members of the Senate are millionaires; a "soak the rich" tax policy may not be irresistibly appealing to them.)

Also, the powerful groups resisting tax reform are better organized, better financed, more politically skilled, have better connections, and work night and day to protect their interests. They not only understand the intricate structure of power in Congress, the subtleties of the political process, and the sensitivities of particular congressmen and senators, but congressmen know that they speak for the big campaign contributors. And, many congressmen, who feel heavily dependent on these contributors for the bulk of reelection campaign funds, are understandably sympathetic to their points of view. If campaign expenses were paid largely or wholly from public funds, reformers could feel more optimistic. As for the reform-minded, they are largely unorganized, except for ill-financed organizations like Common Cause. (Whether the AFL-CIO would mobilize to support reforms which could be construed as threatening to the economy remains to be seen.) They cannot afford to hire the expensive legal and lobbying talent that the National Association of Manufacturers, the Chamber of Commerce, and the variety of specialized business organizations can recruit. They must depend, for the most part, on the liberal magazines and newspapers for educating public opinion and needling congressmen, and, of course, on a president who shares their objectives. If an aroused public opinion were involved, the reformers would be immeasurably strengthened. But the general public, at least up to now, has been far more interested in tax reductions for the middle-income groups than in "soaking the rich."

The nature of Congressional organization and the legislative process also plays into the hands of those who would obstruct tax reform. Congress has always been an obstacle course, which tends to sustain the interests of the negative rather than the positive forces of society. (Note the author's subtle semantic technique of identifying tax reform with the "positive forces" of society!) The obstacles are numerous. If those interested in sabotaging legislation cannot persuade a chairman to pigeonhole a bill, they may be able to kill it in a subcommittee; if not in a subcommittee, then in the full committee; if not in the full committee, then perhaps the House Rules Committee will agree either to sit on the bill or to issue orders reducing its chances on the floor; if not killed or mutilated in the House, perhaps a Senate subcommittee chairman will be responsive to their pleas; or the full Senate committee; or a filibuster may be mounted; or the bill may be killed or mangled on the Senate floor. The conference committee which reconciles divergent bills may perform the desired surgery; or the conference-approved bill may be killed on the floor of either House or Senate; or the president may be amenable to veto pressures. In brief, a bill either can be nibbled to insignificance in the labyrinthine catacombs of Congress or can be given the coup de grace at any one of a number of legislative hurdles. Anyone who thinks men of wealth do not have powerful and determined friends stationed at many of these passes does not know much about American politics.

Finally, as we have indicated, the American people are probably not very unhappy about the current distribution of wealth. In the first place, almost none of them knows how much income and how much wealth are controlled by a tiny percentage of the American people. If they did know, would they care very much? Probably more than they do now. But most Americans seem to prefer a country in which people can become millionaires; their envy of the wealthy seem less pronounced than their admiration of them. Americans are also prone to believe, without much skeptical questioning, that adequate economic incentives demand enormous income differentials. How enormous? Well, about the way things are! Like most people, Americans have a tendency to approve that which is familiar. Major tax reform and significant income redistribution smack of socialism and Marxism, moreover, and that is normally enough to doom any proposal.

Having put forth and briefly examined the awesome difficulties which confront tax reform, it would still be imprudent to rule it out altogether. Suppose a President deeply believed in tax reform and gave his utmost to bring it about. Suppose, in a series of television addresses, he set forth the facts about income and wealth distribution, argued the inequities thereof, appealed to the populist impulse that often slumbers but never dies in a democratic society—what then? Would the president, if skillful, resourceful, and resolute, arouse enough public support to put his program across? No one knows because no president has tried. If the President used all of the marvelous array of leadership tools at his disposal, if he employed the veto and threat of veto with maxmimum effect—what might he accomplish? This much is clear: If he succeeded, it would be one of the greatest political coups of all time. The battle would be bitter almost beyond belief, the animosities engendered would jeopardize the rest of his program, and only a president with the strongest convictions and the greatest courage would dare make the attempt. Still, it would be interesting if . . .

NOTES

1. Sources are Robert J. Lampman, "Measured Inequality of Income: What Does it Mean and What Can it Tell Us," *Annals,* September 1973, p. 82; Herman P. Miller, "Inequality, Poverty and Taxes," *Dissent,* Winter 1975, pp. 40–49; "TRB,"*New Republic,* January 1, 1972, p. 6.
2. Miller, "Inequality, Poverty and Taxes," pp. 44–45.
3. Stanley S. Surrey, "The Sheltered Life," *New York Times Magazine,* April 13, 1975, p. 60.
4. Miller, "Inequality, Poverty and Taxes," p. 43. Miller says the top 1 percent pay 29 percent or 38 percent, depending on "eight different variants regarding the incidence assumptions of the various kinds of taxes."
5. Ralph C. Deans, "Redistribution of Income," *Editorial Research Reports,* pp. 650–651.

6. Sanford Rose, "The Truth About Income Inequality in the U.S.," *Fortune,* December 1972, p. 172.

7. Miller, "Inequality, Poverty and Taxes," p. 49.

8. *Time,* January 5, 1973, p. 69, and Robert J. Lampman, "What Does it do for the Poor?—A New Test for National Policy," *The Public Interest,* Winter 1974, p. 71.

9. Lampman, "Measured Inequality of Income: What Does it Mean and What Can it Tell Us," p. 82.

10. Irving Kristol, "Of Populism and Taxes," *The Public Interest,* Summer 1972, p. 10.

11. For an interesting commentary on equality, see Alan Fox, "Is Equality a Necessity?," *Dissent,* Winter 1975.

12. Robert J. Lampman, *Ends and Means of Reducing Income Poverty,* Chicago, Markham, 1971, pp. 37–42. Reprinted by permission of the publisher.

13. John Rawls, *A Theory of Justice,* Cambridge, Massachusetts, Harvard University Press, 1972, passim.

14. Lampman, *Ends and Means,* p. 37, n. 35.

15. Lampman, *Ends and Means,* p. 38.

16. Lampman, *Ends and Means,* p. 38–39.

17. Lampman, *Ends and Means,* p. 39.

18. Irving Kristol, "About Equality," p. 47. Reprinted from *Commentary,* by permission; Copyright © 1972 by the American Jewish Committee.

19. Quoted in Lampman, *Ends and Means,* p. 39.

20. Kristol, "About Equality," p. 44.

21. Richard A. Easterlin, "Does Money Buy Happiness?" *The Public Interest,* Winter 1973, p. 10.

22. Miller, "Inequality, Poverty and Taxes, p. 44.

23. Richard Armstrong, "The Right Kind of Tax Reform," *Fortune,* December 1972, p. 186.

24. Miller, "Inequality, Poverty and Taxes," p. 49.

25. Lampman, *Ends and Means,* p. 42.

26. Armstrong, "The Right Kind of Tax Reform," p. 180.

27. Armstrong, "The Right Kind of Tax Reform," p. 182.

28. Jerry Jasinowski, "Mr. Nixon's Tax Mythology," *Nation,* October 30, 1972, p. 402.

29. Robert W. Dietsch, "Knowing a Loophole When You See One," *New Republic,* May 27, 1972, p. 13.

30. Philip Stern, "Uncle Sam's Welfare Program—For the Rich," *New York Times Magazine,* April 16, 1972, p. 66.

31. Peter Barnes, "Earned v. Unearned Income," *New Republic,* October 7, 1972, p. 16.

32. Barnes, "Earned v. Unearned Income," p. 16.

33. Philip Stern, *The Rape of the Taxpayer,* New York, Random House, 1973.

34. Joseph Pechman, "The Rich, the Poor and the Taxes They Pay," *The Public Interest,* Fall 1969, p. 27.

35. Surrey, "The Sheltered Life," p. 60.

36. Stern, *The Rape of the Taxpayer.*

37. Surrey, "The Sheltered Life," p. 50.

38. Surrey, "The Sheltered Life," p. 58.

39. Surrey, "The Sheltered Life," p. 52.

40. Surrey, "The Sheltered Life," p. 52.

41. Elizabeth Brenner Drew, "Comment: Washington," *Atlantic,* April 1972, p. 30.

SIX

National Health Insurance: Is This the Time?

America, it seems, is verging on a historical decision about national health insurance. The nation has been comsidering the issue, off and on, since the British adopted compulsory health insurance for its working class in 1911. We have moved, intermittently, toward a more comprehensive health insurance system but have always drawn back when faced with the final plunge. The time finally may have come.

The rising interest in extending our limited system of public health insurance stems from a number of deficiencies in and dissatisfactions with the existing system. These are not the product of any niggardliness in spending on health needs. America devotes a higher percentage of its gross national product to health care than any other nation—over 8 percent ($118 billion in 1975). And Washington expenditures for health care rose from $3.5 billion in 1961 to $35 billion in 1975. But while inflation raised the cost-of-living index 112.5 percent from 1950 to 1974, medical care costs rose a stunning 191 percent. A hospital bed cost $16 per day in 1950 compared with about $120 in 1975 (in the larger cities). And costs continue to rise, creating the kind of political pressure to which Congress normally responds.

Doctors' incomes were also causing a lot of muttering around the country. Average physicians' earnings, thanks partly to income from Medicare and Medicaid, had soared to over $50,000 per year, an amount far above that of other professional groups. Although the United States had approximately 160 doctors per 100,000 persons, compared with less than 120 per 100,000 persons in England and Sweden, many poor or sparsely populated areas were in desperate need of doctors' services. New York, for example, had almost twice as many doctors per 100,000 persons as Mississippi was able to attract. In general, rural areas and inner-city areas were in the worst straits. Thousands of communities have no doctors at all. Because of inadequate income, facilities, or the doctor shortage, from 30 to 45 million Americans were believed to be receiving inferior medical care.[1] Most of these people were poor. Moreover, in the words of one writer:

Health services for the poor . . . suffer from depersonalization, disorganization, and inadequate emphasis on health counselling or preventive care. Although private physicians provide some of their care, few poor patients have sustained personal relationships with their physicians. . . . In addition, the old attitudes toward charity patients still prevail, with the result that services are frequently inconvenient to use or personally degrading.[2]

Conservative Senator Wallace F. Bennett noted that 50 percent of poor children aren't immunized against childhood diseases. He added, "Those who need care most often get care least." A million persons per day (especially the poor) are forced to seek medical aid at emergency wards, which are usually badly understaffed and involve an average waiting time of five hours.

Professional students of medicine complain that the American system in general places insufficient stress on preventive medicine while overinvesting in equipment for the more dramatic types of surgery and overrewarding doctors performing such surgery. America is an excellent place for getting high-quality treatment of the more unusual maladies but less good for persons with the garden variety of diseases and ailments. We need more outpatient care and less hospitalization; studies show that in some areas 25 percent of the beds are occupied by persons who didn't need them, except to qualify for insurance payments. Other criticisms allege that our current system does not encourage management economies, especially in hospitals, that group medical practice should be given a strong and continuing stimulus, and that better regional planning of medical facilities is needed; private medical insurance has too many loopholes; far too many unnecessary operations are performed.[3]

No nation's medical system, of course, is without defects; the indictment listed above, even if wholly valid, would not ipso facto condemn our system as second-rate. Harry Schwartz, editorial writer for the *New York Times,* insists that not only is there no "medical crisis," but that America need not be ashamed of its medical system. Although detractors deplore the facts that America is only thirteenth in infant mortality, twenty-second in male longevity, and eleventh in female longevity, Schwartz emphasizes more encouraging facts. U.S. infant mortality is about the same as in Great Britain and Canada, lower than in Belgium, West Germany, Israel, and the Soviet Union and fell 20 percent from 1965 to 1970. The U.S. death rate dropped from 9.0 per 1,000 in 1947 to 7.3 per 1,000 in 1967. Although conceding the maldistribution of doctors, he says the United States has one of the highest ratios of doctors to population of any country in the world. The number of U.S. medical doctors increased almost 50 percent from 1950 to 1970; by 1971, 40 percent more students were being admitted to our burgeoning medical schools than in 1965. He warns that turning American medicine over to a "bureaucratic monster" will not benefit the American people.[4]

Still, everyone believes America can and should do better. Critics believe that other countries—especially in Western Europe and the British Commonwealth—spend less per capita and get more for their money. They argue that ours is a jerry-built system, a "nonsystem system," haphazard, unplanned, and responding to random factors and pressures rather than representing a rational organization and application of our medical resources. It's time, they say, to pull up our socks and get to work.

Before presenting the alternatives from which the nation may choose, a bit of historical background will help place the problem in a better perspective. Although Bismarck introduced the first national health insurance program in Germany in 1883, American interest in health insurance was minimal until David Lloyd George, then chancellor of the exchequer, pushed through his famous National Insurance Act of 1911 in Britain. This legislation provided compulsory sickness insurance for most British workers, assuring them of doctors' services and hospital care financed by workers, employers, and the general tax-paying public. The bill precipitated a tremendous furor in Britain, with doctors threatening to strike. A few years later a Social Insurance Committee of the American Medical Association (AMA) undertook a study of national health insurance. Although the committee made an affirmative recommendation, no supporting action was taken by the AMA's House of Delegates. During the war the question was largely shelved, although opponents of health insurance were apparently able to make some headway with charges that health insurance had originated with the hated Germans, was more developed in Germany than elsewhere, and was a typical "Hun" measure. At any rate, the health insurance issue faded, and little was heard of it for the next twenty years.

During the formulation of the Social Security Act of 1935, serious consideration was given to including medical costs among the financial hazards to be insured by the act. The President's Committee on Economic Security recommended that compulsory health insurance be incorporated into the Social Security program. The proposal was set aside, however, lest its controversial character jeopardize the passage of the Social Security bill.

Interest in health insurance was renewed during World War II, spurred on by Lord William Beveridge's famous report outlining a sweepingly comprehensive plan to protect Britons against most of the fiscal hazards that lead to destitution. The Beveridge Plan was warmly received in Britain, partly because the depression had caused the most acute distress among the working classes and partly because the wartime mood made Britons more responsive to collective measures seemingly related to the national welfare. The National Health Service Act of 1948, enacted by the Labour Party, insured the entire nation against the costs of doctors' bills, hospitalization, medicines, eyeglasses, special appliances, and dental services.

In effect endorsing the Wagner-Murray-Dingell bill of 1943, President Harry S Truman proposed in 1949 that a system of compulsory national health insurance be established in the United States. Truman's plan, following a similar proposal in 1945, called for insuring the costs of surgery, hospitalization, laboratory fees, dental care, and home nursing care. The program was to be financed by a payroll income tax of 1.5 percent each for employer and employee. As in Britain, doctors would be free to enter or stay outside the system. If they chose to be included, however, they were to have a choice of payment by salary (to attract doctors into "underdoctored areas" where population was sparse and income prospects bleak), by a fee-for-service arrangement (earnings to be dependent on the amount and kind of doctors' services provided), or by a panel system. Under the last, a doctor would be paid in proportion to the number of persons who agreed to select him as their "family doctor." Persons would be free to select a doctor and free to change doctors when they wished. Doctors who wished to have a private practice on the side or a completely private practice would be permitted to do so; the percentage who have found a completely private practice profitable have been small, however.

A Gallup poll had earlier shown that about 70 percent of the American people favored the general principle of national health insurance. Mr. Truman's proposal nevertheless ignited one of the most crackling political battles of the century. The AMA violently opposed the plan, and it mustered a formidable group of allies. Enlisting the services of a famous public relations team, Whitaker & Baxter, the AMA carried out one of the most massive and successful campaigns of public persuasion in the nation's history.[5] Truman's plan failed to emerge from committee, and its reputation became so tarnished that even Adlai Stevenson, though sympathetic with the health insurance principle, declined to endorse it in his 1952 and 1956 campaigns. Instead, he contented himself with vague, general statements about the need to study more effective means for dealing with health costs.

In 1957, Representative Aime Forand of Rhode Island proposed the precursor to Medicare. He recommended an increase in Social Security taxes to finance hospital and surgical care for Social Security beneficiaries over sixty-five years of age. The Forand bill, strong supported by then-Senator John F. Kennedy, was defeated in a postconvention congressional session in 1960.

Following President Kennedy's assassination and Lyndon Johnson's landslide election in 1964, a heavily Democratic Congress passed the historic Medicare bill, which insured all Americans over age sixty-five with sixty days of hospitalization for each "spell of sickness" and provided for the payment of surgical bills if the elderly matched Washington's contribution toward the payment of private insurance premiums. Congress also enacted Medicaid, whereby Washington heavily subsidized state programs that paid medical costs for low income families.

THE AMA'S INCREDIBLE TRACK RECORD

Almost from the beginning, the American Medical Association has opposed federal legislation designed to facilitate the payment of medical bills or provide different forms of medical service. As already noted, over a half century ago the AMA declined to support its Social Insurance Committee's favorable report on national health insurance. Although the AMA offers no apologies on that score, it presumably is not proud of its initial opposition to the American Red Cross blood bank, federal aid to medical schools, public venereal disease clinics, free diagnostic clinics for tuberculosis and cancer, public school health services, federal aid to state public health agencies, group medical practice, private health insurance, and Medicare.[6]

In the course of its opposition to governmental initiatives in the medical and social insurance field, the AMA resorted to some interesting semantic ploys. Its spokesmen called the Social Security tax "a compulsory socialist tax" in 1963 and followed this up with a charge that Social Security and unemployment compensation were definite steps "toward either Communism or socialism."[7] The extension of Social Security benefits to cover the disabled was not only a "serious threat to American medicine," but another step toward "socialization." Federal aid to state health organizations for maternal and child welfare care was branded as "wasteful and extravagant, unproductive of results, and tending to promote communism."[8] The editor of the *Journal of the American Medical Association* said group medical practice "savors of communism" and was the equivalent of "medical soviets."[9] In 1932, the *Journal* charged that voluntary health insurance was "socialism and communism" when a distinguished committee recommended the promotion of voluntary prepayment plans.[10] The latter was labelled an "incitement to revolution" by the *Journal*'s editor.

John Knowles, whose appointment by President Nixon as Secretary of Health, Education and Welfare was withdrawn because of furious AMA opposition, wrote in 1970 that "The AMA . . . has resisted every major social change in medicine over the past 50 years. It is an incredible track record."[11] He added that "the situation has degenerated to the point where AMA opposition to any program relating to the nation's health means there must be something good in it for the people."[12]

What accounts for the AMA's patently deplorable history? For several decades the *Journal of the American Medical Association* was edited by Morris Fishbein, whose ideological opposition to government involvement in medicine strongly colored the influential *Journal*'s editorial position and article selection, as well as its handling of letters to the editor. Letters friendly to public health insurance at home or abroad were rarely printed. Fishbein left his mark on an entire generation of doctors, many of whom are now highly placed in the AMA hierarchy. Critics charge that the leaders of the AMA are usually munificently paid specialists who fear that government health insurance will bring controls over doctors' remuneration. Any powerful interest group, moreover, is reluctant to share its power, whether with other interest groups or with representatives of the general public. Finally, fear of the unknown acts as a conservative social force in circumstances such as those confronting the AMA. The AMA leadership is still conservative but less hidebound than in the past. As for American doctors, 51 percent of them now favor a limited form of national health insurance.

Most proposals to improve our medical system assume the inadequacy of our private health insurance industry. The statistics on private health insurance are subject to a "see the doughnut—see the hole" interpretation. Such insurance has increased its coverage over the past forty years; almost 90 percent of the population now has some of its benefits. Of persons over sixty-five, 94 percent have some kind of private health insurance. On the other hand, only about one-third of those under sixty-five who earn under $3,000 a year have any hospital or surgical insurance. Only about half of the American people enjoy the protection of major medical insurance, which usually has a reimbursement ceiling of about $5,000. About one-third of the hospital insurance plans limit their coverage to not over sixty days. Less than half of the population has coverage for doctors' office calls and home visits; private insurance, overall, pays less than half of the money personally expended for health care. In the words of *Consumer Reports*, "Health insurance coverage, in short, is nonexistent for many of the poor and inadequate for almost everyone else.''[13]

Critics of the private health insurance industry also contend that it returns a much smaller percentage of its gross income to the consumer than do public insurance plans and that it fails to encourage cost-consciousness on the part of the medical profession. In the words of the AFL-CIO, ''They have acted simply as a pass-through mechanism, paying for whatever care was offered, good or bad, needed or unneeded, efficient or inefficient.''[14]

THE *CONSUMER REPORTS* GUIDELINES

Consumer Reports offered the following guidelines for developing an adequate system of national health insurance:

1. Everyone's health-care needs should be covered, and the entire population should be included within the system.

In insurance terminology, that's called *universal* coverage. With universal coverage, the risk of loss from illness can be shared equitably. Coverage should be *mandatory,* not voluntary. Otherwise, those who most need coverage, the poor, are likely to risk, or be forced to risk, allocating their meager resources to more immediate needs, such as food. There should be a single policy and program for everyone (*a unitary plan*), not several plans offering one set of benefits to the poor and another to the nonpoor: It guarantees coverage between jobs, for example, and it protects against higher rates that may result from an illness in the family. But the basic argument for a unitary plan is social fairness. The inevitable outcome of separate programs is discrimination against the poor in the receipt of health services. . . .

2. There should be no connection between a patient's income and the extent or quality of care dispensed by doctors, hospitals, and others.

Financial hardship resulting from illness should be ended. Benefits should include: all hospital charges; doctor bills, whether incurred in the office or a hospital; preventive services, such as prenatal care, well-baby care, and eye examinations; short-term care for mental illness; and long-term nursing-home care. In insurance language again, these are called *comprehensive, balanced benefits.* Any "cost-sharing" between the insurance plan and the patient should be arranged in such a way that no patient is tempted to neglect needed care or is faced with financial hardship as a result of some medical need. Cost-sharing usually takes the form of a *deductible* (a minimum amount paid by the patient before insurance payments begin) or *coinsurance* (a percentage of the bill charged directly to the patient). It is argued that some form of cost-sharing is desirable to discourage overburdening the health-care system with trivial or unnecessary demands for service. . . .

3. The plan should be financed progressively and in a manner open to public scrutiny.

All the national health insurance proposals under consideration in Congress involve public spending. The money to finance the plan should be raised through a form of progressive taxation—those who can afford less should pay less, and those who can afford more should pay more. In addition, the cost of the program should be visible to the public, so that the public can decide through democratic processes the place of health insurance in national spending priorities. . . .

4. The program should provide incentives for efficiency, control over the cost and quality of services, and encouragement of alternative or innovative systems for delivering health care.

The new system should end "cost-plus" payments to medical providers. (When a hospital or nursing home knows an insurer will pay all costs incurred, plus a premium, there is no incentive to control costs. Such institutions should be held to negotiated budgets and rewarded for their efficiencies.) Physicians who participate in the system should be paid according to fee schedules negotiated through their professional societies. The system should encourage formation of such alternate modes of practice as health maintenance organizations (HMOs). . . . And it should subsidize the training of more health professionals, since more will be needed to provide appropriate care to everyone. . . .

5. The administrators of the program should be accountable to the public, and consumers should have a voice in administration.

The organization administering national health insurance will disburse tens of billions of publicly raised dollars each year. This organization should owe its allegiance to taxpayers, not to health-care providers. The administering organization should be accountable to the Congress and to consumers through well-defined review, grievance, and appeal mechanisms. Consumers should have a say at all levels of administration, preferably through elected representatives. . . .[15]

FOUR FORKS IN THE ROAD

Where then, do we go from here? Our choices are apparently among a program recommended by the AMA; major medical or *catastrophic* health insurance; a stripped-down Republican version of national health insurance; comprehensive national health insurance. (If the Republicans retain control of the White House, we are likely to get a compromise between the latter two options.)

The AMA plan relies heavily on voluntary public purchases of private health insurance policies. The government would pay for the health insurance premiums of the poor while granting tax credits, inversely related to income levels, for other families and individuals who buy private insurance.

The chances of the AMA *Medicredit* plan passing Congress are slight, however, partly because of the AMA's past record and partly because the plan flunks a number of criteria which are approved by most Democrats and by many Republicans.

Major medical or catastrophic health insurance usually calls for a payroll tax to create a fund for paying family (or individual) medical costs that substantially exceed normal expenditures or exceed, say, 10 percent of a family's income. (100,000 catastrophic illnesses per year cost an average of over $25,000 per patient; most families find this burden financially shattering.) The family or individual usually would pay a portion of the expense involved in order to reduce the tendency toward exorbitant charges, which would probably occur if the government paid the total bill. One of the plan's principal attractions is its relatively small cost compared to more ambitious programs.

Critic Anne Somers believes catastrophic health insurance plans invite purveyors of medical care to raise prices "especially for the seriously ill and dying." They would shift attention and funds from prevention, health maintenance and home care to institutional treatment; because Ms. Somers believes the deductible is likely to be rather high, it would prove disillusioning in practice.[16] Other critics contend it would entail a great deal of family record keeping and governmental checking of those records when claims were presented. It might also encourage longer hospital stays than are really needed, thus exacerbating an already serious problem. (Some way should be found, incidentally, to prevent such insurance from expensively prolonging not life, but the death ordeal of hopelessly ill persons.)

Victor Fuchs, in his excellent book, *Who Shall Live?* (New York, Basic Books, 1974, p. 136), is skeptical of major risk (or catastrophic) health insurance. "In my view, its appeal is extremely deceptive. It seems like a cheap way of getting out of a crisis but it offers little hope of solving the major health care problems now facing the American public."

The Republican plan is likely to stress employer insurance for employees and their families (including catastrophic insurance), along with an emphasis on deductibles and coinsurance to keep costs down. The poor will probably have their medical costs paid wholly or largely from general revenues.

Liberals will criticize it for failing to measure up to a number of the standards set forth by *Consumer Reports.* Even if they do not oppose all deductibles and coinsurance, they will contend that those offered by the GOP are less liberal than they would favor.

Comprehensive national health insurance would cover almost all medical and dental costs (although partial private payments for prescription drugs and office calls might be included in the plan). It would be financed by a payroll tax, perhaps supplemented by general revenues. The government would not own or operate the hospitals, nor would doctors work on a salary for the government; private insurance might or might not survive in the administration of the program. Doctors would not be forced to cooperate with the program but over 90 percent would probably find it in their economic self-interest to do so.

Victor Fuchs endorses compulsory health insurance but wants payments made on a capitation basis—that is, a doctor or group of doctors would be given a fixed number of dollars per year per patients whom they are able to attract and are willing to serve. The capitation system, he says, would tend to prevent unnecessary operations, discourage doctors from keeping patients in hospitals for excessive periods, reduce excessive drug prescribing, and generally encourage maximum cost consciousness in the medical system. At the same time, Fuchs cites experience with group medical practice systems (which use the capitation system) as evidence that doctors do not neglect their patients under this system (*Who Shall Live?* pp. 138–141, 150).

Under group medical practice (often referred to as *health maintenance organizations*) a number of doctors with complementary specialties offer members of the community their combined services on a prepaid, comprehensive basis. The advantages are numerous: The patient can be assigned to the specialist best qualified to deal with his problem without being shunted from one location to another; doctors save money by using the same laboratory, X-ray, and diagnostic equipment instead of duplicating these for each doctor's office; consultation between doctors is promoted, an advantage to the patient and to the maintenance of a stimulating professional atmosphere. Doctors' incomes are divided among themselves on a mutually agreeable basis.

Comprehensive national health insurance faces four major complaints. Skeptics believe a "free" medical service would prompt excessive demands on doctors' services, as patients flocked to their doctors with both trivial and imaginary complaints. This would reduce the doctors' capacity to care for those who really need help.

This system allegedly would produce a kind of "assembly-line" medicine, with doctors giving their patients impersonal and perfunctory attention as they rushed people through their offices. The quality of the doctor-patient relationship would suffer, and with it, the quality of medical care.

Doctors would be swamped with paperwork, since government bureaucrats are notoriously enchanted with reports; to prevent "abuses" of the system and insure that the public was getting "its money's worth," forms would proliferate on every hand, consuming more and more of the doctors' valuable time. As doctors' strikes abroad indicate, doctors are often unhappy with "government medicine;" people rarely do as good a job when they dislike the system under which they operate, and doctors strongly prefer a private practice to "civil-service medicine."

Finally, costs allegedly would soar if we established a national health service or a national health insurance system. If medical costs are high now, imagine what they would be once the system was snarled with bureaucratic red tape and the public was taking full advantage of a "something for nothing" medical service.

THE BRITISH EXPERIENCE

Probably the best rebuttal to these charges is found in the experience of the British system of *socialized medicine,* which went into effect in 1948.

This system involved comprehensive coverage, jointly financed by workers, employers, and the general treasury; most hospitals were taken over and run by the government; general practitioners were paid a flat rate per patient on their "panels," with the patient free to select the doctor of his choice; specialists were paid on a fixed fee-for-service basis, with fee rates reflecting their experience and special training; special "distinction grants" were made to outstanding doctors; doctors were free to practice outside the system if they chose to service comparatively wealthy clientele (3–4 percent did so); patients' only direct costs were a fraction of the charge for drug prescriptions. All of the apprehensions expressed above were voiced in Britain, but the only one which materialized was that of cost—and costs have riven sharply in *all* systems of medical practice throughout the world.

Ten years after the British National Health Service (NHS) went into effect, Harvard's Dr. Harry Eckstein reported that "there is precious little evidence to suggest that patients have abused the service by making inordinate demands on the practitioners."[17] A few years later, Dr. Osler Peterson announced after extensive study that Americans visit their doctors more often than do the British.[18] Dr. Richard M. Titmuss, head of the Department of Social Science and Administration at the London School of Economics, wrote that there was "no evidence of inordinate demands on the family doctor since 1948."[19] Kenneth Robinson, British Member of Parliament, confirmed this in an article for the *New York Times Magazine:* "There is little evidence to show that the problem is any more acute in Britain than elsewhere."[20]

(Nathan Glazer wrote in 1973 that about the same percentage of Englishmen visit a doctor annually as in the United States. Drawing on Odin Anderson's comparative study of the health-care systems of England, Sweden, and the U.S., he notes that England has the happiest public and the unhappiest doctors of the three while America has the happiest doctors and the unhappiest public. The English have been able to keep health costs down to a relatively stable 5.2 percent of the GNP while the U.S. figure has risen sharply to 8 percent. Strict controls over hospital costs receive much credit. Glazer also finds the U.S. fee-for-service system partly responsible for the lower ethical tone of American medicine.[21])

As for the alleged vast increase in paper work, Dr. Paul Gemmill of the Wharton School, University of Pennsylvania, reported that although 39 percent of British doctors thought paperwork under the new system was "burdensome," 61 percent did not. "Both sides agreed that the National Health Service had increased certain kinds of form-filling but that it was largely offset by no longer having to make out bills and prod patients for private fees.''[22] Robinson calculated that doctors spent not over an hour or so per week on paperwork for the NHS. Almont Lindsey, a history professor at the University of Virginia, found that only about one-fourth of the doctors were concerned about their clerical work.[23]

Was the National Health Service swamped with bureaucratic employees? The Service stated, quite surprisingly, that it employed only 32,000 administrative and clerical personnel, or roughly one for every 1,500 persons. Furthermore, administrative costs were running to about 3 percent, quite a remarkable record.

The doctor-patient relationship was said to have improved rather than deteriorated under NHS because the financial barrier had been abolished. Robinson says, ''Most doctors . . . regard the elimination of the fee for service not as a handicap but as a positive advantage to doctor-patient relations. . . .''[24]

Young doctors, it appears, grumbled surprisingly little about the requirement that they set up their initial practice in ''underdoctored'' areas.

As for the overall success of the program, it is difficult to find a responsible account that is not generally favorable. On the tenth anniversary of the National Health Service, the *Journal of the British Medical Association* carried columns of praise for its performance. Don Cook says, ''Opponents who would turn back the clock ten years and return to the old medical system are really nonexistent.''[25] The widely respected *London Times* said, ''If the AMA has any regard for the truth, they should put the record straight: the American people should know that far from being a failure the British service can be counted a qualified success.''[26] Winston Churchill's personal physician declared, ''If consultants were asked whether they desired to go back to the old days, I believe the overwhelming majority would prefer the conditions of today.''[27] Dr. Eckstein avers that ''[the Service] has made nothing appreciably worse and a number of things appreciably better.''[28] Lindsey says, ''That the Health Service has won its way into the hearts of the British people was demonstrated in every poll taken. . . .''[29] In 1962, a Gallup poll showed that 89 percent of the people were still satisfied with NHS.

In recent years, British doctors have become increasingly unhappy with the system because their salaries (although initially about the same as pre-NHS levels) have fallen to levels that compare poorly with those of doctors in western Europe, the British Commonwealth countries, and the United States.[30] A shortage of hospital beds has also contributed to declining public satisfaction with the system. These developments, however, are by-products of Britain's severe economic crisis rather than being an inherent aspect of national health insurance systems. Most countries with comprehensive systems have not experienced a comparable discontent.

There is no substantive reason why national health insurance would not be a workable system, once the initial kinks were worked out. Experience not only in Britain, but in virtually every industrialized nation in the world has demonstrated that comprehensive national health insurance (or socialized medicine, if the government owns and operates the hospitals as well as pays the medical bills) produces general satisfaction among both doctors and patients. True, doctor opposition is often bitter at first, but it usually dies down in a few years.

Although national health insurance is almost always "successful," the results, predictably, are less gratifying than its proponents prophesy. Martin Feldstein, for example, notes that "detailed controls, fee schedules, and limits on hospital charges might . . . prevent rising costs, but the experience of Canada, Britain, and Sweden suggests that health costs rise very rapidly even in government health programs with extensive direct controls."[31] After an exhaustive study of socialized medicine in sixteen countries, William Glasser observes that "[socialized medicine] enables the poor to get medical care more easily . . . but the quantity and quality of care are never altered as much as its creators had hoped."[32] Some countries have found it necessary or desirable to institute small charges for each call to the doctor's office and for prescriptions.[33] Although advocates of national health insurance often urge that the consumer be given a greater voice in the organization and delivery of medical care, Glasser notes that where administrative decisions are "made by mixed committees with lay and professional members," the doctors' voice tends to prevail.[34]

Whatever the experience abroad, America is unlikely to adopt full-fledged national health insurance for some time. It would *appear* to add a huge amount to the national budget, even though the net cost to the citizen might be only about $10–15 billion, since most of the cost would replace payments rendered for medical care under the existing system. But the health insurance of many employees is now invisibly paid through employer contributions negotiated under collective bargaining agreements or voluntarily granted as a fringe benefit; turning even a portion of this cost over to the taxpayer would not be welcomed. Any attempt to torpedo America's $20 billion private health insurance industry would also meet fierce resistance. The most likely outcome, as suggested earlier, is a compromise between a comprehensive plan and a less ambitious plan favored by conservatives in both parties.

If developments occur as prophesied, they will coincide with the general philosophy of Anne Somers, who sees national health insurance as probably inevitable but prefers moving there by stages. She believes

". . . the most compelling argument for the slower approach is fear that we still do not understand all the factors involved in a total program and could end up with a real monstrosity."[35] (The author believes that if a carefully devised program of catastrophic health insurance were combined with insurance coverage for the medical expenses of children—plus the Medicare program—perhaps the rest of our medical bills could be paid by private action. At a time when the antitax, antispend, antigovernment spirit runs high, this may be the most politically feasible approach now available.) Still, sooner or later, for better or for worse, it appears that comprehensive national health insurance will come. America has always lagged behind Western Europe in enacting social legislation; unemployment compensation, workmen's compensation, old-age pensions, and disability insurance, for example, were enacted only after European experiments suggested their desirability. Once Congress embarks on social welfare programs like Medicare and Medicaid, it has a penchant for broadening those programs. Having reached the ultimate destination, we will be reminded again and again that nothing Washington can do is as important to the nation's health as the health practices of the individual. Ms. Somers writes: ". . . Most of the nation's major health problems—including automobile accidents, all forms of drug addiction including alcoholism, venereal disease, obesity, many cancers, most heart disease, and most infant mortality—are primarily attributable not to shortcomings on the part of [the medical system] but to the living conditions, ignorance, or irresponsibility of the patient."[36]

When people eat less and eat more wisely, exercise more, drink less, smoke less, and worry less, the nation's health will improve rapidly. That is, when people stop acting like people.

NOTES

1. Robert W. Dietsch, "Care You Can't Buy," *New Republic,* May 20, 1972, p. 14.
2. Mary W. Herman, "The Poor: Their Medical Needs and the Health Service Available to Them," *Annals,* January 1972, p. 21, reprinted by permission of the author; also see Peter Isaacson, "Poverty and Health," *New Republic,* December 14, 1974, and *New York Times,* October 27, 1974, p. E9.
3. On unnecessary operations, see Robert D. Wright, "The Immorality of Excellence in Health Care," *Virginia Quarterly Review,* Spring 1974, p. 183.
4. Harry Schwartz, "Health Care in America: A Heretical Diagnosis," *Saturday Review,* August 14, 1971. This theme is more fully developed in Harry Schwartz, *The Case for American Medicine,* New York, McKay, 1972.
5. Irwin Ross, "The Supersalesmen of California Politics: Whitaker & Baxter," *Harper's,* July 1959, pp. 55–61.
6. *Toledo Blade,* May 31, 1962.

7. Speech by Representative Cecil R. King to House of Representatives, March 5, 1962 (reprint), p. 1.

8. King, Speech to House of Representatives, p. 1.

9. Milton Mayer, "The Dogged Retreat of the Doctors," *Harper's*, December 1949, p. 29.

10. James H. Means, "The Doctors' Lobby," *Atlantic*, October 1950, p. 57.

11. John Knowles, "Where Doctors Fail," *Saturday Review*, August 22, 1970, p. 22. For a defense of the AMA, see Dr. Max H. Parrott, *Vital Speeches*, April 15, 1975.

12. Knowles, "Where Doctors Fail," pp. 22–23.

13. "National Health Insurance: Which Way to Go?," *Consumer Reports*, February 1975, p. 118.

14. Wallace F. Bennett, "Controversy Over National Health Insurance Proposals," *Congressional Digest*, February 1972, p. 45.

15. "National Health Insurance: Which Way to Go?," *Consumer Reports*, February 1975, pp. 119–122. Reprinted by permission.

16. Anne R. Somers, "Catastrophic Health Insurance? A Catastrophe?," *Medical Economics*, May 10, 1971, p. 213.

17. Harry Eckstein, *The English Health Service: Its Origins, Structure and Achievements*, Cambridge, Massachusetts, Harvard University Press, 1958, p. 222.

18. Osler Peterson, "Medical Care in the U.S.," *Scientific American*, August 1963, p. 22.

19. Richard M. Titmuss, "What British Doctors Really Think about Socialized Medicine," *Harper's*, February 1963, p. 24.

20. Kenneth Robinson, "The Case for Britain's Health Service," *New York Times Magazine*, November 18, 1962, p. 49.

21. Nathan Glazer, "Perspectives on Health Care," *The Public Interest*, Spring 1973, pp. 124–125.

22. Don Cook, "Socialized Medicine, Ten Years Old,"*Harper's*, May 1959, p. 36.

23. Almont Lindsey, *Socialized Medicine in England and Wales: The National Health Service, 1948–1961*, Chapel Hill, University of North Carolina Press, 1962, p. 199.

24. Robinson, "The Case for Britain's Health Service," p. 46.

25. Cook, "Socialized Medicine, Ten Years Old," p. 32.

26. London *Times*, July 14, 1962, p. 105.

27. Cook, "Socialized Medicine, Ten Years Old," p. 32.

28. Eckstein, *The English Health Service*, p. 236.

29. Almont Lindsey, "How Socialized Medicine Works," *New Republic*, June 4, 1962, p. 11.

30. "Showdown In British Health Care," *U.S. News and World Report*, March 3, 1975, p. 63.

31. Martin Feldstein, "A New Approach to National Health Insurance," *The Public Interest*, Spring 1971, p. 98.

32. William Glasser, " 'Socialized Medicine' in Practice," *The Public Interest*, Spring 1966, p. 104.

33. Note a similar admission by a group-health official, reported by Schwartz, "Health Care in America," p. 55.

34. Glasser, " 'Socialized Medicine' in Practice," p. 94.

35. Somers, "Catastrophic Health Insurance?," p. 173.

36. Somers, "Catastrophic Health Insurance?," p. 161. A similar observation was made by Schwartz, "Health Care in America," p. 55.

SEVEN

Crime: The Dark at the End of the Tunnel?

America has become a crime-ridden and fear-ridden society. Americans commit over 10 million recorded crimes a year; if all crimes were reported, the figure might be 50–100 percent higher. Serious crime has risen 125 percent in the last ten years; the United States has fifty times as many murders as Japan, the United Kingdom and West Germany combined. Violent crime is committed so casually in many big-city areas that even professional criminals are uneasy about working there. Over 100 murders are committed in the public schools each year, and teachers are assaulted 70,000 times annually.[1] 70,000 times!

From time to time, polls find Americans regarding crime as the number one problem in this country. The market for German shepherds, Doberman pinschers, pistols, and padlocks could hardly be better. Almost as many private guards as policemen are on the lookout for crime. But despite vast increases in spending for crime prevention, the figures keep rising; in our best years, we congratulate ourselves if the rate of crime *increase* seems to be slowing down.

As for the costs of crime, an informed estimate in 1976 placed this figure at over $95 billion. Organized crime was believed to exact a toll of $40 billion; crimes against property totalled over $25 billion; other crimes exceeded $10 billion; the costs of law enforcement itself (police, corrections, courts) were nearly $15 billion; the cost of private efforts to prevent crime amounted to about $6.5 billion.[2] America has about 500,000 ''career'' criminals, earning anywhere from $20,000 to well over $100,000 a year—all tax-free!

If it provides any satisfaction, urban crime was also scandalously high from 1850 to 1900.[3] In 1855, the New York gang population was estimated at 30,000; one gang posted warnings that police entering its territory would be shot. Police frequently dared not enter many urban zones alone. Newspapers deplored the fact that six-year-olds were roaming the streets, armed with guns and knives. Chicago saloonkeepers expected to be robbed several times a week, and San Francisco's streets were unsafe at night. Statistics were so poorly kept, however, that accurate comparisons with today's crime rate are impossible.

Why is crime far more prevalent in America than in any other industralized nation? The root causes of individual crimes are obscure, criminologists agree. Most experts believe, however, that crime would be rare if children were raised in homes where love and sensible discipline were present. (Why, however, does one child become a criminal and others from the same family become law-abiding citizens?) William and Joan McCord, in *Origins of Crime,* find the deepest roots of crime in the "absence of parental affection" in conjunction with inconsistent discipline, family conflict, and "parents who themselves rebelled against the standards of society."[4] Harvard's James Q. Wilson, perhaps the nation's foremost authority on crime, cites a similar conclusion from distinguished sociologists Sheldon and Eleanor Glueck and expresses his own hunch that they are right.[5] Common sense agrees, whatever the difficulty of establishing empirical proof. But having conceded this elementary point, why has crime risen so rapidly since 1960? Presumably the quantity of family love and of rebellion-prone parents has not altered materially, (though family discipline may have declined).

Among the general stimuli to crime are (or may be!) the following:

1. Crime pays! The risks are small. An adult burglar stands only one chance in 412 of going to jail for a particular job; for juveniles, the chances are one in 659. Norval Morris finds that out of every 100 crimes committed in America, only about half are reported to the police, twelve arrests are made, six convictions are won and only two persons are sent to jail.[6] Insofar as property crimes are concerned, only 0.5 percent of them lead to jail sentences. With these odds and the confidence of most people that they are a little sharper than the next guy, it is no wonder that the criminally inclined are little deterred by our law enforcement system.

Wilson views the attractions of crime from this perspective: "One works at crime at one's convenience, enjoys the esteem of colleagues who think a 'straight' job is stupid and skill at stealing is commendable, looks forward to the occasional 'big score' that may make further work unnecessary for weeks, and relishes the risk and adventure associated with theft. The money value of all these benefits . . . is hard to estimate but is almost certainly far larger than what either public or private employers could offer to unskilled or semi-skilled young workers.''[7]

2. The high birth rate that followed World War II is one of the major contributors to our high crime rate. Adolescents are far more crime prone than adults, and 14- to 17-year-olds are at the top of the list. As the population curve has risen, the percentage of the population that commits a disproportionate amount of crime has also risen.

3. An urbanized society generates more crime than an agrarian society, particularly when the urbanizing process has been rapid. Crime rates are five to ten times higher in the congested areas of the inner city than in rural regions. The reasons for this are fairly obvious: Young people on farms work harder and longer than city children; they have less leisure time for getting into mischief; there are fewer gangs and fewer tempting goods (often alluringly advertised by television) readily available to the thief. Black crime rates are much higher than white, and this can be largely attributed to the heavy influx of southern blacks into large cities since 1940. Uprooted from an established rural culture and its values, placed in an environment challenging their parents' folkways and mores, often jobless and immersed in the harsh milieu of street life where delinquent behavior is often considered normal and nondelinquent behavior abnormal, it would be remarkable if they were not prone to crime. The sharp rise in fatherless black families has accompanied the migration to the cities and contributes appreciably to a family atmosphere conducive to undisciplined and unruly behavior. A further and often unremarked factor is the waning of those religious influences that are an important part of southern black culture but that tend to dissolve in northern ghettoes.

Although widespread black poverty is often cited as the major cause of black crime, this seems to be an overly simplified explanation. Black families were just as poor, or even more so, in rural America than in the inner city, but the factors cited above produce more crime among the urban poor than the rural poor. Moreover, the huge increase in black crime between 1960 and 1970 coincided with the period when blacks were making the greatest economic gains in their history. It is hard to believe, however, that the high rate of involuntary unemployment among urban black youths, a rate several times higher than that of white teenagers, does not contribute to youthful black crime.

(Although blacks comprise about 11 percent of the population, they commit over half of the serious crimes and about 60 percent of the murders. This is not fully explained by the fact that more blacks than whites are lower class; at every socioeconomic level, black crime greatly exceeds that of whites.)[8]

4. In the most profound sense, the prevalence of black crime is the

bitter harvest of centuries of injustice. The problem of black crime is, to a significant extent, the problem of the black father. All too often he either leaves his family or fails to provide the model which male children badly need. This failure goes back to the slavery era when the disorganization of the Negro family gave rise to the familial characteristics that plague it today. The male slave had no opportunity to assume normal parental responsibilities; he could not legally marry, own property, sign contracts, or even testify in court against a white man. In the eyes of the law, he was a cipher; at any time he might be wrenched from his family and sold to another master. He had to surrender his "wife" to his master's lust and often had to accept the fact that his "children" were not his own.

After the Emancipation Proclamation had "freed the slave but ignored the Negro," fresh difficulties arose. Lacking a job or land (in many cases), the sense of responsibility that only freedom can fully develop, and strong family ties, the Negro male often became a drifter— rootless, promiscuous, and covering up his insecurities and lack of self-esteem with a happy-go-lucky air.

Necessarily, then, the Negro mother became the family's mainstay, the one stable element in the children's life. She earned the family bread in the husband's absence, cared for the children, and assumed the dual role of mother and father. Aside from the economic and emotional insecurities generated by this pattern, the children could not look up to their father as a loved, trusted, dependable masculine figure. The absence of such a relationship wreaked heavy psychological damage on the children, especially the boys.

The condition that this background generated will not soon be corrected. It may take several generations to undo the damage wrought by white supremacy.

Black crime rates are so extraordinarily high that a further question should be asked: Why are the parental admonitions and restraints in the typical urban black family so frequently incapable of coping with the destructive influences of the street culture?

To a considerable extent, the street culture has a dynamic of its own —a self-generating, self-perpetuating character which creates its own milieu. But it is also fed to some extent by attitudes brought to the street from the family. This crucially important matter is not well understood. Sociologists have not made the urban black family an object of sustained critical inquiry since Daniel Moynihan's ill-fated memorandum in 1965 brought a storm of abuse upon him.[9] Both blacks and liberal whites excoriated Moynihan for daring to imply that there might be something about black family cultural patterns that needed attention. His critics took the position that whatever unique problems blacks have were wholly the product of white racism, and it was racist to assume anything else. Because the subject is so sensitive and the hazards so great if a researcher arrives at unpalatable conclusions, some scholars believe the job can probably be done only by sociologists from black societies abroad which lack comparable rates of crime.

The high rate of urban black crime cannot be regarded as altogether unique, however, because American slums have always produced high crime rates, whether those slums were inhabited by Irish, Poles, Germans, Italians, or blacks.

5. The heavy influx of heroin into our major cities in recent years can be listed as another important cause of crime. From 35–50 percent of serious crime in many inner-city areas is charged to heroin addicts' efforts to support their costly habit.

Why the sharp increase in heroin usage in the past ten years? James Q. Wilson cites four possible reasons: (1) Greater affluence makes expensive habits more feasible; (2) "the cult of personal liberation among the young may have led to greater experimentation with heroin as it led to greater freedom in dress and manners and the development of a rock music culture;" (3) the Vietnam war gave soldiers easy access to heroin and an incentive to use it; (4) the continued disintegration of urban black family life enhances the role of "street life" influences. Wilson notes, incidentally, that from one-fourth to one-third of heroin users apparently do not resort to the drug to compensate for personal problems.[10]

6. Permissive gun laws are widely and properly blamed for much crime. Unlike the situation in many modern countries, almost any American who wants a gun can get one. Somewhere between 150 million and 200 million guns are in private hands in America, a situation not duplicated in any country in the world. Since 1900, an estimated 800,000 Americans have died from privately owned guns—not far from the number killed in all American wars. (Many of these deaths were accidental, of course.)

In the words of a *Wall Street Journal* writer, "It seems self-evident that the reason guns are involved in so many acts of violence is that there are so many guns in so many hands."[11]

In the United States there are 35–40 million handguns; in Canada there are only one-tenth as many per capita, and in Great Britain, only 2 percent as many. In Britain and West Germany, gun homicides are only one-thirty-fifth as common as in the United States. Tokyo, which has strict gun controls, had only three gun murders in 1970, compared with 500 in New York City alone. Although many factors other than gun possession are involved in these statistics, the relative ubiquity of guns is undoubtedly highly significant.

Hand-gun murders have more than doubled (currently 10,000 gun homicides each year) and gun robberies have tripled since 1964.

In America the gun has a special mystique, perhaps because of the recency of our frontier experience and the character of our popular entertainment. As one writer put it, "From the psychological perspective, guns variously symbolize a source of power, pride, control, independence, strength . . . manliness, virility, potency."[12] For those lacking in self-esteem or subject to oppressive social pressures, the gun is "the great equalizer." Mere possession of a gun (or ready access to it) has subtle but important effects on people. In the ancient Indian epic Ramayana it is written, "The very bearing of weapons changeth the mind of those that carry them." A modern writer noted that "far too many guns, innocently bought, ultimately are turned on other people. One reason, obviously, is that a gun may simply be at hand at a moment of deadly passion. But there is also evidence that the mere presence of a gun can itself stimulate violence under certain conditions."[13] Professor Leonard Berkowitz, psychiatrist at the University of Wisconsin, conducted an experiment with several hundred angry students. One hundred students who saw a gun lying about reacted much more aggressively than one hundred students who did not see a gun. Professor Berkowitz noted, "The finger pulls the trigger, but the trigger may also be pulling the finger."[14]

7. America's huge private gun arsenal must be seen, some writers believe, in light of the nation's entertainment fare. Surveys show that the average child between the ages of five and fourteen witnesses 13,000 violent deaths on television, to say nothing of uncounted other examples of violence and mayhem. "It is as though we delivered our children to someone who took them away for four or five hours every day in their formative years to watch police interrogations, gangsters beating enemies, spies performing fatal brain surgery, and demonstrations in how to kill and maim," wrote Ben Bagdikian, one of the nation's foremost authorities on mass media. He ridicules the notion that five or ten years of exposure to these atrocities will not adversely influence children's view of life.[15]

The Surgeon General's Scientific Advisory Committee on Television and Social Behavior issued a major report early in 1972, which found that more than half of the youngsters who watch television violence become more aggressive after watching it (contrary to an earlier assumption that only "abnormal" children reacted in this fashion). The report also noted that children do not distinguish accurately between fantasy and real-life violence and that the more and the longer children watch television violence, the more socially aggressive they become.[16]

If Aristotle had been correct in his belief that witnessing violence vicariously drains away our aggressive impulses, we could be more complacent about our television (and movie and fiction) entertainment. However, as long ago as 1968, *Editorial Research Reports* concluded that "there is ample clinical evidence that all children exposed to acts of violence are overexcited by them and will tend to imitate what they see, rather than being drained of their aggressions."[17]

Still other factors must be fed into this picture. Years ago young men found outlets for their violent impulses by hunting, chopping wood, and other forms of vigorous activity. Psychiatrist Karl Menninger thinks it significant that "today the routine of life, for most people, requires no violence, no fighting, no killing, no life-risking, no sudden supreme exertion . . . no tearing, crushing, breaking, forcing. And because violence no longer has legitimate or useful vents or purposes, it must all be controlled today."[18] William James said society needs to find a "moral equivalent to war." Do we also need to find a "moral equivalent" to more ordinary forms of violence?

8. The permissive spirit of recent years and the general decline of the traditional sources of moral authority also provide a backdrop against which crime-producing influences must be seen. When home, church, and school are disparaged as sources of moral authority, when most social restraints are under attack, when parents are reluctant to apply the forms of parental discipline that were routine in the past, when moral and social inhibitions are seen as barriers to self-expression and self-development, when self-discipline is downgraded as a desirable characteristic, when the mood of the young is expressed by "do your thing" and "let it all hang out," when the most profound subliminal message of the entertainment world is "let's go" and "let 'er rip," and when many blacks believe that "ripping off" is a legitimate way to get even with "Whitey"—who should expect that this social atmosphere would not weaken the forces of order? Although youngsters from good homes, with good parental examples to draw upon, will rarely turn to crime because of this social environment, and although strongly crime-prone youngsters will commit crimes in the absence of this milieu, it is altogether probable that many marginal youngsters—who might or might not become law-abiding citizens, depending on the pressures and stimuli of their environment—would slip into crime because the social environment weakened the restraints which ordinarily prevent such behavior. It would be extraordinary, indeed, if an atmosphere of unrivaled social freedom should not bring both constructive and destructive results. Among the destructive consequences of our recent tendency to elevate freedom over responsibility may well be an acceleration of crime.

9. A further factor *may* have something to do with the greater propensity for crime in our age. Erich Fromm writes:

Harold Esler has observed a number of young people in an institution for juvenile delinquents. Those adolescents seem to have acted criminally because it was the only way to overcome their boredom and to experience their existence, to "make a dent." Some, reporting their experience of stabbing or killing people, described a feeling they had never had before. They had felt the excitement of making somebody respond to them; the response was the victim's anguished face and his groan of pain. Reading the statements of some of the defendants in the Manson murder case, I have the impression that one of the main motivations for the stabbings was the sensation of making one's self feel alive in the act of killing, a feeling that was connected with sexual excitement for one of the girls. There are other examples of spontaneous killings by previously well-behaved and seemingly normal young persons in which it seems that uncompensated and extremely painful boredom was the root of the unexpected destructive behavior.[19]

Fromm notes that most work is boring today because of its monotony and repetitiveness. ''Among the answers to the question of how violence —and drug consumption—can be reached, it seems to me that perhaps one of the most important ones is to reduce boredom in work and in leisure . . . . I believe that the further study of what has become the illness of the age—boredom—could make an important contribution to the understanding of aggression.''[20]

10. Finally, the impersonality and vastness of the modern corporation may contribute to crime. Some people feel a large corporation will not miss a few shoplifted goods; besides, the corporation is probably cheating the customer in various ways anyhow! It is one thing to steal from a neighborhood grocer whom you know and another to pilfer from an absentee-owned, faceless corporation, which is making millions whether you lift a few items or not. Such is the specious reasoning of some of our growing army of shoplifters.

The more we delve into the causes of crime, then, the more complex they become and the more difficult our task of dealing with them. In trying to prevent crime, we are dealing with a phenomenon as mysterious and little understood as man himself.

WHAT HASN'T WORKED

What, if anything, can be done to curb crime? It would be logical to devote society's major energies to the prevention of crime rather than to the punishment and rehabilitation of criminals. But that is easier said than done. James Q. Wilson writes, ''I have reviewed virtually every major effort (for which I could discover evidence) to reduce crime by removing its causes and find little support for the view that any presently known strategy, consistent with our civil liberties, works.''[21] He adds, ''. . . there is little society knows about how to make bad families into good families or otherwise eliminate the roots of crime.'' In an even more pessimistic vein, he states that ''. . . nobody is very optimistic that the underlying social forces that cause crime are going to show much improvement over the next generation or two.''[22] Unhappily, his pessimism is shared by most other students of crime.

If we don't know what will eradicate the root causes of crime, what about deterrent law enforcement strategies? Well, we are learning about many of these that *don't* work! Or don't help much.

The number of squad cars patrolling an area seems to make little difference. So does the number of police assigned to a given area, exasperating though that fact may be.[23] Assigning policemen to neighborhoods for prolonged periods so that they get to know the area and the people—and hopefully win their confidence—seems to help a little but not much. Better street lighting helps temporarily, but the gains are soon lost.

Would better police training and more effective use of police services substantially reduce crime? Our hopes are doused again. Wilson insists that not even the most professionally operated police departments can ''bring about a substantial, enduring reduction of the crime rate.'' He adds, ''I doubt that any deployment, any strategy, or any organizational principles will permit the police to make more than a slight or temporary reduction in the rate of most common crime.''[24] Police administrators, he says, agree that police cannot do very much to reduce crime, however efficient they may be.

(Unhappily, police often engage in criminal practices themselves. A notable study by Albert J. Reiss, Jr., reports on 36 trained observers who accompanied almost 600 policemen on their daily rounds. Even though the police knew they were being watched, one-fifth of them were ''observed in criminal violation of the law.'' This included theft of goods following burglaries, accepting bribes for not issuing traffic tickets or for altering sworn testimony or accepting money or goods from businessmen. In addition, 40 percent of the officers broke important departmental regulations. In 43 percent of the situations in which the observers saw felonies being committed, no arrests were made.)[25]

How about appropriating more federal money to enable local law-enforcement agencies to do a better job? Congress tried this when it passed the Omnibus Crime Control and Safe Streets Act of 1968, which called for appropriations of $300 million per year to help the states with training, crime research laboratories, experimental programs, and certain salary payments. Apparently the program has been almost a total fiasco. Much of this money was misspent for showy crime-fighting and antiriot equipment, or wasted in other ways.

James Vorenberg writes that:

The principal justification for federal aid was that it would provide an incentive for cities and states to make changes in criminal justice agencies. But with block grants the federal government cannot directly push for reform. It simply gives a lump sum to each state to be distributed in accordance with the state's own written plan. These plans are the products of large new state bureaucracies, many of which are controlled by old-line representatives of the state and local police departments, courts, prosecutors, and correctional agencies that need to be changed. Since the state plans are rather general and require only superficial changes in the agencies, much of the money has been spent to preserve the status quo.[26]

Why not block the importation of heroin, the demand for which triggers so much inner-city crime? The Nixon administration worked out an agreement with the Turkish government to subsidize Turkish poppy producers over a period of years while Turkish farmers switched to other crops. Elaborate efforts were also made to apprehend heroin smugglers. The results were minimal. The agreement with the Turkish government expired and was not renewed. Heroin was available from other countries, and the ingenuity of heroin smugglers is awesome; the reader, in fact, could probably think up some pretty tricky methods for whisking heroin past customs inspectors. When profits are fabulous, people are willing to take risks. While the supply of heroin has varied from time to time, drying up the supply has proven beyond the capability of the government.

A Report to the Ford Foundation by the Drug Abuse Survey Project estimates that:

. . . the entire U.S. demand could probably be met by cultivation of about five square miles of opium and concludes that a program based on suppression of opium production seems no more likely to succeed than the program based on the prevention of importation.[27]

Maybe we can reform the prison system so that convicts are rehabilitated instead of returning to crime at such a high rate (said to be 70 percent). Certainly our prisons desperately need reform.

Karl Menninger, one of the nation's more respected psychiatrists, has made one of the most sweeping indictments of the American prison system since the days of Dorothea Dix. Prisons, he says, are "unhealthy, dangerous, immoral, indecent, crime-breeding dens of iniquity."[28] Their principal contribution, most criminologists believe, is to embitter their members, turn them into homosexuals, and train the less experienced in the fine points of crime. In 1969, an Arkansas judge declared the entire state penal system to be unconstitutional; a number of judges in other states have ruled that state prisons violate the Eighth Amendment's injunction against "cruel and unusual punishment." Many judges refuse to send prisoners to jail, unless they seem to be a positive menace to public safety, lest prison have a detrimental rather than a correctional effect. As a result, although crime has increased at a staggering rate and population has grown rapidly, the total prison population has been falling. All this, despite a belief, as a *Wall Street Journal* writer put it, that ". . . American prisons probably have never before done as effective a job in caring for and rehabilitating convicted criminals as they are now doing. . . ."[29]

Prison directors have tried almost every conceivable method of incarceration and treatment, and these experiments have been studied intensively. Robert Martinson summarized the findings which emerged from 231 academic studies of correction treatment techniques from 1945 to 1967:

On the whole, the evidence from the survey indicated that the present array of correctional treatments has no appreciable effect—positive or negative—on the rates of recidivism (relapse into crime) of convicted offenders.

The present list of treatments is not lengthy. For example, Americans believe strongly in the value of education, so no self-respecting prison can be without formal classroom instruction. Or since many Americans find salvation in therapy groups, why not try them on inmates? The list includes small caseloads in probation or parole which have no effect (with the interesting exception of *youthful* offenders given "intensive" probation supervision). Group counselling or therapy has no effect, although "group" supervision reduces costs. Psychiatric treatment may actually be "harmful" if it is given to younger "nonamenable" offenders. Formal education increases reading and writing skills, but those who benefit go on to recidivate at the same rate. Early release (90 days) does not increase recidivism for adult offenders and may decrease rates slightly for young people. Early release also saves money. The highly touted halfway houses actually *increased* recidivism slightly, probably because offenders perceived their stay as an additional period of deprivation of liberty, but there are only a handful of studies on this. The picture is little different for cosmetic surgery for facial defects (by itself), specialized caseloads for addicts or chronic drunks, job training (a little hope), prison vocational training and for programs resembling these in the intensity of the treatment.[30]

Martinson observes that "we hear it said that if correctional treatment of prisoners hasn't worked yet, that is because it hasn't really been given a chance. The claim begins to wear thin, since treatment has been the official ideology of corrections for over half a century."[31]

David J. Rothman agrees. Writing in *The Public Interest*, he asserts:

The record on criminal reform, past and present, is dismal—if by reform one means transforming criminals into law-abiding citizens. That existing persons do not rehabilitate anybody, or produce lower rates of crime, or decrease recidivism, is beyond dispute. Would newer programs like increased staff for probation, or halfway houses, or intensive prison counseling, or liberalized bail accomplish these ends? Probably not. Research findings on the effectiveness of these procedures demonstrate all too unanimously that no one procedure has a better effect in reforming the criminal or lowering recidivism rates than any other. Social science has not reached the point of being able to fulfill these aims.[32]

Rothman makes an interesting suggestion. He would reduce the number of persons in jail, largely eliminate the funds spent for prison correction, and "invest these funds in broadening probation, parole, bail, and halfway houses—not because they offer a hope of redeeming the criminal or of ridding our society of crime, but because (1) they will do no worse than our present system in terms of prevention, and (2) the price we pay for them, in terms of human and financial and social costs, will be considerably lower."[33] Perhaps, but for recidivists?

WHAT MIGHT WORK

Maybe we could urge teenage marriages and apply a heavy tax on bachelors! Why? George Gilder cites the intriguing statistic that single men are 13 percent of the population over the age of 14 but they constitute 60 percent of the criminals and commit 90 percent of major and violent crimes. Gilder is convinced that wives have a civilizing effect on their husbands and tend to keep them on the straight and narrow path.[34] (Since some citizens will object to *anything,* there may be political difficulties in getting this legislation passed and rigorously enforced!)

What about a less "permissive" Supreme Court? Millions of Americans (and Richard Nixon) were inclined to blame the Warren Court for much of the nation's crime problem. They believe that the Court was so eager to protect the criminal's rights that it lost sight of society's right to be protected from the criminal. *Mapp* v. *Ohio*—which held that evidence obtained by illegal search and seizure could not be entered as evidence in court—and *Miranda* v. *Arizona*—which required that arrested persons be promptly notified of their constitutional rights and which made even voluntary confessions inadmissible as court evidence if those rights were not protected[35]—led many to believe that the indictment and conviction of criminals was being seriously hampered by the Court. The constitutional reasoning which defends and attacks these decisions need not concern us here, but their impact on law enforcement does. Vorenberg points out that law-enforcement officers are dependent on confessions in not over 1–2 percent of their cases. Since many suspects did not confess before the *Miranda* decision and almost as many confessed after the *Miranda* decision, "the result is that the maximum direct statistical impact of this much reviled decision is on the order of a fraction of one percent."[36] Vorenberg concludes that "what the Supreme Court does has practically no effect on the amount of crime in this country. . . ."[37]

Longer prison sentences for those committing felonies? Most Americans strongly endorse this position, and most students of crime have dissented. The latter contend that America imposes longer prison sentences than almost any nation in the world, but our crime rate is among the world's worst. They point out that European countries once castrated rapists, cut off the hands of thieves, and tore out the tongues of perjurers. England had 200 offenses for which hanging was the penalty; public hangings were long a popular form of entertainment in the "emerald isle." There was little evidence, however, that these barbaric penalties deterred crime. When penalties are extremely severe, prosecutors are reluctant to indict and juries reluctant to convict.

Several decades ago a study of over 300 confirmed recidivists revealed that long imprisonments did not deter further crime more than shorter periods of imprisonment.[38] A recent review of relevant research concluded that ". . . there is no evidence that severe penalties deter crime more effectively than less severe penalties."[39] Whether the prison term is long or short, about the same percentage of convicts return to crime.

LOCK 'EM UP?

But while all this may be true, more and more "authorities" are swinging toward imprisonment for more offenders. Their reasoning runs as follows: Perhaps severe prison sentences do not deter prisoners from reverting to crime when they are released, but at least they are not committing crimes while they are in jail. And since a high percentage of serious crimes are committed by recidivists, identifying these persons and imprisoning them for substantial but not extreme periods of time should reduce the commission of crime materially. Wilson cites one study showing that three-year jail sentences for everyone committing a serious crime would reduce serious crime to one-third of what it is today.[40] His personal estimate is that a sensible sentencing procedure requiring mandatory incarceration for a larger fraction of convicted serious robbers would rapidly reduce robbery by 20 percent—or by 60,000 robberies a year.[41]

The growing trend to reconsider the utility of imprisonment in reducing crime also draws upon the behalf that it may be a stronger crime deterrent than previously has been conceded. Gordon Tullock asserts that a series of scholars attempted to disprove an article by Jack Gibbs in 1968, which argued that punishment *does* deter crime, "and all ended up agreeing with him."[42] Tullock adds that "multiple regression studies show that increasing the frequency or severity of punishment does reduce the likelihood that a given crime will be committed."[43] Wilson tends to concur, arguing that it is unreasonable to believe that criminals ignore the costs associated with their occupation. They will take greater risks than the average citizen, but to assume that they are indifferent to the prospects of imprisonment is to assume that they are a different order of being from the rest of us.[44] Wilson agrees, however, that severe sentences do not deter more successfully than do more moderate sentences.

Several states are experimenting with ''shock therapy'' of short prison sentences for first offenders, hoping these will have a sobering effect without having imprisonment becoming the school for crime that more prolonged incarceration often represents.

President Ford's recommendation in 1975 that mandatory prison sentences be given virtually all persons committing violent crimes under federal jurisdiction was thus compatible with the direction in which many thoughtful students of crime had already moved. The president was hopeful that state laws, which cover most of the crimes committed in this country, would follow suit.

PLEA BARGAINING AND JUDICIAL DISCRETION

The trend toward mandatory imprisonment for serious offenses is accompanied by growing national discontent with the discretion prosecutors enjoy in seeking indictments, the discretion judges enjoy in imposing sentences, and the indeterminate sentence itself.

In 90 percent of convictions, the defendant has pleaded guilty, thus avoiding the necessity for a court trial. And in 85 percent of the cases involving a guilty plea, plea bargaining has taken place, usually involving a scaling down of the offense with which the defendant was initially charged. In plea bargaining, the prosecutor confronts the defendant with the most serious charge(s) of which he is apparently guilty (often adding a number of related charges for further bargaining purposes) and then agrees to whittle this down to a lesser offense (or offenses) in return for a plea of guilty. In some cases, the prosecutor may not reduce the charge but promises to recommend leniency to the judge if the defendant pleads guilty.

Although a guilty plea enables law enforcement officers to cover up any abuse of power committed in connection with the case—such as unreasonable search and seizure, a failure to notify the accused of his rights, the use of coercive interrogatory tactics—defendants usually cooperate with the plea-bargaining process because they learn that conviction following a court trial usually involves a much more severe sentence than a plea of guilty to the same offense. Indeed, the risks of a tougher sentence following trial are so great that an innocent person is sometimes persuaded that it is prudent to plead guilty to a lesser offense than to the charge that the prosecutor initially brandished before him.[45] Often, too, he faces the prospect of a long stretch in jail awaiting trial if he continues to profess innocence, whereas a pleas of guilty may bring no more than probation. If he had planned to fight the case in court, moreover, the legal expenses of employing a private lawyer would be high.

The shortcomings of the system are obvious. A criminal is typically convicted of a less serious crime than that of which he is guilty, to the disgust of the arresting officer and of other citizens who know about the case. Innocent persons may find it in their self-interest to plead guilty rather than languish in jail awaiting trial. It encourages sloppy and incomplete investigatory work by law-enforcement officers, since a case need not be nearly as airtight for effective plea bargaining as is needed to persuade a jury that a person is guilty "beyond a reasonable doubt."

The entire process diminishes respect for the law; it involves the kind of deals plus the arbitrary use of discretion that are repugnant to the concept of justice under law.

Bernard Feder notes that the severity of punishment is determined less by guilt or the nature of the offense than by "the condition of the court calendar, the vacancy rate in jails and prisons, the work burden of the prosecutor's office staff, the efficiency of the local police, the negotiating skill of the defense attorney and his relationship with the judge and the prosecutor. The innocence or guilt of the accused plays a relatively minor role in determining the severity of the sentence. It is plea bargaining, rather than the oft-cited 'softness' of the courts or the rigid adherence to the procedural protections built into the Constitution, that is responsible for the fact that the courts turn criminals loose on the streets. The other side of the coin is that the same process operates to the disadvantage of those who may be innocent of wrongdoing but who are not able to resist the pressures to cop a plea."[46]

The defense of plea bargaining is threefold: (1) It is a practical necessity for an overburdened criminal court system. We simply don't have the judicial manpower to handle all the cases that would have to be processed if a high percentage of guilty pleas were not obtained via plea bargaining. The entire system of criminal justice would break down in its absence, since the courts would be hopelessly inundated with cases. Delays in reaching trial would become preposterous; a classic judicial axiom holds that "justice delayed is justice denied." (2) Defendants will sometimes implicate higher-ups in return for the reduced charge which accompanies plea bargaining. (3) Although this is not officially conceded, prosecutors favor plea bargaining because it enables them to obtain a high conviction rate—which makes their records look good.

In rebuttal, it is contended that guilty pleas would still occur in a high percentage of cases if the prosecution did a more careful job of collecting and sharpening the evidence so that a guilty defendant recognized that the odds against him were formidable. If this requires more detectives, lawyers and judges, so be it. This nation can afford an adequate supply of law-enforcement officers—and the law schools are already turning out more lawyers than the current system can use. Let's put these lawyers to good use as prosecuting attorneys, defense attorneys and—ultimately judges. As for the utility of a reduced charge to encourage turning state's evidence against a defendant's criminal superiors, critics do not ask the elimination of plea bargaining but only its restriction to narrowly limited categories of cases that clearly require it.

(The courts could also be decongested to a considerable degree if we redefined crime to exclude *victimless offenses*. The Crime Commission pointed out that about one-third of all arrests are for drunkenness, and many people do not regard drunkenness as a crime. Instead of sending drunks to jail, they could be sent to detoxification centers. Moreover, by declining to arrest people for minor cases of disorderly conduct, vagrancy, possession of marijuana, gambling, and sex acts between consenting adults, another large chunk of crimes could be eliminated. Overall, about half of the persons in jail are there because of victimless crimes. Most professional students believe the law-enforcement system should concern itself with more serious public offenses.[47] Such a policy would also go far toward reducing the long delay in bringing a defendant to trial.)

Judges now exercise wide discretion in imposing sentence and in deciding whether someone should go to jail or be placed on probation. A crime which might carry a sentence of one to ten years may bring a one-year sentence in one court, five years in another, ten in a third, and probation in a fourth—even though the circumstances are roughly comparable in each case.

Willard Gaylin, after interviewing 40 judges, concluded that there is no semblance of uniformity in the sentencing of convicts.[48] To one judge, a year is a tough sentence, to another it is light. A convict's period of imprisonment (or whether he goes to prison at all) depends not only on the factors Feder cites but also on the temperament, values, mood, philosophy, and experience of the judge who chances to sentence him. The problem is compounded by the widely divergent criminal laws and practices in our 50 states, one of the least-admirable aspects of American federalism. Little wonder that citizens who are aware of the cruel inequities in our sentencing system are indignant at the perversions of justice so commonplace in the American system.

Judges were initially granted sentencing discretion so the punishment could fit the criminal rather than the crime. If a shorter sentence would help rehabilitate one offender while another offender seemed a poorer risk, the judge would rule accordingly. The judge could also take family background and various "extenuating circumstances" into account. But we are increasingly aware that judges engage in a vast guessing game when they exercise this discretion; they are not really capable of probing the defendant's mind and psyche and of ascertaining the probabilities of reform in this person as compared with that one. A judge, someone has said, is a lawyer who knew a governor. Or someone who is a sufficiently good politician to win a popular election. He is not someone uniquely qualified to foresee the future behavior of those who come before the bench. Parole boards probably do little if any better, judging by the high rates of recidivism.

If sentencing discretion were reduced considerably, the tendency of the courts to give much more lenient treatment to middle-class offenders than to the less educated, less well-dressed, less nicely mannered, less artic- ulate lower-class defendants would be reduced, also. This would be a ma- jor contribution to even-handed justice even though middle-class persons would continue to get a break when police were deciding whether to ar- rest, when prosecutors were deciding whether to indict and when juries were deciding whether to convict.

Wilson (and others) would not eliminate a judge's discretion entirely, since there are occasions when mitigating or aggravating circumstances are clearly relevant to a sentence. But they would impose sharp limits on it, to avoid the kind of unconscionable inequities which now blot our judicial system.

Wilson has suggested that *every* nontrivial offense should involve a deprivation of liberty. For minor offenses, this might mean as little as a week, perhaps served on weekends. For most crimes, this deprivation of liberty would be limited to, perhaps, between six months and a year, with longer sentences imposed for the most serious offenses. Deprivation of liberty, however, would not necessarily mean confinement in prison. It might mean "enrollment in a closely supervised community-treatment program; referral to a narcotics treatment program or confinement in a well-guarded prison."[49] But *some* deprivation of liberty would always ac- company conviction for all but minor offenses, and the period of restraint would be increased with each subsequent offense.

As for the indeterminate sentence, it was initially conceived as an en- lightened and humane measure, enabling authorities to release a person as soon as he or she was deemed ready to assume the role of law-abiding citizen. But, again, the authorities were unable to discern who was and who wasn't rehabilitated, and their capacity to control the length of sen- tence gave them enormous power over the lives and behavior of convicts. Inmates uniformly and deeply resented this power and saw little rhyme or reason why some prisoners were released before others, except that some "played the game" more skillfully than others or were the bene- ficiaries of either favoritism or purely arbitrary judgment. In general, then, the leading students of crime are proposing that criminal justice be based on more objective criteria, with roughly similar penalties for similar offenses (modified, of course, by the recidivist record) and the element of human guesswork be pared to a minimum.

Criminologists believe that the certainty of punishment has a much more deterrent effect than the severity of the sentence. People commit crimes of passion without making rational calculations concerning the probable results, and they commit other crimes because they do not expect to be caught. (They seldom are!) If we were able to apprehend and convict a much larger percentage of criminals, this doubtless would do far more to reduce the commission of crime than any conceivable penal measure. But no one knows how this can be done.

In one area of crime prevention we could do far more than is now being done. The official crime statistics show that Americans commit about 20,000 murders a year. But well over 10,000 additional murders are committed annually by drinking drivers who are responsible for at least half of our 45,000 annual auto fatalities (as well as half of our half-million or so traffic injuries). This incredible massacre produces an astonishingly small amount of public indignation. The nation was convulsed with a (legitimate) sense of outrage when less than 10,000 American soldiers were annually and senselessly killed in Vietnam but is only mildly concerned about the equally senseless slaughter of more than 10,000 persons each year because drinkers do not have the judgment or decency to refrain from driving. The Scandinavian countries have reduced drunken driving sharply by close surveillance of drivers and by handing down much more severe penalties than we impose. If police were authorized to conduct spot-checks of auto drivers, especially after 10 P.M. on weekends, and if the courts routinely imposed prison sentences and drastic license withdrawals on those with over 0.10 percent alcohol in their blood, the carnage on the highways could be vastly lessened. Probably the nation could do more to reduce human suffering (and the volume of serious crime) by this rather simple and feasible policy *than by any single measure available to it*. But so many Americans, including otherwise responsible and conscientious citizens, want to drink and drive that there seems little likelihood that we will do what commonsense pleads with us to do.

GUN CONTROLS: IS THE PUBLIC READY?

There is consensus among students of crime that strict control of handguns could make a substantial *long-range* impact on the volume of crime. Four presidential commissions have recommended such controls. Because of the difficulty of enforcement, we recognize that it might take years for the full impact of handgun controls to be felt, but as the Committee for Economic Development (CED) states, ''Wherever handguns are forbid den by well-enforced laws, abroad and in some American cities, murder rates are far lower.''[50] Great Britain licenses the ownership of guns and strictly controls the sale of guns and ammunition. (The Lord Chief Justice of England believes gun-control laws are the principal reason Britain has so many fewer murders per capita than the United States. See *U.S. News and World Report,* Jan. 27, 1975, p. 49.) Italy, France, and Germany have established equally rigorous controls. In Japan only the police and a few dozen other persons may own handguns.

However, in America similar controls have been blocked, in part by the lobbying activities of the National Rifle Association (NRA), a million-member organization with a $10 million budget supported by 12,000 local and state gun clubs, which has boasted that within seventy-two hours it can flood Washington with half a million letters opposing gun control. The Association fires off a curious assortment of blanks in its efforts to prevent Congress from enacting strong handgun legislation. It contends that the Second Amendment forbids such legislation: ''A well-regulated Militia, being necessary to the security of a free State, the right of the people to keep and bear Arms, shall not be infringed.'' The courts, however, have long interpreted this amendment to refer to state militias, not to the private possession of firearms. The NRA also seeks to blur the distinction between handgun control and control over long guns in an effort to arouse sportsmen's opposition to gun controls in general; no Congressmen, of course, wants to deny sportsmen the privilege of hunting with rifles. (Handguns are rarely used for hunting.) The NRA insists that tough laws would, in effect, disarm the law-abiding citizen seeking to protect his home and family from intruders, while leaving the criminal in possession of his weapons. This ignores the fact that the average citizen would still be able to keep a rifle on hand for household protection. It also ignores the fact that, as the crime commission reported, for every robber frustrated by a gun, four persons are killed by handgun accidents. Householders, moreover, only succeed in shooting home burglars less than two-tenths of 1 percent of the time.[51]

The NRA contends that people will commit as many crimes whether guns are readily available or not; if they don't use one weapon, they will use another. ''People kill, not guns.'' But as former governor of California Edmund Brown says, ''The quarrels which most frequently trigger murder might well result in nothing more than bloody noses or a lot of noise, absent a deadly weapon—handy and loaded.'' Moreover, it is logical to assume that although most criminals who use guns would become involved in crime even if guns were harder to obtain, an appreciable number of young people whose backgrounds and propensities make them borderline criminals do become involved because handguns are so readily available when temptation beckons.

Probably the NRA's best argument is that since current gun controls (forbidding mail-order sale of guns in interstate commerce and over-the-counter sale of such guns to persons from out of state or under the age of twenty-one) are so poorly enforced, why pass more such laws? It is unhappily true that the more effective a gun control law would potentially be, the more unlikely that strict enforcement would follow, given the American people's passionate attachment to their firearms.

There is good reason to doubt that the NRA is as politically potent as it claims; its alleged defeats of various Congressmen who dared cross its path have been challenged by Robert Sherrill in his fascinating book, *The Saturday Night Special and Other Guns with Which Americans Won the West, Protected Bootleg Franchises, Slew Wildlife, Robbed Countless Banks, Shot Husbands Purposely and by Mistake, and Killed Presidents—Together with the Debate Over Continuing Same.*[52] (Yes, that's its title, and it is the most absorbing book on a politically significant subject that this author has ever read.) But, whatever the actual power of the NRA, Congress believes it to be a dangerous adversary, and that belief confers power on it. It also has heavyweight allies in the $2 billion gun and ammunition industry, which puts up a terrific squawk when restrictive gun legislation is proposed. Sherrill notes that the "gun industrialists . . . know the right social nerves to touch, the right patriotic ligaments to twang, the right slogans to keep repeating. 'God made man, but Colonel Colt made him equal.' It's a cheap, flip, simplistic, wahoo, strutty way to view life. It's the kind of sloganeering that has made us the most violent major nation in the history of the modern world."[53]

The gun merchants' lobbying activities are supplemented by those of hunting and wildlife journals and even by conservation organizations, improbable bedfellows though they may be. Many police chiefs oppose gun legislation, many Congressmen own and treasure their handguns, and even Chief Justice Warren Burger of the U.S. Supreme Court once greeted late-night callers with a pistol at the ready. But the NRA's major ally has always been the American people. While polls have repeatedly shown that the majority of Americans favor more restrictive gun legislation, the legislation most of them have favored is an innocuous brand that would not accomplish very much. Those who oppose meaningful handgun legislation (meaning strict controls on the right to own or carry handguns) have been more vociferous and politically active than those who have favored it. A psychiatrist correctly observed that many American males would rather give up their wives than their guns. Since Congress almost always vindicates the squeaky-wheel theory of politics, prospects for real reform have previously been regarded as dim.

Recently, however, public opinion seems to have stiffened. California has enacted a law which requires a mandatory and substantial jail sentence for anyone who uses a gun while committing a felony. Massachusetts passed a statute which requires anyone carrying a gun outside his or her home to have a license; anyone convicted of carrying an unregistered gun in a car or on the streets automatically gets a year in jail. No plea bargaining and no judicial discretion! And a Gallup poll revealed that 53 percent of the people approve of this legislation while only 21 percent disapprove. Maybe, miracle of miracles, Congress will yet acquire the guts to enact a meaningful law. But a law that severely limits *possession* of handguns! That will be the day!

THE COSA NOSTRA

What about organized crime? Interest in it waxes and wanes, depending on the state of the headlines. But from time to time Americans become very excited about it—as well as being perennially fascinated by it. (The success of *The Godfather* was virtually assured by its theme.)

Federal law defines organized crime as "those unlawful activities in which a highly organized, disciplined association supplies illegal goods and services." Professor Thomas C. Schelling finds this definition somewhat unsatisfactory, noting that the essence of organized crime is its attempt to monopolize certain types of crime within a given area, forcing intruders to join and share their profits or else get out of town. When monopoly occurs and the organization "collectively negotiates with the police," we have organized crime.[54]

Organized crime in America primarily means the *Cosa Nostra* (often called the *Mafia* before aggrieved Italians raised a clamor). The Cosa Nostra and some other "mobs" control much of the illegal gambling in America and are heavily involved in narcotics, loan-sharking, and the jukebox and vending machine businesses, as well as in various bars, cafes, and nightclubs. A few unions also seem to be involved. Henry E. Peterson, former head of the Justice Department's criminal division, said his division identified 3000 members of Cosa Nostra (also called *the Syndicate*), who rely upon "cooperation" with a far larger number of subordinates.[55]

Although some people think the Cosa Nostra usually engages in crime without victims, Schelling dissents. The victim is usually the local bookie, who does not need Cosa Nostra, which badly needs him.[56] By forcing the bookie to pay a percentage of his profits in return for "protection," Cosa Nostra leaders became fabulously wealthy. (Extortion money is also obtained from some legitimate businesses.) The Committee for Economic Development estimates that organized crime's gross annual receipts from illegal gambling range from $20 billion to $50 billion,[57] with its net profit placed at about one-third of these figures. Winnings, of course, are seldom taxed.

Peterson says there are 26 *families* (mostly Sicilian) that run the

Cosa Nostra. Each family controls a metropolitan area, and a *national commission* of from nine to twelve of the most influential families meets from time to time to decide jurisdictional problems and other questions of common concern. Since organized extortion demands monopoly, the gang wars which sometimes make the headlines usually involve jurisdictional disputes. The national commission, Peterson believes, has the authority to decide if a mobster is to die.

The Commission on Law Enforcement and the Administration of Justice contends that the typical crime syndicate is organized as follows: The boss is the chief executive, the principal organizer, planner and strategist. He represents the organization when the rare *summit meetings* are held to iron out differences with other criminal organizations. The underboss is the chief lieutenant, always a major figure although his authority varies from gang to gang. He may mediate between gang members, make important decisions or decide that they should be bucked upstairs. He is the boss' probable but not certain successor.

Both the boss and the underboss often rely on a counselor, a staff member who furnishes technical advice in addition to handling many problems arising with other gangs. Each family will probably also have a *corrupter,* who arranges police and judicial protection, and an *enforcer,* who handles disciplinary problems where gang members get out of line or competing gangs seek to muscle in. Gang violence is normally directed at gang members rather than at members of the general public.

The *lieutenants* are overseers of particular gang activities or sometimes are in charge of all gang functions in a particular area. They hold positions corresponding to that of plant managers. As the supervisor of a facet of gang operations, each lieutenant is responsible for the profits or losses of his jurisdiction. One of his principal responsibilities is to keep his mouth shut if the police grill him about gang operations or the identity of his superiors. This code applies to all members of the organization, of course.

The gang's infantry, appropriate enough, are referred to as *soldiers.* They actually operate the illegal enterprises, whether these be gambling, drugs or houses of prostitution (which nowadays play a minor role). They may receive a salary, or they may turn over a percentage of their earnings to the lieutenant. Many of them may be unwilling accomplices of the gang, but cooperation has proven essential if they are to have a "license" to operate.

David Caputo declares that while this describes the usual organized crime structure, "the complexity of any criminal operation should not be overlooked; the manpower needs for actual operations vary according to the service involved. . . . This labor need results in the recruitment of personnel who are employed by the organization but who are not actual members of the organization."[58] These personnel may outnumber the members by 300 percent. The president's crime commission noted that in large-city gambling, "the profits that eventually accrue to organization leaders move through channels so complex that even persons who work in the betting operation do not know or cannot prove the identity of the leader."[59]

Since gangs are organized hierarchically, with each member ordinarily having contact only with his immediate superior, this reduces the chance that higher-ups will be identified when police crackdowns take place.

An American Bar Association report on organized crime declared, "The largest single factor in the breakdown of law enforcement dealing with organized crime is the corruption and connivance of many public officials." The president's Commission on Law Enforcement and the Administration of Justice said, "All available data indicate that organized crime flourishes only where it has corrupted local officials."[60] A *New York Times* reporter wrote, "The history of the New York Police Department can be read as one long story of corruption. Every 20 years or so, there is a new scandal, followed by a brief flurry of reform, followed by the long, gradual slide back into what seems to be the Department's normal state of discreet but all-pervasive corruption. . . ."[61] The Committee for Economic Development (CED) notes sadly that "new recruits hesitate to report gambling 'payoffs' made to colleagues and superiors [and soon learn that] the easy path is toward participation."[62] And adds, "Conspiracy is screened behind token arrests and arrests to extort pay-offs, with occasional mild penalties for minor figures."

This situation levies a heavy toll in public respect. Donald Cressey, a foremost student of organized crime, says it is common knowledge among street youth in the cities that the cops are "on the take" from organized crime and that this contributes heavily to their disrespect for "law and order."[63]

Caputo asserts that organized crime spends from one-fourth to one-third of its gambling "take" on such things as legal fees, bail money, expenses for the families of members temporarily doing time, payoffs and protection.[64]

Much of the difficulty in stamping out organized crime lies in its provision of services desired by significant portions of the general public. Many ordinary citizens want to be able to gamble, or to buy narcotics, or to borrow money through illegal channels if they cannot obtain it otherwise. Being beneficiaries of a gang's services, they are not eager to cooperate with law-enforcement officials seeking to drive it out of business.

What can be done to curb organized crime in America? Congress passed the Organized Crime Control Act of 1970, which provided for the establishment of special grand juries to hear organized crime cases and return indictments, granted immunity from prosecution for certain witnesses, and made them subject to contempt of court if they would not testify. The act also guaranteed protection by the attorney general for witnesses who did testify, extended federal jurisdiction over major forms of illicit gambling, made it a federal offense for organized crime to buy or operate a legitimate business, and set up a special class of "adult special offenders," with jail sentences of up to 25 years for "professional criminals" convicted under its provisions.

Recently the Justice Department has been experimenting with *strike forces* composed of representatives from the Customs Bureau, the Bureau of Narcotics, the Department of Labor, the Internal Revenue Service, the U.S. Postal Service, the Secret Service, and the Federal Bureau of Investigation. This coordinated effort helped produce a 50 percent increase in convictions over a three-year period.

Many authorities are not optimistic that the government will be able to make major inroads into organized crime as long as gambling is largely illegal in America. The CED observes that "gambling is at the same time both the main source of illicit revenue for organized criminal syndicates and the primary channel to corruption of police and other officials. Until this country comes to grips with the gambling issue, organized crime will prosper."[65] The CED frankly recommends that:

All statutes and ordinances that make unorganized (and charitable-religious) gambling criminal should be repealed; efforts to prohibit conduct socially acceptable to tens of millions of citizens are unjustifiable as well as unenforceable.

We recommend extensive experimentation with governmental ownership and operation of gambling arrangements that substitute effectively for the numbers rackets, horse rooms, and betting pools that now form the main source of income for organized crime. Experiments monitored and found successful should be widely copied by other states."[66]

Many states are now following this recommendation.

In recognition of the widespread opposition to public gambling enterprises, the CED also recommends "in the public schools and elsewhere, an educational campaign designed to portray the financial hazards and disadvantages of participation in gambling activities, stressing the odds and probabilities against the player."[67]

Finally, the CED notes:

One major obstacle to broad national reform lies in the complex nature of American federalism as it relates to crime and justice, making evasion of responsibility easy. Citizens who desire better protection for persons and property become confused over which level of government or which agencies are primarily at fault. Wherever they turn, they find a resistance to change traditional in both bureaucratic and political circles. The result is continuing deterioration—a trend that must be reversed, promptly and decisively, to secure a viable society. . . .

The main constitutional responsibility for crime prevention and control rests upon the states, an assignment they have botched. They have failed to keep their criminal codes up-to-date, and they have turned responsibility for enforcement over to a welter of overlapping counties, municipalities, townships, and special districts. Despite the obvious and urgent need, the states have neither straightened out their tangled and ineffective patterns of local government nor assumed direct responsibility for law enforcement.[68]

Although the constitutional power to make indispensable reforms rests with the states, "past experience indicates that few if any of the 50 states will, either on their own behalf or through their local units, take the wide range of measures needed to meet the present crisis."[69]

NOTES

1. *Time,* June 2, 1975, p. 39.
2. *U.S. News and World Report,* February 9, 1976, pp. 50–53.
3. *Time,* August 11, 1975, p. 14.
4. William and Joan McCord, *Origins of Crime,* Montclair, New Jersey, Patterson Smith, 1969, p. 179.
5. James Q. Wilson, "Crime and the Criminologist," *Commentary,* July 1974, p. 49.
6. Norton Long, "The City as Reservation," *The Public Interest,* Fall 1971, p. 4.
7. James Q. Wilson, "Lock 'em Up," *New York Times Magazine,* March 9, 1975, p. 46.
8. Fred P. Graham, "Black Crime: The Lawless Image," *Harper's,* October 1970.
9. See T. Meehan, "Moynihan of the Moynihan Report," *New York Times Magazine,* August 14, 1966.
10. James Q. Wilson, et al., "The Problem of Heroin," *The Public Interest,* Fall 1972, pp. 6–8.
11. *Wall Street Journal,* May 19, 1972, p. 1.
12. *Wall Street Journal,* June 9, 1972, p. 1.
13. *Wall Street Journal,* June 9, 1972, p. 21.
14. *Wall Street Journal,* June 9, 1972, p. 21.
15. Ben Bagdikian, quoted in *Time,* December 27, 1968, p. 58.
16. *Newsweek,* March 6, 1972, pp. 55–56.
17. Joan S. Gimlin, "Violence in American Life," *Editorial Research Reports,* June 5, 1968, p. 413.
18. Karl Menninger, "The Crime of Punishment," *Saturday Review,* September 7, 1968, p. 22.
19. Erich Fromm, "The Erich Fromm Theory of Aggression," *New York Times Magazine,* February 27, 1972, p. 86.
20. Fromm, "The Erich Fromm Theory of Aggression," p. 86.
21. James Q. Wilson, Letters to the editor, *New York Times Magazine,* April 13, 1975, p. 70.

22. James Q. Wilson, "The Crime Commission Reports," *The Public Interest,* Fall 1967, p. 67.

23. James Q. Wilson, "Do the Police Prevent Crime?," *New York Times Magazine,* October 6, 1974, p. 18.

24. James Q. Wilson, "Dilemmas of Police Administration," *The Public Administration Review,* September 10, 1968, p. 415.

25. Albert J. Reiss, Jr., *The Police and the Public,* New Haven, Connecticut, Yale University Press, 1971, pp. 164–171.

26. James Vorenberg, "The War on Crime: The First Five Years," *The Atlantic Monthly,* May 1972, p. 67. Copyright © 1972, by The Atlantic Monthly Company, Boston, Mass. Reprinted with permission.

27. Quoted by James M. Markham in the *New York Times Book Review,* May 21, 1972, p. 33, in a review of *Dealing with Drug Abuse,* New York, Praeger, 1972.

28. Karl Menninger, *The Crime of Punishment,* New York, Viking Press, 1968, p. 21.

29. *Wall Street Journal,* September 16, 1971, p. 1.

30. Robert P. Martinson, "Can Corrections Correct?," *New Republic,* April 8, 1972, p. 15. Reprinted by Permission of THE NEW REPUBLIC, © 1972, Harrison-Blaine of New Jersey, Inc.

31. Martinson, "Can Corrections Correct?," p. 13.

32. David J. Rothman, "Prisons, Asylums and other Decaying Institutions," *The Public Interest,* Winter 1972, p. 16. Reprinted by permission.

33. Rothman, "Prisons, Asylums and Other Decaying Institutions," p. 17.

34. George Gilder, "In Defense of Monogamy," *Commentary,* November 1974, pp. 32–33.

35. *Mapp* v. *Ohio,* 367 U.S. 643 (1961); *Miranda* v. *Arizona* 384 U.S. 460 (1966).

36. James Vorenberg, "Is the Court Handcuffing the Cops?," *New York Times Magazine,* May 11, 1969, p. 33. Reprinted by permission.

37. Vorenberg, "Is the Court Handcuffing the Cops?," p. 32.

38. Norval Morris and Frank Zimring, "Deterrence and Corrections," *Annals,* January 1969, p. 141.

39. "Crime and Punishment," *New Republic,* March 30, 1968, p. 8.

40. James Q. Wilson, "Lock 'em Up," p. 44.

41. James Q. Wilson, *Thinking About Crime,* New York, Basic Books, 1975, p. 199.

42. Gordon Tullock, "Does Punishment Deter Crime?," *The Public Interest,* Summer 1974, p. 107.

43. Tullock, "Does Punishment Deter Crime?," p. 109.

44. James Q. Wilson, "If Every Criminal Knew He Would Be Punished if Caught," *New York Times Magazine,* January 28, 1973, p. 54.

45. Bernard Feder, "Plea Bargaining: The Used Car Lot of Justice," *Nation,* October 26, 1974, p. 399.

46. Feder, "Plea Bargaining: The Used Car Lot of Justice," p. 400.

47. See Norval Morris, "The Law Is a Busybody," *New York Times Magazine,* April 1, 1973 and Alexander B. Smith, "Crimes Without Victims," *Saturday Review,* December 4, 1971.

48. Willard Gaylin, *Partial Justice,* New York, Knopf, 1975, Chs. I, IX, X.

49. James Q. Wilson, "If Every Criminal Knew He Would Be Punished if Caught," pp. 55–56.

50. Committee for Economic Development, *Reducing Crime,* p. 59. Also Carl Bakal, "The Failure of Federal Gun Control," *Saturday Review,* July 3, 1971, p. 15.

51. Robert Sherrill, *The Saturday Night Special,* New York, Penguin Books, 1973, p. 10.

52. Sherrill, *The Saturday Night Special,* p. 10.

53. Sherrill, *The Saturday Night Special,* p. 324.

54. Thomas C. Schelling, "What is the Business of Organized Crime," *American Scholar,* Autumn 1971, p. 644.

55. "Winning the War Against Organized Crime," *U.S. News and World Report,* June 5, 1972, p. 64.

56. Schelling, "What is the Business of Organized Crime," p. 647.

57. Schelling, "What is the Business of Organized Crime," p. 50.

58. David Caputo, "Organized Crime and American Politics," University Programs Modular Studies, Morristown, New Jersey, General Learning Press, 1974, p. 4.

59. The President's Commission on Law Enforcement and the Administration of Justice, Task Force on Organized Crime, *Task Force Report: Organized Crime,* Washington, D.C., Government Printing Office, 1967, p. 3.

60. Donald Cressey, "Organized Crime," *New Republic,* July 18, 1970, p. 12.

61. *New York Times,* August 29, 1971, Sec. 4, p. 6.

62. Committee for Economic Development, *Reducing Crime,* p. 51.

63. Cressey, "Organized Crime," p. 13. Cressey is the author of *Theft of the Nation: The Structure and Operations of Organized Crime in America,* New York, Harper & Row, 1969.

64. Caputo, "Organized Crime and American Politics," p. 20.

65. Committee for Economic Development, *Reducing Crime,* p. 55.

66. Committee for Economic Development, *Reducing Crime,* p. 56.

67. Committee for Economic Development, *Reducing Crime,* p. 14.

68. Committee for Economic Development, *Reducing Crime,* p. 15.

69. Committee for Economic Development, *Reducing Crime,* p. 72.

EIGHT

The Twenty-seventh Amendment and the Feminist Movement: A Dialogue

The proposed Twenty-seventh (or Equal Rights) Amendment reads—

Section 1. Equality of rights under the law shall not be denied or abridged by the U.S. or by any State on account of sex.

Section 2. The Congress shall have the power to enforce, by appropriate legislation, the provisions of this article.

Section 3. This amendment shall take effect two years after the date of ratification.

The amendment, approved by two-thirds of the Congress in 1972, was ratified by more than 30 state legislatures but had been unable, through 1975, to win approval by the constitutionally required three-fourths majority of the state legislatures. On several occasions, its determined supporters appeared on the verge of success, only to lose to an equally determined group of opponents. A good deal of passion has been invested in the issue by both sides, primarily because of the amendment's symbolic relation to the larger issue of women's liberation. When the Vietnam war, the counterculture and environmental issues lost their emotional steam during the Great Political Apathy following President

Nixon's resignation, women's liberation remained the one major socio-political-moral movement which continued to arouse deep feelings on the college campuses and among a substantial number of American women (and men). For many women it was *the* issue of the twentieth century, since for them it involved the basic right to equality for half the human race, a half which had never come close to enjoying that right throughout the long sweep of history. For other women, the movement contained some constructive elements that were being overridden by feminist ideologues and extremists, whose views constituted a threat to fundamental values dear to their hearts.

To deal with these questions, an imaginary dialogue will be carried on between spirited defenders of the two camps—feminist and antifeminist (for lack of more satisfactory terminology). It is conceded that a wide spectrum of views are to be found on both sides and no brief dialogue can do justice to them. But it is hoped the debate will illuminate some of the principal issues at stake.

Feminist: The Twenty-seventh Amendment is long overdue. The reluctance of almost all societies in all ages to give women the equal status they deserve is one of the most depressing chapters in human experience. That half of the human race should have been consistently denied the opportunity to develop fully its talents and fully share in the economic, social and political life of societies everywhere has to be the most wasteful, suffocating and inhuman phenomenon of all time. Even societies supposedly dedicated to the democratic proposition of human equality have systematically excluded half of their citizens from that vision. The drafters of the Declaration of Independence stated their position precisely when they phrased it, "All men are created equal." They certainly didn't mean women any more than they meant blacks. Just men. Well, the time has come to accord women full membership in the human race rather than the second-class citizenship they have always known.

The Twenty-seventh Amendment will not mean instant and total victory for this cause, but it will signal the fact that this nation formally, specifically and constitutionally recognizes women's right to full equality before the law. That would be a magnificent step forward, one laying a solid foundation from which we could battle the remaining elements of sexist discrimination in American life.

Antifeminist: Very eloquent—and of course I agree with some of your sentiments. Women have not received a fair shake in most societies; I don't condone that for a moment. But noble goals are one thing, and the best way to reach them is another. Behind your lofty and inspiring rhetoric lie some dubious premises—and a lot of fine print. I have read the fine print and don't like all that I see.

Feminist: Just how does "Equality of rights under the law shall not be denied or abridged by the United States or by any State on account of sex" contain fine print objectionable to you? That's about as simple, direct, straightforward and principled a statement as you can find. What rights *should* be denied or abridged for women?

Antifeminist: Someone has shrewdly observed that "I care not who writes the laws so long as I can interpret them." It's some of the interpretations you place on the law that worry me and some of the interpretations that the courts, under pressure from the feminist movement that dominates the mass media, are likely to make.

Feminist: What's this about the feminist movement dominating the media?

Antifeminist: You surely know what I mean. The people who write the articles and editorials and books and the radio and TV scripts are either female writers who, as professional women, have the views regarded as appropriate for today's professional women, or they are men who know that it is intellectually chic to hail the feminist movement. These men know they will be branded as philistines or male chauvinist pigs if they don't toe the line you and your crowd has drawn. But these people don't represent the average American woman; laws affecting women should reflect the views of most women rather than of a vociferous, militant and unrepresentative minority.

Feminist: If the leading figures in the media are enlightened enough to perceive the patent injustice of denying equal rights for women, I wouldn't disparage them by insinuating that some ominous kind of feminist coercion has whipped them into line. It was intellectually chic, as you put it, to espouse the cause of equal rights for blacks in the late 1950s and early 1960s. Did that make it wrong or somehow discreditable? Were the leading figures in the mass media insincere or intimidated by black pressures because they favored full equality for blacks?

Antifeminist: You keep placing the issue on a high moral plane that evades the grubby, down-to-earth details of its actual application to American life. It's those interpretations, I remind you, which disturb me.

Feminist: Would you please be specific? Are you opposed to equal pay for equal work?

Antifeminist: Of course not.

Feminist: Do you oppose women's equal right to be hired for any governmental position, or for any position in a firm that has governmental contracts, if their training and qualifications are as good as men's? Are you against an equal right to be promoted to any position for which a woman is as well qualified as a man?

Antifeminist: No, no, equal opportunity is only fair, as a general proposition.

Feminist: I wish you hadn't added that qualifying phrase, but let me proceed. An equal right to sign contracts, establish credit, borrow money, run a business, administer an estate, serve in the armed forces?

Antifeminist: I'm certainly not opposed to all of those, but I don't think women's place is in the military. And I strongly oppose that aspect of the Twenty-seventh Amendment which makes women equally subject to a draft.

Feminist: Why shouldn't women help protect their country as well as men? The notion that women are weak, timid, and helpless creatures, whose job is washing pots and pans and knitting socks for the boys on the front lines, is part of the mythology we're trying to eradicate. If the occasion requires, women can fight modern wars as well as men; if they can, they should. I do not flinch at the full implications of equal rights and equal opportunities.

Antifeminist: Well, I don't want to see women drafted unless it's absolutely essential to national survival. In the first place, I don't think women are as well adapted to a combat role as men. It has always made sense and it makes sense today for men to bear the main burden of combat because, first, pregnant women and nursing mothers are obviously not suitable for fighting; second, men are physically stronger and better able to perform many combat operations; third, men are by nature more aggressive than women.

Feminist: You have been taken in by propaganda that has permeated the warp and woof of our society. That propaganda has stereotyped women's roles in a narrowly restrictive way. There are innumerable military positions that most women can perform fully as well as men, and they should be given both the chance to serve on equal terms in a volunteer army and to be drafted on equal terms if compulsory military service is again required. As long as women do not serve equally in the armed forces, they cannot expect to have much influence on military policy. And look at all the side benefits women have been denied through their virtual exclusion from the armed forces: GI educational benefits; GI housing loans; GI in-service training.

Antifeminist: I notice that even the egalitarian Israeli army reserves branches like the tank corps, combat infantry, and aircraft squadrons for the males. That, plus the virtually universal practice of all societies throughout history of assigning combat responsibilities to males, ought to impress you if anything can penetrate your thick ideological defenses. Of course, it is very nice to have every benefit men receive from military service while being able to avoid really hazardous duty.

Furthermore, you can look forward to all that military service will do for women; I suspect it will bring out the worst in many of them just as it often does in men. I want women to retain the femininity you probably despise.

Feminist: Three points. First, it is what women *can* do, not what men are willing for them to do, that matters. If their abilities are properly recognized, the benefits accruing from military service will be equal. Second, military jobs are pretty technical these days and don't differ that much from civilian jobs. Third, yes, men do behave more aggressively than women at present, but this is because society has conditioned girls and women to believe that they should be passive; boys are conditioned to believe that aggressive behavior fits the male role. If girls and boys were raised in a nonsexist society, in which girls were not taught that a meek and mild posture is appropriate for them, the aggressiveness differential would soon disappear.

Antifeminist: Now you are becoming the ideologue that all true feminists, at heart, tend to be. All the evidence, for those willing to face it, points to a greater innate aggressive drive in men than in women. Boys engage in more rough-and-tumble play than girls; young male animals play more aggressively than their female counterparts; male primates are more aggressive than females. Cultural conditioning can't explain all of these. Adolescent boys generate far more aggression-stimulating testosterone than females; injection of male hormones into women makes them more aggressive, while emasculation makes men and male animals more passive. Cultural conditioning, my eye! There is such a mass of scientific evidence in support of this view that even feminists Eleanor Maccoby and Carol Jacklin in their definitive work, *The Psychology of Sex Differences*[1]—in which they summarize and evaluate the results of all the studies about innate male-female differences—had to concede that males were inherently more aggressive than females. Your common sense should have told you that anyway, if it weren't obscured by what you are determined to believe.

Feminist: I suspect the evidence is not all in on that question.

Antifeminist: The evidence is *never* all in on any issue, but it is as convincing as scientific evidence is ever likely to be.

Feminist: Well, aggressive tendencies can be modified by the culture; we aren't honor-bound to accept every primitive impulse and give it free rein. Part of civilization's job is to restrain the destructive drives and impulses or channel them into more constructive patterns.

Male dominance, I should point out, has been based largely on men's greater physical strength. That quality is almost irrelevant to modern society. How many jobs or functions depend on sheer brute strength these days? Male dominance is thus an anachronism, resting as it does not on real male superiority in significant respects but on bulging muscles. It's time men faced up to that and put bicep measurements in their proper and extremely insignificant place.

Antifeminist: Maybe pure physical strength isn't as important as it once was, but it is still relevant to some roles, such as firefighting, police work, stevedoring, various loading and unloading operations, many farm jobs, professional athletics and many more. Greater inherent aggressiveness will remain an important factor in many occupations requiring daring, physical courage and various kinds of risk. I think women are a little more conservative when it comes to risk-taking than men, and that has many social and economic implications.

Feminist: Pure speculation, lacking all empirical support.

Antifeminist: We shall see, we shall see. Anyhow, once your Twenty-seventh Amendment is passed, there would be a presumption of discrimination in every field where men outnumber women or get the top jobs. Then there will be a demand for quotas, and heaven knows what headaches and absurdities those create. What I most object to is your doctrinaire assumption that there really aren't roles more appropriate for men and others more suitable for women. You are trying to indoctrinate children with this point of view by textbook pressures and media presentations in your determined drive toward a unisex society.

Feminist: What a ridiculous conclusion! Who said we wanted a unisex society?

Antifeminist: A lot of feminist leaders may deny it, but that's the sum and substance of their attacks on what they call a sexist society. Their disclaimers, when pressed, are unconvincing to me and seem to be tacked on for debating purposes.

Feminist: Utter nonsense. Of course a few feminists may sound that way, but they are not representative. You can discredit any movement by pointing to some of the more extreme statements issued by its most radical members—and by putting the most farfetched interpretations on those statements. The predominant majority of spokespeople for women's rights do not advocate unisex or even its first cousin. They only want to eliminate those behavioral differences between male and female that have no relationship to authentic differences between the sexes, that society has arbitrarily imposed because of false concepts of what is properly male and female behavior, and that tend to stunt women's development. You misunderstand so many things, it almost seems deliberate. The Twenty-seventh Amendment does not require that women be equally numerically represented in *any* particular field. Only about half as many women work as men, so there couldn't be numerical equality in most occupations. Besides, and I hope this registers with you, the Equal Rights Amendment will only forbid employers to discriminate against an individual woman, not women as a class, who is able to compete on equal terms with a man. Whether it be firefighting, police work, the military, or weight lifting (assuming a governmental job or a private job having a federal relationship, of course), if an individual woman can do a job as well as a man, I cannot for the life of me see why you find any objection to protecting her right to compete on an equal basis. Do you believe in equal rights for women or don't you?

As for your fears that the courts will interpret the amendment unreasonably, you could raise that objection to any law. In any case, male judges will be interpreting the law, since they occupy most of the judgeships. Are they going to issue a lot of irrational rulings?

Antifeminist: You feminists keep switching back and forth, as convenience dictates, between asserting that male-female differences are outgrowths of mere cultural conditioning and then claiming that you only want equality where women can compete with men. I wish you'd make up your mind.

IS THIS AMENDMENT REALLY NECESSARY?

Feminist: Your point is irrelevant to the Twenty-seventh Amendment. We are saying, please listen, that women should not be denied equal access with men to any job at any rung on the ladder.

Antifeminist: That right was established in the Civil Rights Act of 1964. It forbids employers or trade unions involved in interstate commerce to discriminate in any way against a person because of sex, religion, age or national origin. And, lest you forget, the Equal Pay Act of 1963 requires equal pay for work requiring equal skill, effort and responsibility. Since these are already the uncontested laws of the land, why restate them in the Constitution? If the public won't obey a federal law, why will they obey the Constitution?

Feminist: A constitutional amendment carries more moral and psychological weight than a law. It provides a more solid basis for resisting discrimination in employment, as well as in other areas such as the administration of estates and various business relationships. A constitutional amendment would represent a national commitment to the goal of equality between the sexes, which would have a profound effect on national attitudes as well as enable cases to be more effectively prosecuted in the courts. We could rectify wrongs much faster with a constitutional amendment than by attacking inequities in each of fifty states.

Antifeminist: Did you ever notice how ineffectual the Fourteenth Amendment's equal protection clause was for blacks? It was one of your vaunted constitutional amendments, with all the symbolic value and deep national commitment you attribute to constitutional amendments, but it was virtually a dead letter from 1876 to almost 1950. A law or an amendment has force and vitality only to the extent that it is supported by active public opinion. If the public believes in it, it will acquire meaning; if it doesn't have that support, it won't. The Fourteenth Amendment, incidentally, says that no state shall deprive any person of the equal protections of the law. Women are persons, aren't they? Why add a constitutional amendment saying that the Fourteenth Amendment means what it says? I suppose if you are not satisfied with the results of the Twenty-seventh Amendment you will want a twenty-eighth saying that the twenty-seventh *shall* be obeyed, by golly. I'm against cluttering up the Constitution with unnecessary amendments, and that's precisely what the Twenty-seventh does. And any suit which you can bring under the Twenty-seventh Amendment can be brought under the Fourteeth or the Civil Rights Act of 1964. The Supreme Court even said, in *Frontiero* v. *Richardson*,[2] that sex classifications in our laws are "inherently suspect," meaning there is a presumption of illegality attached to every law which sets forth sex classifications. Unless you think all sex classifications are inherently wrong, that ought to satisfy you.

Feminist: It certainly does not. Only four members in the *Frontiero* case came out clearly against sex classification as a "suspect" category.

Since *Frontiero,* the Court has repeatedly declined to go all the way by nailing down the "suspect" presumption. We want an amendment, moreover, that is not dependent on the shifting opinions of an unpredictable court. And I still believe that passage would give the Equal Rights Amendment the foundation and impetus it needs to really do the job that needs to be done. Remember that the equal protection clause, even though it applies to "persons," didn't give women the right to vote until the Nineteenth Amendment specifically granted that right. Nor did it abolish the poll tax, which was discriminatory against poor people; it took the Twenty-fourth Amendment to accomplish that. We need an amendment that is squarely on target, which directly attacks and unequivocally condemns sex discrimination.

Antifeminist: A weak argument but maybe it's the best you have. That brings me back again to the matter of interpretation. You want, I understand, no judicial presumption that mothers shall have custody of the children, even small children, in case of divorce because you reject the idea that mothers have a more important role to play with even small children than fathers have.

Feminist: That's right. We believe each has an equal obligation toward the children and each should be assumed equally capable of giving the children the love, security and support they need. The divorce courts should review each case on its own merits and, without any presumption based on male or female, decide in favor of the parent whose characteristics in that case suggest a preference is justified.

Antifeminist: While granting that men are sometimes better qualified to give children the care they need, I believe the mother normally should continue to receive preference, other things being roughly equal. In giving birth to children and in nursing them (I am a firm believer in breast feeding as consistent with Nature's intentions), a special relationship is created with children, which can be disregarded only at our peril. In every society we know about, women have the major responsibility in caring for small children. That goes back not to any male sexist plot but to the fact that a nursing mother needs to be near her child, for nutritional purposes and logically to meet its other needs as well, while the male works in the fields, hunts or whatever. Furthermore, only about half as many women as men are in the work force, you said. If women can keep their children in case of divorce, this enables them to continue a domestic role, which you may scorn but which many women prefer to working outside the home. I think they should continue to have that privilege if they want it.

Feminist: We are rapidly moving toward a society in which men and women will equally seek careers outside the home. Now, I am perfectly content, under ordinary circumstances, for women to stay home and care for the children if that is what they want, but I believe the premise that women are uniquely qualified to rear children is rubbish. Most men can do the job just as well or better, and divorce courts should accept that for the fact it is. The belief that a woman is singularly equipped by Nature to change diapers, wash men's socks, make beds and dust the furniture is an idea which may die hard, but die it will. That myth has crippled the lives of millions upon millions of creative women. For those who want housework, fine. But away with the belief that this is woman's divine mission and that if she doesn't fulfill it she is somehow violating Nature's plan. Women are just as intelligent and just as capable of doing the world's work as men, and some of us are determined that women's horizons shall be as unlimited and wide-ranging as men's.

Antifeminist: Just as I thought. You say if women want to stay home and rear children, that's fine with you. But the language you use to describe that role speaks all too clearly of your contempt for it. You feel that if women don't leave home, have a career and make money, they are living a shrivelled and rather pathetic existence. Well, many women as intelligent as you don't feel that way at all. They feel that if they do a good job of raising physically healthy, emotionally sound and morally upright children, they are doing work as valuable as anything society requires. And I agree with them 100 percent. To me, no work people do is more constructive or more supremely vital to society than providing the right environment for children in their most impressionable years. That's far more significant work than typing invoices, selling bras, or even writing most of the trash I see in the drug stores and in some of the professional journals.

Feminist: I flatly reject your allegation that I don't regard homemaking as a worthy role of great value. Maybe my description of housework did involve some unfortunate phrasing, but most feminists readily acknowledge the dignity and importance of homemaking.

Antifeminist: They acknowledge it in footnotes, or when pressed in an argument, to fend off criticism.

Feminist: I do not challenge the sincerity of your views, and I would thank you for not challenging ours. Of course we emphasize the importance of female careers, because that is where women have been most frustrated in their quest for equality. Helping women see the breadth and fullness and richness of their human potentialities is the essence of our movement, so naturally we stress careers. But that means no lack of respect for the roles of mother and housewife.

EMPLOYERS AND YOUNG WOMEN

Antifeminist: Maybe. But that brings me to my next point. One of the interpretations of the Twenty-seventh Amendment which men—speaking for their interests now—have reason to fear pertains to strict equality in hiring and firing. Your amendment would doubtless forbid employers to prefer young men over women of equal qualifications. Yet employers are not engaging in rank discrimination if, for many jobs requiring extensive training and leading to major responsibilities, they prefer young men. Young women often work awhile and then drop out to have a baby or two or three, requiring extensive leaves of absence. And many of them may opt for a rather permanent leave until their kids are all off to school. If employers choose to take this into account and, where qualifications are about equal, to prefer hiring young men, they are only being prudent. I don't think that is an unreasonable or arbitrary discrimination, but the courts will probably declare it so.

Feminist: Now we're getting down to bedrock. If you want to ignore the facts that many women won't get married and many others won't have children, and you want young women as a class to be viewed as potential occupational dropouts, you are dooming women to a permanently inferior economic position. If they cannot get an equal start in the business and professional world, they will never be able to compete on equal terms and win their share of the best jobs our society offers. You really don't want that to happen, or do you? What a prospect for young women everywhere, knowing that their child-bearing ability, whatever their life plans may be, will be used as a club to keep them in permanent economic subservience. What a "champion" women have in you and people like you!

Antifeminist: I don't see it that way. If two men were being considered for a job and there were objective reasons for believing one would be much more likely to give the employer uninterrupted service than the other, the employer would properly prefer the former, and he wouldn't face legal penalties for acting on his preference. He would be making a wholly rational decision. Of course, some women won't be dropouts, but no employer can determine that reliably in advance. Single women do change their minds and get married from time to time, married women do change their minds and have children, mothers do decide to stay home instead of working, and there is no way under heaven employers can tell who will and who won't. They have to play the odds, and the odds favor men. This doesn't mean women are being treated that unfairly. They won't be occupying the most dangerous wartime positions, whatever you feminists may say. They won't be doing much of society's most dangerous work, such as operating farm machinery, apprehending burglars, mining coal, and so forth. Men deserve some compensation in return for these.

Many women find homemaking and child rearing infinitely more satisfying and worthwhile than dreary office labor or repetitive factory work. You feminists forever picture careers as exciting, creative, and responsible when most jobs aren't that way at all. Most men dislike their work, and most women do, too. But they like the money. Women have the choice of homemaking or a career, a choice men don't realistically have. Many women who work away from home (like Alice Lafuze) welcome the opportunity society now accords them to take a break from year-in, year-out paid employment by occasionally taking a few months or years off from the grind. They can do this without incurring a social stigma, where men cannot. I'd hate to see them lose this advantage. Finally, many young women have been and will continue to be hired on an equal basis because many employers are willing to establish that policy; many female applicants are *better* qualified than their male competitors and will get the good job on that basis. A really superior and highly creative female will make her mark in today's business world, Twenty-seventh Amendment or no. Women shouldn't expect to have every advantage men have, plus many advantages men don't have. Women aren't that bad off, when you survey the total scene.

Feminist: Let me draw a deep breath and have at you. We want women to be treated as individuals, not as members of a class. A single woman should be treated precisely the same as a single man, and a married woman the same as a married man. That's not very much to ask—but it is at the heart of justice and equality. And lest you are in any doubt, we will settle for nothing else. Working women who are pregnant should be granted brief leaves of absence from their jobs, just as ill or injured men and women are given leaves, without any loss of seniority when they return. Women should not be penalized economically because they bear the necessary burdens of pregnancy and childbirth. Being pregnant for nine months and giving birth to a child is not an experience men envy women, believe me. The least society can do in return for this service is grant women full equality in the business world. Once children arrive, if women choose to have them, there is no reason why the husband shouldn't be granted a work leave, at least half of the time, so the wife can carry on her career rather than be forced to give primacy to her husband's career.

Antifeminist: Men's breasts don't yield much milk.

Feminist: You can go on your breast-feeding kick if you wish; most women prefer using the bottle.

Antifeminist: The baby doesn't.

Feminist: The evidence, please, the evidence!

Antifeminist: I don't think the author of *Challenge and Decision,* faithfully recording this historic conversation—with a sly look on his face—wants me to recite the evidence in detail for his readers. His book is in the area of political science.

Feminist: Some political science!

Antifeminist: So, women need some kind of social rewards in return for pregnancy and childbirth? To borrow one of your phrases, ''utter nonsense.'' For most mothers, motherhood is the most deeply rewarding experience in their lives. Nothing else can compare with it. And how many good mothers do you hear whining about their fate and demanding social compensation for their great sacrifices? As for your vision of men taking work leaves to care for the children so women's careers won't be interrupted, there's no law against dreaming. We can have what we want in our dreams, which is nice when the hard world of reality proves intractable. Oh, a few ''liberated'' men may cooperate in your idyll, but not many. It does make interesting speculative material for feminist books and magazines, of course.

Feminist: You and your realism! If some people didn't dream of a more just world and work toward that goal, we'd never make any progress. I can never, never accept your assumptions that everything will always be the same and that women must forever face a male-oriented and male-dominated economy, with women fighting an uphill struggle to develop their abilities and win their share of the money, the power, the glory and the challenges that men have monopolized up to now. You can resign yourself to that world and even revel in it, if you wish. But many of us feminists will fight that prospect with every ounce of our strength.

Antifeminist: Brace yourself, you haven't heard the worst. I don't blame employers, when recessions come and layoffs are required, if they give men retention preference over women. Especially married men. In our society women who don't work or can't find work are not regarded as failures; a man who can't find work or support his family goes through a much more psychologically devastating experience than does a woman. For millennia, men have been expected to be the breadwinners; successful breadwinning is the primary criterion by which a man's life is judged. If he is a failure here, he is a failure period. No matter how unfair this may be, it is a crucially important cultural fact. As a product of his culture, the male cannot avoid feeling a deep sense of humiliation, worthlessness and defeat if he can't find work for prolonged periods. Of course women suffer, too, when they lose a job, but the pain is not that intense and the social stigma is largely absent. If employers are humane and seek to minimize human suffering when they discharge or lay off employees I don't think that should be regarded as an antisocial act.

Feminist: Your attitudes have all the modernity of a brontosaurus. There is no remaining doubt in my mind; you are thoroughly content with keeping women in a position of second-class citizenship. Maybe third-class. Are you sure women should have the right to vote? Didn't that upset a lot of men at first, who had been culturally conditioned to believe politics was for men only? Weren't their feelings wounded and psychological scars incurred when women marched to the polls? And whites were culturally conditioned since time immemorial to regard themselves as superior to blacks. Blacks were supposed to keep their place, be humble, do menial work, and be grateful for whatever crumbs came their way. It must have been painful for whites to see blacks granted equality and competing with them on equal (or, should I say, more equal) terms. How could we disregard their tender, bruised feelings? You were surely opposed to the entire civil rights movement, weren't you?

Antifeminist: I don't regard the situations as comparable. Men's irritation at female voting was trivial compared with their feelings about breadwinning. And unlike blacks, women have not been regarded as an inferior order of being. . . .

Feminist: You're so wrong. They most certainly have been.

Antifeminist: Different but not inferior. I think most men have regarded the mother's contribution to society as highly as the man's.

Feminist: Not all women are mothers or want to be. I keep telling you that, but you won't listen. Why should nonmothers be viewed as inferior creatures, undeserving of equal status with men? In an overpopulated world, they should be honored. A lot of men are nonfathers, too, you know. Do you realize how hard it is to be patient with people like you?

Antifeminist: Yes, you red-hot women's liberationists are so convinced of the total righteousness of your cause that you can hardly tolerate dissent. Everyone must agree with you or be consigned to the status of brontosaurus. Well, I think more women agree with me than with you.

Feminist: As if that settled anything! The root question is whether you believe in equal rights for women or whether you don't. And you don't. It's as simple and as clear-cut as that.

I'd like to return to employer preference for males. Since studies have shown that older women have less absenteeism, less alcoholism and less illness than older men, shouldn't employers give older women employment preference over men? According to your reasoning, they should.

Antifeminist: You may have an arguable point there. But if you believe that, then you should accept my point about preference for younger men.

Feminist: Certainly not. I have said, and I repeat, employers should treat applicants as individuals and not as members of a group. That's the only principle that makes sense.

Antifeminist: I'm not through with the Twenty-seventh Amendment. It would weaken women's rights to alimony and cause many legal protections for women to be lost. Laws involving safety requirements, rest periods, overtime, and the like. Most women would like to keep the protection they now enjoy.

Feminist: One of the virtues of the Twenty-seventh Amendment is the obligation it will create to review all of our laws containing sexual classifications and to eliminate those not based on empirically defensible evidence. If safety rules are needed, they should apply to both sexes; that goes for all the other work rules as well. Many times, please note, gender work rules have been designed to reserve certain better-paying jobs for men—jobs that many women could do as well as men. Laws should apply to persons, not to men or to women, unless there are incontrovertible reasons, scientifically supported, that demand different rules. I can't think of what those might be. It would be such a tremendous step forward for the human race if we could see men and women first as persons, sharing a common humanity and only secondarily as sexually diverse people. The latter aspect of human nature should be confined to its proper place, a place that has little to do with the economy. We are persons before we are black or white or yellow or red or male or female. That perspective would go so far to remove senseless barriers to human achievement and understanding. If only you could see that!

Antifeminist: As I said, you feminists lean strongly toward a unisex society.

Feminist: I never said that. I said we should restrict sexual differences to the realm where they are relevant. That isn't in the economy—except for a very, very few instances. When are you going to start talking about common restrooms and showers? I know it's coming, so go ahead and get it over with.

Antifeminist: Many women do fear that the Twenty-seventh Amendment will lead to precisely that. Jails and mental institutions and military barracks and public buildings in which men and women are treated only as persons and their sex characteristics and needs are disregarded. It's all the uncertainties about just how the amendment *will* affect all sorts of economic and noneconomic relationships and requirements that have led many legislatures to decline ratifying what might look like an innocuous amendment. As for common restrooms and things like that, I've never been that worried. I think common sense will prevent some of those indignities from taking place.

Feminist: It's nice to know you don't think we will collectively take leave of our senses once the amendment has passed.

Antifeminist: As for reviewing our laws for obsolete gender provisions, there is nothing to prevent us from doing that right now. In fact, it is going on all the time. One more example of the superfluity of the Equal Rights Amendment.

Feminist: It's going forward on a fitful and inadequate basis. The amendment would spur it along on a broader front.

Antifeminist: We shouldn't pass constitutional amendments just to energize political causes that need a shot in the arm. I don't blame crusaders for trying to use the Constitution in this manner, but more objective, level-headed people shouldn't be stampeded that way.

DO MEN NEED THE FEMINIST MOVEMENT?

Feminist: We should pass constitutional amendments that are needed to reach democratic goals—like equality for all persons—even if these amendments do provide a fillip for worthy causes. This discussion has stressed careers too much and given too little attention to women's rights in noncareer situations like marriage and divorce laws, equal access to education, the need for child-care centers, to name just a few. I wish I had time to go into these more fully, but, even more importantly, I think men need the feminist movement as much as or more than women. If men could come to see women primarily as people rather than as sex objects or China dolls or domestic servants, they would gain a perspective that would be not only far healthier for them but would promote infinitely more satisfying male-female relationships. And if men could come to see women primarily as persons, with the same complex range of aspirations, feelings and fears as they have and with the same desire for and right to self-realization, what a profound change for the better that would be.

Males may or may not be more inherently aggressive than women, but that aggressiveness, whatever its origin, reinforces a male-dominated world. In the world we feminists envision, male aggressiveness will decline and the male ego, which our culture fosters, will shrink. That is something most devoutly to be desired. Most of the political disasters of history have come about because inflated male egos drove men on to butchery and oppression and destructive self-aggrandizement. Look at Lyndon Johnson's monumental ego and the monumental tragedy it produced—the Vietnam war. Look at the pharaohs and their ego-hunger for pyramids. The Roman conquests, to feed the vanity of Roman emperors. Napoleon, Hitler, Mussolini—all men with diseased egos, which male-dominated cultures accepted because war was seen as such a virile and red-blooded business. Males have even found war attractive because boys are conditioned to be tough, aggressive, and supercompetitive. Our movement aims at demasculinizing society in certain crucial ways. We want men to see that gentleness and compassion are human characteristics rather than bearing a distinctively female flavor. We want to deemphasize the dog-eat-dog competitive world and move toward a more humane society. All of us, not least the men, would be better off if this were done. And we can do it if we reorganize our educational system so that children are not grooved into the kind of gender-stereotyped attitudes and behaviors that have deformed our society for so long. We need your help—but doubtless we won't get it.

Antifeminist: We may be closer on this point than on many others. I admit to getting a little disgusted with some manifestations of machismo, myself. And I have entertained some heretical thoughts about the role of the male ego in history's darker pages. But, alas, that ego—which may be the byproduct of all that testosterone—drives men on both to great achievements and to great disasters. Maybe you can't have one without risking the other. Every human quality has within it the seeds of good or evil; everything depends on how it is channeled. We may be able to educate males somewhat to the hazards of the overweening ego but I doubt we can go very far if it has hormonal roots. Our emotional drives are often so much more powerful than our reason. The latter may well be more the servant of our passions than their master.

Feminist: I don't buy your biological basis for the male ego at all, but otherwise there is something to what you say. Still, we must do what we can, and I am less pessimistic than you. I think women have made considerable progress in recent years and that many young men today share the vision of a society in which demeaning, constricting and destructive gender differences will have been phased out.

Antifeminist: Do you know what I fear most? It's that women won't hold firmly to those qualities that have characterized them at their best but almost unconsciously will be drawn to imitating whatever seems masculine, because the masculine life-style seems more exciting or more liberated or somehow superior. In other words, I fear that your movement, despite the hopes of people like yourself that you will change society for the better, will produce a powerful trend toward women's becoming more aggressive, more supercompetitive, more power-driven, more ruthless than they have been. They will seek political success by trying to demonstrate how closely their political behavior resembles that of men. They will tend to use the crude and vulgar language associated with masculinity, drink as hard as men, use as many hard drugs, be as sexually promiscuous, commit as much crime as men. What we least need are developments like those. Yet, these trends seem to be already strongly in evidence. If only "liberated" women could hold to the best that women have represented, including women's historic role with small children, while striking down the senseless barriers to self-fulfillment, which I must agree do exist, then yours would be the glorious movement you believe in. But history is full of paradoxes and ironies, and crusades rarely achieve what their leaders hope for. If they do, a lot of evils they didn't anticipate come rushing in.

Feminist: I share some of your fears, too, but I see the constructive potential of our movement as more significant and the destructive as less probable than you do. Anyway, it's good to see us coming closer together as this discussion draws to an end. I see the author looking anxiously at his watch and muttering something about Harper & Row production costs. I wonder where *he* stands on this issue?

NOTES

1. Eleanor Maccoby and Carol Jacklin, *The Psychology of Sex Differences,* Stanford, Stanford University Press, 1974, Ch. 7.

2. Frontiero v. *Richardson,* 411 U.S. 677 (1973).

NINE

Pornography, the Sexual Revolution, and the State

Censorship of pornography? Don't be ridiculous! This isn't Victorian England. Or even the 1950s. This is the America of the 1970s and it's a bit late, Grandpa, to be talking about censorship. We've come a long way since Puritan times and, make no mistake, there will be no turning back here. If you can't get with it, step aside and let the world go past.

Certainly most intellectuals, the entertainment industry, most of the younger generation, and a surprisingly large percentage of older people are opposed, by and large, to the censorship of pornography. Although most of them might have difficulty articulating their reasons—beyond a few simple statements—those who have given the most attention to it would argue something like this.

The history of censorship is not a pretty picture. Works that are now recognized as literary classics were often censored in the past; the censors merely end up looking silly when the mature judgment of history is brought to bear. Who is wise enough to survey the world of literature and entertainment and say what you should be permitted to read and see and what you should not? It is preposterous arrogance to make such a claim, and those who are willing to act as censors are probably the psychologically twisted souls least qualified for the job. The effort to censor is invariably an exercise in stupidity and futility. Can we learn nothing from our past?

The would-be censors cannot even define, with sufficient precision to properly meet the due-process-of-law test, that which they would forbid. They have to fall back upon fuzzy, ambiguous terms like "prurient interest,'' ''filfth,'' ''patently offensive,'' ''lustful,'' ''disgusting,'' ''indecent,'' and so forth. But these terms are subject to such wildly varying interpretations, depending on the tastes of the interpreter, that they are of little value to a court or a jury.

Pornography, it is said, is protected by the First Amendment (and the Fourteenth Amendment ''due process'' clause) which says Congress shall make ''no law . . . abridging the freedom of speech or of the press.'' To some students of constitutional law, no law means no law; the language is as clear as the founding fathers could make it. And others who are not First Amendment ''absolutists,'' believe that the state should at least enact no law proscribing any form of speech or press unless the latter creates a ''clear and present danger'' that some behavior will follow that the state has a right to forbid.

But there is no solid empirical evidence that pornography does anyone any harm—or leads to antisocial behavior of legitimate public concern. Indeed the National Commission on Obscenity and Pornography, after surveying the available evidence and conducting numerous experiments on pornography's effects, concluded that scientific research had failed to establish that pornography adversely affected adults.[1]

As for ''corrupting'' the morals of the people, critics of censorship insist that moral values are formed overwhelmingly by the family and the schools, with pornography having no more than a minute impact. Our personal value systems are solidly established before exposure to pornography (in any important degree) takes place.

Although children may need protection from pornography, adults should be free to see and read what they please. That is part of what being an adult in a free society should mean. If you do not like pornography, the remedy is simple and painless: don't look at it. But don't set yourself up as a moral judge of what other people should read or see. Who made you the high priest of the nation's morality? Who are you to impose your moral views on others, even if you might be a member of a majority? Since when are majorities supposed to tyrannize minorities?

When you get to rock-bottom it's really a matter of taste, and as Stanley Kauffmann put it, ''I disbelieve in the legislation of taste.''

The sexual revolution has come and has triumphed. Although many old-timers and moral conservatives find it distasteful, they have been made uncomfortable by many social advances. The younger generation is not troubled by pornography; it welcomes the freedom from Puritanical restraints and taboos that mark this era. Be grateful, if you can, that the young lack the sexual hang-ups that have afflicted, deformed, and constricted previous generations. Freedom is something to be cherished, not feared.

The issue of pornography is actually a tempest in a teapot; with all the serious problems this world faces, it is rather absurd to become exercised about a matter of such minor importance as pornography. If it is a problem at all, it is only a trivial one. The likelihood is that people will soon become bored with sexually explicit entertainment, and turn elsewhere for amusement.

This, then, is a brief summary of the principal arguments against the censorship of pornography. The balance of this chapter will concentrate on the other side of the case—in much greater length and detail—because (1) it is a case almost completely unfamiliar to college students since the public college environment is unremittingly hostile to anything remotely smacking of censorship; (2) if presented in this manner, it should trigger a lively debate in the classroom (if not incite to violence!); (3) the author (who thinks social scientists should not conceal their ideological or moral biases) believes pornography is a serious problem; (4) the author would like to test college students' capacities to deal soberly and rationally with a point of view they will find thoroughly unpalatable but which is supported by a line of reasoning that deserves some attention. It may be unconvincing, it may be wrong, but perhaps it should be faced squarely rather than dismissed with jeers and jibes about "Puritanism."

(*Note:* To professors who find what follows beyond the outer limits of the most elastic concept of academic tolerance, a comforting word: You don't *have* to assign this chapter. You have my gracious permission to assign the other chapters—crammed as they are with wit and wisdom— and consign this chapter to limbo. Of course, it would be a rotten thing to do. . . .!)

SOCIAL SCIENCE AND PORNOGRAPHY

Is there any evidence, from academically respectable quarters, that the so-called sexual revolution poses a threat to society? If so, does pornography contribute in a significant manner to behavior that ought to concern the law? If the answer to that question is affirmative, can we deal with the threat within the limits of the Constitution?

Let us first concede that modern social science cannot definitively determine whether pornography does either short- or long-run damage. The Commission on Obscenity and Pornography carried out and reported on numerous studies on pornography's effects, finally concluding that proof of adverse effects was lacking. But the Commission report is seriously flawed. Both the chairman and chief counsel were associated with the American Civil Liberties Union, a highly respectable and useful organization but one with a fixed antagonism toward censorship of pornography (children excepted). Had these men been members of an organization long identified with pornography censorship, the outcry in the universities and the publishing and entertainment worlds would have been deafening. But most of America's intellectuals tend to be rather selective about their indignation. Bias from the Left is treated with tolerance and understanding but bias from the Right can count on a stern reception. There are reasons to believe, moreover, that American intellectuals' views on sexual mores and sexual entertainment are considerably different from those of the average American.

Only the most unsophisticated social scientists would deny that *when crucial and controversial moral values are involved,* personal bias frequently affects scientific experiments and the conclusions drawn therefrom.

Leonard Berkowitz, a distinguished social scientist, observes: "It seems to me that the general conclusions drawn in both the Violence and Pornography Commissions . . . have been influenced as much by values, ideologies, suppositions, and biases as by the actual findings."[2]

Harvard's Professor James Q. Wilson, one of America's foremost political scientists, agrees. He also declares, "In the cases of violence and obscenity, it is unlikely that social science can either show harmful effects or prove that there are no harmful effects."[3]

The Commission's findings are suspect on less general grounds, also. Most of its studies involved volunteers; volunteers for sexually related studies are almost certainly not representatives of the general population. Nor are self-reporting techniques, when sensitive matters like sex are involved, always that reliable. The laboratory experiments, moreover, took place in a highly artificial atmosphere, sometimes with gadgets attached to the body to measure reactions to pornographic stimuli. This environment is obviously much different from that of the "real" world. The experiments involved short duration; none were made on children. Finally, where different interpretations of data were possible (the usual case), the more liberal interpretations were generally made.[4]

It is not suggsted that the social scientists involved were dishonest or unprofessional. They were probably doing a conscientious job—in an area where truly scientific judgments are almost unattainable. Their tools were simply not equal to the task, and where subjectivity enters in, personal values cannot be kept out.

While many social scientists do defend the research of the Pornography Commission, there is little disagreement over social scientists' incapacities to scientifically measure the *middle-range* and *long-range effects* of pornography. Professor Wilson says, ". . . it seems plausible that the media and other forces have contributed powerfully over the last generation to changes in popular attitudes about sexuality, political action, and perhaps even violence. But for lack of a control group it is unlikely that this will ever be proved scientifically." He concludes that "social science probably cannot answer the questions put to it by those who wish to rest the case for or against censorship on . . . proved effects of exposure to obscenity.''[5]

If science cannot tell us how dangerous pornography is, especially over the longer run, the public must rely on its own judgment and intuition, and on the considered judgments of those who have studied the sexual behavior of many cultures and of various civilizations over a prolonged span of time.

Those students of behavior are remarkably united in their view that declining sexual standards lead to a deteriorating society. Cambridge scholar J. D. Unwin, surveying the sexual practices of 80 primitive and many more advanced societies, concluded that sexually permissive behavior led to less cultural energy, creativity, individualism, and a slower movement toward advanced civilization: ''. . . throughout the world and throughout history, a greater or lesser mental development has accompanied a limitation or extension of sexual opportunity.''[6] Unwin says there is no known instance of a society that retained as high a cultural level after relatively permissive sexual standards replaced more rigorous ones. (He conceded it might take several generations before the debilitating effect was fully manifested.) Unwin arrived at his views, interestingly, through intensive anthropological research which he had hoped would disprove the thesis he finally accepted. William Stephens, after studying 90 cultures, wrote that the tribes lowest on the scale of cultural evolution have the most sexual freedom.[7] (Those with ''maximal freedom'' show ''little connection between sex and love,'' he also states.) Harvard sociologist Pitirim Sorokin's extensive studies convinced him that societies that disapprove of sex outside of marriage ''provide an environment more favorable for creative growth'' than those that do not.[8] Sorokin concedes that the relaxation of unusually severe and prolonged sexual repression may be accompanied by a temporary increase in a group's creativity. But if permissive sexual standards continue, creativity soon declines. Arnold J. Toynbee, the most celebrated student of world civilizations, asserts that a culture that postpones rather than stimulates sexual experience in young adults is a culture most prone to progress.[9]

Sigmund Freud observed: ''We believe that civilization has been built up by sacrifices in gratification of the primitive impulses and that it is to a great extent forever being recreated as each individual repeats the sacrifice of his instinctual pleasures for the common good. The sexual are amongst the most important of the instinctual forces thus utilized. . . .''[10] (Asked by students if they should abstain from sexual activities, Freud replied, ''It is my opinion that you should abstain. But not without protest!'')[11] Bruno Bettelheim, a foremost psychologist, noted that ''a society which does not have sex taboos will be one in which culture and civilization will not advance.''[12] Will and Ariel Durant, after a lifetime writing *The Story of Civilization,* declared that sex in the young "is a river of fire that must be banked and cooled by a hundred restraints if it is not to consume in chaos both the individual and the group."[13] (It may not be unimportant that both the Christian and Jewish religions have historically condemned both fornication and adultery.) Warnings like these raise the possibility that the sexual revolution, although not generally recognized as such, may be one of the greater dangers to our civilization. Concern with that revolution may be of as legitimate interest to our society as poverty, inflation, unemployment, crime, and most of our other problems. There is no reason why we should be preoccupied by immediate dangers but indifferent to long-range perils.

If there is, not proof, but respectable reason to believe that a decline in sexual standards can cost a society dearly, should pornography itself concern us? Why assume that its presence materially contributes to the alleged dangers?

Before answering this question, pornography must be placed in today's context. "Dirty" pictures, literature, and graffiti have been around for centuries. But the pornography of the past does not remotely compare in volume to that which exists today. In previous eras most people were exposed to it infrequently, in secrecy, and an aura of social disapproval generally surrounded it. The situation is wholly different today. We are virtually deluged with pornography and near-pornography in drugstore and supermarket magazines, and in well-advertised books and motion pictures. Many of these are aimed directly at the adolescent market and they are reaching their target with growing accuracy. Judging by all we have seen in the last fifteen years, material of increasing raunchiness will continue to invade our regular theatres, moving from there, step by step, to television. This is no far-fetched fantasy. Five years ago we would not have tolerated scenes that now appear on television and in the theatre, and each year finds both media offering more daring material than the year before, with the enthusiastic approval of entertainment critics. Nothing suggests we are at the end of the road.

We are thus confronted with a totally new phenomenon in human history. Never before has an entire nation, and especially the young, been exposed to such an outpouring of pornography and near-pornography as America (and some other countries) is now experiencing. The dimensions of this flood, together with its apparent acceptance by more and more people (thereby reducing the stigma associated with it) creates a social environment apparently unlike that which any major nation has experienced before. It must be emphasized, then, that all which follows should be assessed in the light of this condition—one which renders obsolete most of the pornography discussions that have appeared in the past.

WHAT EFFECTS, IF ANY?

William James, the celebrated psychologist, reminds us that every experience of our life becomes a part of us; it registers in our cells, whether we know it or not, leaving its subtle but enduring imprint on us. Nothing bounces off, leaving us wholly untouched.

For most young people who come from homes with healthy parental examples, exposure to pornography and near-pornography is likely to do little harm. Its influence will be heavily outweighed by the salutary family training they have received and by the example of their parents. For young people who have had little moral training and lack sound parental models, pornography can probably do little harm also. For them, there are almost no moral standards to be corroded; the ethical guidelines of their lives are so blurred they barely exist. That brings us to the most critical category—the (here one must guess) 10 to 20 percent of young people who come from borderline homes. Their parents provide some but not much moral instruction. Their example is neither very good nor very bad. A moral structure is erected within these children but it is weak and fragile. Whether it will sustain a life of responsible moral behavior depends largely upon the influences of their peers and of society as a whole. They can be drawn in either a positive or a negative direction, depending upon the nature and strength of the social currents that beat upon them. These are the vulnerable ones—*for now*. What about the longer run? If the younger generation is regularly exposed to an entertainment media that seems indifferent to its moral responsibilities, that is hostile to sexual restraints, and that annually confronts its customers with more uninhibited sexual entertainment than the year before—what then? This will leave the young unscathed? Ernest van den Haag logically asserts that "Most persons probably do not emulate pornography directly, . . . yet it exercises a cumulative influence on their lives by affecting . . . their own attitudes, values and ambitions. Any model of action attractive to some part of the average person (even if rejected otherwise), when presented often enough, will influence his attitude and make what is modelled . . . more acceptable."[14]

The Surgeon General's report on television violence came to the common-sense conclusion that heavy and prolonged exposure to television violence was bound to have detrimental effects on young people.[15] That study, it is admitted, was not scientifically pure and does not provide definitive evidence, but it is curious how many people now believe violent entertainment can adversely affect the young but pornography, mysteriously, cannot. As Leonard Berkowitz wrote in *Psychology Today*, "We Can't Have It Both Ways."[16]

Anyone, it should be noted, who thinks young people under eighteen don't have access to pornographic materials doesn't know much about what's going on in this country.

PORNOGRAPHY'S MESSAGE

What is the pornography "message"? Pornography presents sexual activity divorced from love, from personal commitment, from morality, and from responsibility. For people, as for animals, sex is designed to satisfy a purely physical desire. No more and no less. Women are typically treated in pornography as little more than sex objects. They are not presented as intelligent, responsible, loving, *whole* persons but as creatures whose significance is found in their sex organs—which are fair game for whoever is able to exploit them. Worst of all, pornography presents women as if *they* see themselves in this light; or as weak, spineless persons unable to resist the sexual advances of aggressive males. No wonder the feminist movement hates pornography!

But if sex is nothing but fun and games, to be indulged without shame as impulses dictate, why be faithful to one's spouse if someone more attractive—and willing—is at hand? Why not follow your lust wherever it leads?

Pornography also attacks the concept that sexual experience should be a private matter. Do animals worry about privacy? They have intercourse wherever and whenever they wish—in the joyous manner appropriate to creatures unspoiled by unhealthy sex repressions. If you would live the good life, free from crippling, guilt-producing, puritanical, life-destroying inhibitions, go and do likewise. Group sex? Why not? Wife-swapping? Why not? Invite the children to witness the fun when Mom and Pop are having sex? Why not? What's so private about sex?

The author recently testified on the social effects of pornography in a federal pornography case. The film *Mountain Girl* contained long stretches of vivid, close-up scenes of genital-fondling and sexual intercourse in various postures. These scenes included fellatio and group sex. A sex murder occurred along the way. To further spice things up, some messy scenes were included involving coitus interruptus and other forms of sexual behavior that are best not described in these pages.

When the writer told the jury that if this sort of thing found community acceptance today in the more inconspicuous theatres, experience indicates it will become acceptable for drive-in theatres tomorrow, the defense attorney commented, "Would you believe it already is being shown in some of them?"

Of course we can get used to it. The Marquis de Sade reminded us that we can get used to anything, even cruelty, if exposed to it long enough. Our sense of shame can be dulled to the point where it barely flickers, no matter what we see. But do we want to become this way?

Most of the future entertainment in movies and television will not be like *Mountain Girl,* presumably. Much of it will involve drama similar to that presented in the past *except* that explicit sex scenes will probably be included with increasing frequency. People will come to expect it, to want it, and an entertainment industry that recognizes no value higher than the dollar will give it to them. We cannot be sure of this but it seems like a reasonable prophecy.

Will these explicit sex scenes involve sex between married couples? Of course not. They will involve illicit sex, generally presented in an indulgent and permissive light.

Perhaps it becomes clear why, if current trends continue, the family itself is threatened. As Professor Harry Clor puts it, "The arts, for good or ill, are teachers. What if they . . . teach many that love is reducible to sex, that people are objects to be used for self-centered gratification, that moral restraints upon self-centered gratification are outmoded, and that there are no intimacies that one is bound to respect as sacred or private?"[17] The family cannot long survive unless marital partners view their sex relations in a responsible manner, with due regard for the emotional demands of love. And if society has any institution of greater significance than the family, what is it?

What about the other effects of free-flowing pornography and near-pornography? For the millions of young people from marginal homes, pornography encourages experimentation with various deviant forms of sex. Because these are represented as supremely adventurous and exciting, why won't many of them (especially those whose sexual identities are not clearly established) be prompted to take the plunge and see for themselves? Lacking strong moral restraints, at an age which thirsts for adventure and readily yields to peer pressures, it would be surprising if many did not succumb to the enticements of pornography and sample sex deviations which, in practice, may have traumatic emotional effects and leave them with ugly images for life.

Those familiar with the behavior and development of the young know that 18 (especially for many males) is far from the age of maturity. Innumerable persons from ages 15 to 20 are passing thru a rebellious stage —challenging parental restraints and parental values. At a time when they are eager to demonstrate their adulthood and independence by flouting parental standards, pornography and other influences that beckon them to dubious sexual adventures are sometimes particularly appealing. For some, then, pornography may be more dangerous at this phase of their life than at any other.

Because pornography and near-pornography encourage impulsive sex, they promote *careless sex.* We can expect, from those with inadequate moral foundations, more sexual experience before they are ready to handle it. This, in turn, will bring still more venereal disease, more abortions, more 16-year-old mothers, and more fathers unwilling to assume responsibility for their children. Recent sharp increases in these phenomena have already cast doubt upon our vaunted "sexual revolution," as has the sharp rise in rape—another by-product of our growing sexual "freedom." To assume that sexual restraints can be generally loosened in society without reducing individual restraints against rape is irrational. And to assume that premarital sex barriers can fall while extramarital fidelity is unaltered is equally irrational. Defenders of the sexual revolution typically appraise it from the standpoint of those presumed to have the greatest maturity and judgment in coping with the freedom it offers. But the wisdom of a social code cannot be judged by its impact on its most responsible members; it must be judged by its effect on the collective behavior of all those affected by it. This commonsensical truth is curiously avoided by most of those who so ardently defend the sexual revolution. Does anyone seriously doubt that vast numbers of young people do not have the maturity and judgment to responsibly handle their newfound freedom?

Those who initially sought a sexual revolution wanted a healthier view of sex than the Victorian legacy, more realistic sex education, acceptance of premarital sex between deeply committed adults, and more literary freedom in dealing with sexual themes. But revolutions, as all students of history know, have a way of getting out of hand. They move from modest goals to increasingly radical ones that jeopardize the values and institutions the early revolutionaries themselves cherished. Certainly the sexual pendulum has now swung as far to the left as the Victorians had moved it to the right.

And has all this produced a happier generation of young people? That's not what youth counsellors tell us. This is, instead, a deeply troubled generation—one that is unsure of its values, fearful of its sexual adequacy, and uncertain of its capacity to cope with its problems. In our eagerness to please the young, we have denied them sources of strength essential to their own sense of well-being. We have done this in tandem with an entertainment industry that tells young people precisely what they want to hear, and which increasingly shapes their values and lifestyles.

Sex is central to human existence as well as being one of our most powerful emotional experiences. It would not be surprising, then, if sexual morality were crucial to man's entire value structure. It may, indeed, be the centerpiece, as some anthropologists believe. Loosen the center of a moral system and you weaken the entire structure.

Some specific examples will illustrate this point. Those who engage in extramarital sex usually find themselves drawn into a network of practices at odds with sound ethical values. A pattern of deceit emerges, of coverup, of hypocrisy, and of lies to avoid painful disclosures. Once people get caught up in activities of this kind, it is easier to engage in deceit, hypocrisy, and lies in other aspects of life. Every act of moral strength adds moral stature to our lives; every betrayal of our values tends to weaken our capacity to live up to them.

If there were no sexual taboos, it may be said, there would be no need for lies and deceit. But without sexual taboos, there will be no family—at least, not the family as we know it. Instead there will be sexual chaos and the crumbling of one of the central pillars of society. Yet even the most revolutionary societies have ultimately been forced to respect the family and its significance to orderly social life.

DEMOCRACY, THE CONSTITUTION, AND PORNOGRAPHY

As many writers have suggested, democracy is heavily dependent on the self-discipline of its citizens. The more self-discipline the citizen exhibits, the less constraints society needs to impose. And the opposite is also true. This is, indeed, one of the iron laws of life. Professor Clor, a political scientist, observes that "liberal democracy and the constitutional system of government depend, for their vitality if not for their sheer survival, upon the character of citizens. A political order that relies heavily upon citizen responsibility and judgment requires citizens who respect each other and are capable of self-discipline."[18] He finds pornography's effects to be ultimately subversive of a free society. Another political scientist, Walter Bern, came to a similar conclusion in a widely noted article in *The Public Interest,* "Pornography vs. Democracy: The Case For Censorship."[19] It will be the supreme irony if the movement for maximum sexual freedom promotes personal behavior that indirectly shrinks our freedoms because society cannot endure the disorder and moral chaos that sexual license brings in its wake.

Adults, it is said, should be able to see what they wish since individuals supposedly have a right to do what they wish so long as they do not injure others. Irving Kristol has pointed out that we did not bar cockfighting and bearbaiting only because of humaneness to birds and animals. They were barred because they were believed to debase and brutalize the spectators.[20] No doubt a host of Americans would tune in to their television sets (with shades drawn) if the networks were to televise executions —whether by electric chair, cyanide gas, or hanging. But a self-respecting nation will not tolerate this, even if it took place after the children were safely in bed, for perfectly obvious reasons. Nor would we demand scientific proof of societal damage before applying the ban. Nor would we protest that the majority shouldn't impose their moral views on the minority. Almost all laws have a moral-ethical dimension to which a minority of society disapproves. Why give pornography a privileged position?

Will people finally weary of pornography? Will the flood recede thru pure boredom? We have been told this for years, but the nation is annually exposed to a greater volume of ever-more explicit material. Kristol notes that "those who masturbate do not get bored with masturbation, sadists don't get bored with sadism, and voyeurs don't get bored with voyeurism."[21] E. J. Mishan agrees, adding that "people do not tire of their fantasies, least of all their sexual fantasies."[22] Did the Romans weary of the gladiatorial contests, of the death struggles between wild animals, or of animals pitted against people? They did not; instead, they sought ever-more lavish spectacles, with more violence, more bloodshed, and more excitement. People seem not to weary of dramatized sex and violence; they just want the voltage stepped up.

The boredom theory is also challenged by Stephens' anthropological studies, which showed that tribes with the greatest sexual freedom display the "*greatest* interest in obscenity."[23] This is the most convincing evidence of all.

Where does this bring us? Justice Harlan, in *Alberts* v. *California*, made the wholly sensible observation that "the state can reasonably draw the inference that over a long period of time the indiscriminate dissemination of materials, the essential character of which is to degrade sex, will have an eroding effect on moral standards."[24]

But greater freedom for pornography is only a part—and a secondary part at that—of the sexual revolution. It may be, and sometimes is, the cutting edge of society's future course, but the recent outpouring of unquestionably legal sex-oriented literature, the media's eagerness to publicize and provide a platform for every challenge to previously accepted sexual standards, is at the heart of the matter. And no democrat believes the Constitution permits the censoring of this material.

The risks of free speech we must take, wherever they lead us. But the additional risks of pornography we need not take. Alexander Bickel put it this way: "The role of law, in this as in some other areas, is to make a moral statement about the kind of society we wish to live in. This concerns the tone of society, the mode, the style and quality of life, now and in the future."[25]

If a firm stand were taken against some of the grosser manifestations of pornography, it would be only a first step toward reexamining the course we are pursuing. But it would be saying something important: that this nation is not without some concept of decency that it is prepared to uphold.

Suppose, for the sake of argument, that pornography is regarded as inimical to important social values. Can the state, while respecting the Constitution, do anything about it? Here is one way to view the question. No matter what it says, the First Amendment does not mean "no law" and never has. We have a score of well-established laws limiting freedom of speech and press, many dating back to the earliest days of the republic. A few of these forbid libel, perjury, contempt of court, incitement to violence, disrespect toward commanding officers, divulgence of military secrets, plagiarism, fraudulent advertising, picketing in a context of violence, certain kinds of profanity and blasphemy on television, anonymous threatening or obscene phone calls, and partisan speeches by civil servants during a political campaign. Indeed, the First Amendment itself limits free expression; by implication, the "establishment of religion" clause forbids the advocacy of religious doctrines in public schools. And since the earliest days of our Constitution, laws forbidding obscenity have been accepted by the courts as constitutionally unobjectionable.

The drafters of the Constitution probably and properly intended an absolute ban on efforts by the government to forbid the dissemination of any political, economic, religious, or social ideas. John Stuart Mill and others have made an overwhelmingly cogent case for such freedom; no equally persuasive case has been made for the unlimited freedom of commercial entertainment. There is a right, therefore, to advocate the most bizarre forms of sexual perversion (fornication with billy goats, for example) so long as the proponent is clearly attempting to persuade rather than to entertain commercially. But in the words of Chief Justice Burger, in *Miller* v. *California* (1973), "to equate the free and robust exchange of ideas and political debate with commercial exploitation of obscene materials demeans . . . the First Amendment and its high purposes in the historic struggle for freedom."[26] The Chief Justice could not have hit the mark more squarely.

What about the due process issue? First, it is interesting that those who insist pornography cannot be adequately defined to meet the clarity test of due process usually agree children deserve protection from pornography. But if you can't define it for adults, how do you define it for children? As a matter of fact, we have hundreds of laws that are no more vague, or even much more vague, than the Supreme Court's pornography criteria. The Sherman antitrust law forbids monopolies. What is a monopoly? When one firm—or an oligopoly—controls 50 percent of the output in a field? 75 percent? 90 percent? No one knows for sure. What is an "unfair trade practice?" What is a merger that "substantially" reduces competition? What is "negligent" manslaughter? The list is endless. Yet those indignant over the lack of specificity in obscenity laws are quite complacent about vagueness in laws they approve.

Perhaps those who seek the lush profits that flow from explicit sex entertainment (like the Mafia, who have a heavy involvement in the traffic) deserve whatever uncertainties they experience when testing the limits of the law. If they are uneasy about the shadow of the law, there is a simple remedy: stay away from the danger zone!

In *Miller* v. *California* the Supreme Court permitted the condemnation of materials if (1) "the average person, applying contemporary community standards, would find that the work, taken as a whole, appeals to the prurient interest . . . (2) the work depicts or describes in a patently offensive way, sexual conduct specifically defined by the applicable state law and (3) the work, taken as a whole, lacks serious literary, artistic, political or scientific value.''

The court went on to "give a few plain examples of what a state statute could forbid:

1. Patently offensive representations or descriptions of ultimate sexual acts, normal or perverted, actual or simulated.

2. Patently offensive representations or descriptions of masturbation, excretory functions, and lewd exhibitions of the genitals."

Genuine hard-core pornography, in sleazy magazines, movies, and the like, can be dealt with by this criteria. Books are best ignored, even when they might fall within the purview of the law. They lack the vividness and emotional impact that pornography has in films and on stage. Books are less threatening to adolescents, who are avid movie-goers but not addicted to reading. Besides, seeking to eliminate more than the most egregiously written pornography entails serious risks of abuse as well as mind-boggling enforcement problems. The greatest menace is elsewhere.

Although *Miller* v. *California* was bitterly assailed as a backward step, it was actually more permissive, applied to stage and screen, than may be warranted. It permits customers to watch commercialized displays of explicit sexual behavior, conventional or otherwise, so long as they take place in films, for example, that have artistic merit. This interpretation opens the door to endless protracted litigation and to an endless succession of partially pornographic films and plays having alleged artistic value.

The major question we must answer is this: Are we willing for people to be entertained by portrayals of explicit sexual acts, in all their various forms, or do we regard this as socially unacceptable, whatever the artistic merits of a film or play? Do we really believe artists need this kind of license? Even if they want it, is the price too high? For every film or play that employs explicit sexual scenes in a "sensitive and artistic" manner, a score of films and plays will deal with it in a crude, vulgar, tasteless, and degrading fashion. To have legal access to the former, we must accept the latter. Is this a good bargain? Should responsible dramatists demand a privilege that, in its overall effect, is likely to be destructive to society?

What is needed is a thorough-going national debate on the propriety and permissibility of explicit sexual entertainment in this country. If the pornographers and their defenders win, democracy requires that they have their way. But they should not win by drift and default, without having the issue met head-on. When all sides have spoken, let us make a decision. Let us either say that explicit sexual entertainment deserves neither condemnation nor harassment—or let us stop it in its tracks. Let this nation search its soul and then decide : What kind of people do we want to be?

NOTES

1. *The Report of the Commission on Pornography and Obscenity,* Toronto, Bantam Books, 1970.
2. Leonard Berkowitz, cited in Victor B. Cline, *Where Do You Draw the Line?* Provo, Utah, Brigham Young University Press, 1974, p. 254. Also see Cline's devastating critique of the Commission's objectivity in *Where Do You Draw The Line?,* pp. 203–256. Ernest Van de Haag observes (Cline, p. 270) that the Commission "selectively and prejudicially initiated and presented investigations to bolster conclusions which were determined by its formulation of the problem . . ." Professor Harry Clor observes that "throughout the report, one finds discrepancies or ambiguities in the facts presented and conclusions drawn from them. And where alternative interpretations of data are possible, the report unfailingly chooses the libertarian one . . ." (Cline, pp. 339–340.) Herbert L. Packer asserted that ". . . the behavioral studies, which are at the heart of the Effects Panel case, prove almost nothing . . ." ("The Pornography Caper," *Commentary,* February, 1971, p. 76.)
3. James Q. Wilson, "Violence, Pornography and Social Science," *The Public Interest,* Winter 1971, p. 61.
4. See Cline, *Where Do You Draw The Line?,* pp. 203–256, and Harry Clor, *Censorship and Freedom of Expression,* Chicago, Rand McNally, 1971, pp. 119–129.
5. James Q. Wilson, "Violence, Pornography and Social Science," p. 57. Skeptics are urged to read this article in its entirety.
6. J. D. Unwin, *Sex and Culture,* London, Oxford University Press, 1934, pp. 374, 411, 412. Also see Unwin, *Sexual Regulations and Cultural Behavior,* London, Oxford University Press, 1935, *passim.*
7. William N. Stephens, "A Cross-Cultural Study of Modesty and Obscenity," *Technical Report of the Commission on Obscenity and Pornography,* 1970, vol. 9, pp. 406, 426.
8. Pitirim Sorokin, *The American Sex Revolution,* Boston, Porter Sargent, 1956, pp. 106–107, 113.
9. Arnold J. Toynbee, "Why I Dislike Western Civilization," *New York Times Magazine,* May 10, 1964, p. 15.
10. Reported in Vance Packard, *The Sexual Wilderness,* New York, David McKay, 1968, p. 424.
11. Ibid., pp. 424–425.
12. Bruno Bettelheim, "Parent and Child: Children Must Learn to Fear," *New York Times Magazine,* April 13, 1969, p. 145.
13. Will and Ariel Durant, *The Lessons of History,* New York, Simon and Schuster, 1968, pp. 35–36.
14. Quoted in Cline, *Where Do You Draw The Line?,* p. 264.

15. *Television and Growing Up, Impact of Televised Violence,* Report to Surgeon General's Scientific Advisory Committee on Television and Social Behavior, Washington, D.C., 1972.
16. L. Berkowitz, "Sex and Violence: We Can't Have It Both Ways," *Psychology Today,* December, 1971.
17. Clor, *Censorship and Freedom of Expression,* p. 107.
18. Ibid., p. 109.
19. Walter Bern, "Pornography versus Democracy: A Case for Censorship," *The Public Interest,* Winter, 1971.
20. Irving Kristol, "Pornography, Obscenity and the Case for Censorship," *New York Times Magazine,* March 28, 1971, p. 24.
21. Ibid., p. 112.
22. E. J. Mishan, "Making the World Safe for Pornography," *Encounter,* March 1972, p. 14.
23. William N. Stephens, "A Cross-Cultural Study of Modesty and Obscenity," pp. 406, 443.
24. *Alberts* v. *California,* 354 U.S. 476 (1957).
25. Alexander Bickel, "Pornography, Censorship and Common Sense," *Reader's Digest,* February 1974, pp. 117–118.
26. *Miller* v. *California,* 41 L.W. 4925, 1973.

TEN
Our Federal Budget: The Spigot, the Well, and the Axe (To Mix Metaphors!)

The author has put forward a number of proposals that, if enacted, would prove costly. Very costly, in fact. Refurbishing our long-haul railroad system; returning feedlot manure to the soil; a public-service corps employing several million workers; relocation of blacks from the worst urban slums (the impossible dream!); extended health insurance; an expanded court system; more jails. (Other students of public affairs would compile quite different lists, but theirs would be costly, too. What would yours be?) It is always irresponsible (when inflation is a major concern) to advocate increased federal spending without also outlining either matching reductions in the federal budget, or the additional taxes needed to finance those recommendations, or some combination of both.

First, what defensible policies could increase federal revenues? Closing tax loopholes has already been discussed in Chapter 5. Since the pending shortage of investment capital may make it necessary to grant a larger investment-tax credit to business, overall gains from tax reform will be more modest than seemed feasible a few years ago. An investment tax credit expansion, however, need not apply to all business. It could prudently be limited to investment in energy development and pollution control rather than be available for investment in new shopping centers, resort hotels, gambling casinos, or whatever. Once a larger but sensibly restricted investment tax credit is legislated—if it proves necessary—arguments that the capital-gains tax must not be raised because of our heavy capital requirements will be undercut. (Which doesn't mean those arguments won't prevail, however!) And if various tax shelters were demolished and taxes on earnings of over $40,000 a year were sharply increased, perhaps a net tax increase of over $5 billion could be achieved.

Since cigarette consumption may be the greatest of all threats to the nation's health, a major boost in the cigarette tax would clearly be in the public interest. A 25-cent per pack increase would yield about $7.5 billion if consumption remained at current levels;[1] since cigarette consumption would probably fall, however, a more likely figure might be $6 billion.

If a formula were evolved that restricted large industry from writing off against its tax obligations more than, say, about half of their current volume of advertising (in terms of percentage of sales), the corporation tax would yield substantially more revenue. And, as noted earlier, neither the large corporation nor the economy would be injured one whit.

Unhappily, a good bit of the tax gains realized by this reform would be cancelled out by the necessity of allowing newspapers and magazines to use the mails at greatly reduced postal rates to offset their losses from reduced advertising. Federal revenues would still improve, but it's hard to say how much.

Imposing a federal tax on pollution emissions, along the lines suggested in Chapter 1 by Kneese and Schultze, would initially bring in $4–6 billion a year,[2] but this sum would decline steadily as industry sought to cut its costs by reducing pollution to a minimum.

A higher corporation tax? Most economists believe this tax is passed on to the consumer; in any case, a time of possible capital drought is no time to add dubious taxes to business enterprise.

It appears, then, that during a period in which Congress may be deeply concerned with high unemployment and with unprecedented capital needs for energy, pollution control, and the invigoration of our industrial plants, major new tax sources will be hard to identify. Probably none of the taxes suggested here will be received favorably by Congress. (If higher taxes are voted hereafter, they will probably come in the form of across-the-board increases or a national sales tax.) Since the revenues available even if the author's favored taxes were passed would fall far short of those required to finance needed programs, we turn to possible reductions in federal spending.

We continue to spend nearly half-a-billion dollars annually on *impact aid* for the public schools. During World War II a case could be made for subsidizing districts in which new military camps and installations brought large numbers of servicemen and their families but which lacked the tax base (since federal property is nontaxable) to nourish the schools properly. Some of these districts may still need help, but most of them don't, according to responsible critics. This appropriation has become part of what David A. Stockman calls the *social pork barrel*—superfluous but hard to eradicate because of deeply dug-in vested interests. Indeed, considering the total lack of evidence that federal aid to education is improving our schools at all, that entire massive program should be cut to the bone. Bring out the axe! (I can dream, can't I?)

Also indefensible, Stockman believes, is the $12 billion spent on veteran's programs—''most of which benefits ex-servicemen who do not even have a hangnail to show for their harrowing experiences in uniform. . . .''[3] There is no good reason why servicemen not injured in uniform should receive special benefits from the state. They did their duty, they were lucky, they are making their way just as well as those who did not serve. The benefits they are getting were gratuitously proffered to them by vote-hungry politicians, rather than being a response to the average veteran's conviction that ''I deserve this.'' (If you're wondering, the author is a five-year veteran of military service.) Swing that axe!

We are still spending about $3 billion for space research and spectaculars; a billion would probably be plenty. While almost any multibillion dollar research program produces useful byproducts, space expenditures, which go beyond those absolutely essential to national defense, have to be very, very low on our agenda of national needs. For many years, the outer-space program has been a gaudy frill designed to gratify the national ego and the egos of presidents who preside over it. Its down-to-earth contribution to human well-being is small—and becoming less so year by year. Swing it again!

Charles Peters reports that the administrative costs of a negative income tax program guaranteeing a minimum income for all families would require administrative costs of less than half of those called for by our current complex melange of welfare programs.[4] Alas, supplementary reforms needed to make NIT practicable (see Chapter 4) would probably cost as much as the savings entailed. The federal revenue-sharing program, however, is a fine candidate for the axe. Its value is dubious.

Peters further notes that federal employees now earn far more than employees doing comparable work in private enterprise. Half of the employees in the Department of Transportation, for example, earn over $20,000 a year. There's obviously a job to be done here, although the labor unions will never let Congress do it.

And something had better be done about the fact that retired federal civil servants not only get a justified increase in their pensions when the cost of living goes up but "also get an *extra* 1 percent each time there is a cost of living increase."

There are probably scores of federal programs that could be profitably eliminated or trimmed, but, unfortunately, scholars have devoted very little attention to scrutinizing the federal budget closely for possible savings. True, judgments in this area inevitably are enmeshed in highly subjective personal judgments. And where value judgments are concerned, scholars are not notably wiser than others. But if their own value premises were made clear so others could judge for themselves, a searching analysis of the federal budget for indications of waste, for the presence of anachronisms, and for programs that promise much and deliver little could be one of the greatest services the academic profession could render to this country. The Congressional Budget Office could do likewise, rather than leave the analysis of existing programs to the Office of Budget and Management (OBM), the General Accounting Office (GAO), and the happenstance competence of congressional appropriation subcommittees. While the OBM and GAO are highly useful bodies, their services are no substitute for the kind of unsparing budgetary examination that academe, at its best, could supply. If some of the nation's best newspaper reporters became interested in governmental economy, they could also perform yeoman service.

We have been enacting new programs and passing bigger appropriations bills at a rapid pace for a generation; it is time for a concerted, intensive, exhaustive review of these programs by the top brains in the nation, working from different vantage points and from differing perspectives. Liberals should be just as concerned about economies as conservatives are, because adequate funding for their favorite programs hereafter will be facilitated by economies that release funds from lessvaluable to more-valuable programs. From here on, with financial stringencies bound to bear down heavily upon us, the rule should be—Where the case for new spending is not compelling, resolve the doubts against the spenders. And where promising but expensive new programs are involved, give them a good experimental run (where possible) before committing massive resources to them. Sharpen that axe!

Sharpening the axe is one thing but swinging it is another. Nothing— but nothing—is more difficult in the art of government than withdrawing a benefit once conferred upon a group of voters (and those who administer the program). Usually a semireasonable case *can* be made that any program is performing a useful service. Bureaucrats and their organized allies are ever alert to opportunities to strengthen the political base of their program and to make judicious adjustments whenever it seems threatened. If the threat becomes serious, an unholy clamor is raised by constituents—stimulated by their organization leaders, cultivated by public officials whose jobs are imperiled, and spearheaded by lobbyists who know the tricks of their trade. The counterpressure, organized or unorganized, which might bolster the hands of congressional economizers is largely absent.

As everyone knows, members of Congress tend to respond to pressure, and most of it comes from those who suckle at the federal breast. Since most members run for office on the assumption that the next election will be close and a handful of votes might tell the tale, they tend to do what those who *care most* about an issue want done. Those who care most are those who have the most to lose!

If significant cuts are made at some stage in the legislative process to give members of Congress a chance to point to their records on "economy," the cuts are almost always reversed at some further point—often with the tacit approval of those who voted for reductions in the first place.

Budget cutting is a most frustrating business. The need for a nationally organized, well-financed, skillfully led pressure group, drawing public-spirited support from a wide political spectrum rather than just from the right, is urgent. Is this an idea whose time has come?

THE MILITARY BUDGET

The largest potential federal economies, theoretically speaking, are in the realm of the military budget. Budgetary cuts are always controversial, of course, and the most controversial of all involve national defense. Here's how some of the arguments shape up.

The Pentagon is currently spending about $100 billion a year. It wants more, reminding us that the Russian navy has been outbuilding us by a wide margin since 1955. It contends the Russians are ahead on tanks and catching up on submarines and nuclear missiles. It says we need more money for both submarines and antisubmarine warfare, more ships (including aircraft carriers), more tanks, hundreds of B-1 bombers,[5] low-flying cruise missiles fired by submarines and planes, maneuverable intercontinental ballistic missles (ICBMs, which have more pinpoint accuracy and can change direction in flight to evade possible defensive missiles), less-vulnerable missile silos, mobile ICBM pads and more army divisions. A volunteer army, the Pentagon accurately declares, costs more money than a draft army.

A bloated military budget? How can people say that when the military is spending only 6 percent of the GNP compared with 8 percent in 1964? Its share of the national budget is now only 25 percent, compared with 40 percent in 1964.[6] The military has been starved rather than gorged!

We must maintain parity with or superiority over the Soviets in this perpetually dangerous world, it is said. Vigilance is the price of liberty; preparedness is the price of peace. National security is worth whatever it costs. And so forth. If the Congress or the public becomes complacent, the Pentagon is always prepared to unveil new stories about ominous Soviet military advances. Especially when appropriations are being decided.

The writer makes no claim to being an authority on the military budget (although his bias will soon become clear). But it is necessary to point out that the Pentagon employs a mixture of shoddy logic, shifty footwork and a dazzling display of verbal sleight of hand to bolster its case. There is no logical correlation, for example, between the size of the GNP and the military budget, or the size of the national budget and military spending. If Congress decides to spend more on Social Security or health insurance or pollution control, that has strictly nothing to do with the military needs of the nation. The notion that for every additional billion spent for education or health or highways we should add one-third billion for national defense is specious. And if the auto and construction industries have good years and the GNP rises, that again is totally unrelated to the necessary size of the defense establishment. The Secretary of Defense should really do better than this!

When the Vietnam war was being waged, the Pentagon naturally demanded more money. But with that miserable war over, the Pentagon still wants more, lest our enemies conclude that our will is weakening and we are unable to back up our commitments. If relations with Russia deteriorate, the military needs more money, lest war should break out. If relations with Russia improve and the president and Secretary of State boast of detente, the military needs more money to further detente with a nation that respects only force. If disarmament agreements cannot be reached, the military needs more money to keep pace with the Russians; if disarmament agreements are signed, the Pentagon needs more money to develop new weapons for use as bargaining chips at the next disarmament talks. If America is the world's policeman, we need more money to meet our far-flung responsibilities. If we abandon that role, the Pentagon needs more money, lest the enemy capitalize on our shrunken vision and exploit the more tempting military situation.

Is it any wonder that close Pentagon-watchers develop thick psychological callouses from viewing a slippery performance like this? The Greeks had a word for it: *sophistry*.

As for specific reductions, if the ratio of support troops to combat troops were the same as in World War II (which is about what the Russians allegedly have today) the Pentagon allegedly could save an estimated $13 billion.[7] (This may not be possible, however; a more technically sophisticated army probably needs a higher percentage of support troops. The $13 billion figure is probably much too high.) Is the military top-heavy with brass? We have more three- and four-star generals, admirals, colonels and navy captains today than we had at the height of World War II when far more men were under arms.[8]

As for the Russian navy, it is designed primarily as a defensive instrument rather than as an intercontinental attack force. It is not a standing threat to the United States and need not be viewed as such.

We are apparently spending nearly $10 billion a year collecting military intelligence and financing the Central Intelligence Agency (CIA).[9] The CIA, the Pentagon Defense Intelligence Agency, the State Department's Bureau of Intelligence Research, the Air Force's A-2, Army's G-2 and the Navy's Office of Naval Intelligence are all in on the act. If $10 billion is not the most mind-boggling fiscal excess in the history of our country, it would be interesting to know who holds the record. Is more than two or three billion dollars really needed for gathering military intelligence, and conducting covert operations, especially if we conclude that the CIA's record, when it comes to covert tasks, is so wretched that it has forfeited the right (right?) to continue subverting other governments? Such juicy savings for budget-cutters to feast upon! Bring that axe down hard!

Much of our massive military spending is devoted to maintaining and constantly improving our atomic deterrent forces. Currently we have the so-called triple deterrent; we have over 1,000 ICBMs; 1,640 long-range bombers; and over 30 nuclear submarines, each of them capable of discharging 160 warheads, with each warhead capable of destroying a city. We have a nuclear stockpile equal to nearly 700,000 Hiroshima bombs; one nuclear-armed plane can deliver more explosive power than both sides dropped during World War II. Our explosive stockpile is equal to 50,000 pounds of destructive force for every person on this planet.[10] We are probably capable of destroying Russian cities fifty times over with our nuclear arsenal. To some observers, this is an absurdly excessive commitment of resources to a reasonable goal—that of persuading the Soviet Union that an attack on the United States (or Western Europe) would be a suicidal venture. Since our submarine fleet alone can inflict crippling damage on the Soviets, and this fleet cannot be destroyed by an enemy "first strike" now or in the foreseeable future, why spend so many billions on the pointless *overkill* that the Strategic Air Command and the ICBM jointly represent? If the Soviets should achieve superiority in deliverable atomic warheads (unlikely for years to come, since the U.S., thanks to our big lead in multiple independently targeted reentry vehicles [MIRV], has a clear-cut edge in deliverable nuclear warheads), what difference would that make? Once you can destroy the enemy's major cities, how much greater deterrent is needed? Above all, why spend billions on a new manned bomber fleet in the days of intercontinental missiles? Does not the latter point up the Pentagon's insatiable appetite for more? (The B-1 has been called the "flying pork barrel.")

We are told that bombers, once launched, can be recalled; the decision to launch ICBMs is irreversible. But does this mean the president wants the option of launching atomic bombers in a last-minute intimidation maneuver—a kind of mad brinkmanship—designed to force enemy capitulation while the planes are en route to their targets? And to strike first if they do not yield?

On the other hand, if we do not pull the trigger on our atomic weapons until the enemy has dispatched his ICBMs, there is no need to send recallable bombers. The moment of truth will have come, and if we choose to retaliate, ICBMs are far less vulnerable than bombers.

It can always be argued that we must play safe by having an arsenal of fall-back weapons, just in case. But this game knows no end; its psychology is that of the ceaseless arms race, with perpetual increases in the variety, quantity, complexity, and destructiveness of our weapons. There seems—there really seems—to be only one conclusion to this insanity: an ultimate superdisaster. Enough is enough.

But will the military budget be cut? In all probability, it will not. Americans want their country to be the number one military power in the world, want to keep ahead of the Russians, believe that a huge nuclear arsenal is the formula for peace, and would reject out of hand any proposal that challenged these assumptions.

Finally, a brief comment on the comfortable American assumption that atomic war and the lethal fallout pollution it would create would be so ghastly and so senseless that it will never take place. The assumption is dubious.[11] It assumes that there will be no more Hitlers unrestrained by ethical, moral, or rational principles; that no atomically armed power, backed to the wall in an apparently losing war (Israel? Egypt?), will lash out in one final attempt to prevent the ultimate defeat and humiliation; that no nation at war will ever use small tactical nuclear weapons as a warning to the other side that it means business and that such a warning will not bring an escalated response; that no atomic power will miscalculate what provocation another nation will tolerate; that there will be no frustrated general, prepared to take atomic decisions into his own hands; that in *every* major confrontation between the ever-increasing number of atomically armed powers, rationality will *always* prevail. Perhaps the optimists are right, but they are optimists indeed. Man is really that rational? Always? Murphy's Law reminds us that if something *can* go wrong, sooner or later it *will* go wrong. But perhaps it is best to have blind faith and the peace of mind it brings, since *balance of terror* politics will apparently be with us until the day the lid blows off. Then we will ask, we who live, "How could we be so blind, so complacent, so naive?"

NOTES

1. Dr. Andrew Taylor, *ASH Newsletter,* May–June 1975, p. 4.
2. Allen V. Kneese and Charles L. Schultze, *Pollution, Prices and Public Policy,* © 1975 by The Brookings Institution, Washington, D.C., pp. 95–96.
3. David A. Stockman, "The Social Pork Barrel," *The Public Interest,* Spring 1975, pp. 15, 25.
4. Charles Peters, "We Could Have Saved New York," *Washington Monthly,* December 1975, pp. 42, 45.
5. Peter Ognibene, "Pentagon Prosperity," *New Republic,* February 22, 1975, says that "the case for the overweight and inordinately expensive B-1 is nonexistent," p. 11.
6. Ognibene, "Pentagon Prosperity," p. 10. Drew Middleton (*Can America Win The Next War?,* New York, Scribners, 1975) says the United States would lose a non-nuclear war with the USSR but shoud win in a Soviet–U.S. confrontation in an area like Israel—*if* the American people support the war.
7. Thomas Redburn, "A Platform for the 70s," *Washington Monthly,* October 1974, p. 14.
8. Norman Cousins, "How Not to Fight Inflation," *Saturday Review/World,* November 2, 1974, p. 4.
9. *Time,* February 3, 1975, p. 11.
10. Norman Cousins, "Arms and Madness," *Saturday Review,* July 26, 1975, p. 4.
11. Critiques of our military budgets and posture are found in Richard J. Barnett, *The Economy of Death,* New York, Atheneum, 1969; Philip Green, *The Deadly Logic,* Columbus, Ohio State University Press, 1966; Herbert York, *Race to Oblivion,* New York, Simon & Schuster, 1970; and Edgar M. Bottome, *The Balance of Terror,* Boston, Beacon Press, 1971; Bernard T. Feld, "The Charade of Piecemeal Arms Limitation," *Bulletin of the Atomic Scientists,* January 1975; Reo M. Christenson, *Heresies Right and Left,* New York, Harper & Row, 1973, Chapter 7.

BIBLIOGRAPHY

CHAPTER 1 POLLUTION: THE ISSUE IS SURVIVAL

Anderson, Walt, ed. *Politics and Environment*. 2d ed. Pacific Palisades, Calif.: Goodyear, 1975.

Barnett, John. *Our Mistreated World*. Princeton, New Jersey: Dow Jones Books, 1970.

Baron, Robert A. *The Tyranny of Noise*. New York: St. Martin's Press, 1970.

Berland, Theodore. *The Fight for Quiet*. Englewood Cliffs, N.J.: Prentice-Hall, 1970.

Boulding, Kenneth. *The Economics of Pollution*. New York: New York University Press, 1971.

Clarke, Ronald O., and List, Peter C. *Environmental Spectrum*. New York: Van Nostrand, 1974.

Commoner, Barry. *The Closing Circle*. New York: Knopf, 1971.

Ehrlich, Paul R., and Ehrlich, Anne C. *Population, Resources, Environment*. 2d ed. San Francisco: Freeman, 1972.

Heilbroner, Robert L. *An Inquiry Into the Human Prospect*. New York: Norton, 1974.

Jones, Charles O. *Clean Air: The Policies and Politics of Pollution Control*. Pittsburgh: University of Pittsburgh Press, 1975.

Priest, Joseph. *Problems of Our Physical Environment: Energy, Transportation, Pollution*. Reading, Mass.: Addison-Wesley, 1973.

Roelofs, Robert T.; Crowley, Joseph N.; and Hardesty, Donald L. *Environment and Society*. Englewood Cliffs, N.J.: Prentice-Hall, 1974.

Sax, Joseph L. *Defending the Environment: A Strategy for Citizen Action*. New York: Knopf, 1971.

CHAPTER 2 ENERGY: THE SHAPE OF THE FUTURE

"The Energy Crisis: Reality or Myth?" *Annals*, November 1973.

Davis, David H. *Energy Politics*. New York: St. Martin's Press, 1974.

Ehrlich, Paul R., and Ehrlich, Anne H. *The End of Affluence*. New York: Ballantine Books, 1975.

Energy Policy Project. *A Time to Choose, America's Energy Future*. Cambridge, Mass.: Ballinger, 1974.

Freeman, S. David. *Energy: The New Era*. New York: Walker, 1974.

Goodwin, Irwin, ed. *Energy and Environment*. Acton, Mass.: Publishing Sciences Group, 1974.

Heilbroner, Robert. *An Inquiry into the Human Prospect*. New York: Norton, 1974.

McPhee, John. *The Curve of Binding Energy*. New York: Farrar, Straus & Giroux, 1975.

CHAPTER 3 INFLATION AND UNEMPLOYMENT: THE PERENNIAL SEE-SAW

Friedman, Milton. *Indexing and Inflation*. Washington, D.C.: American Enterprise Institute for Public Policy Research, 1974.

Grayson, C. Jackson, Jr. *Confessions of a Price Controller*. Homewood, Illinois: Dow Jones & Irwin, 1974.

Lekachman, Robert. *Inflation: The Permanent Problem of Boom and Bust*. New York: Random House, 1973.

Okun, Arthur. *The Political Economy of Prosperity*. Washington, D.C.: The Brookings Institution, 1970.

Samuelson, Paul. *Economics*. 10th ed. New York: McGraw-Hill, 1976.

Silk, Leonard S. *Nixonomics*. New York: Praeger, 1972.

CHAPTER 4 POVERTY: A CRUSADE STALLS

Anderson, Martin. *The Federal Bulldozer*. Cambridge, Mass.: MIT Press, 1964.

Banfield, Edward C. *The Unheavenly City*. Boston: Little, Brown, 1968.

Banfield, Edward C. *The Unheavenly City Revisited*. Boston: Little, Brown, 1974.

Coleman, James S. *Equality of Educational Opportunity*. Washington, D.C.: Government Printing Office, 1966.

Donovan, John C. *The Politics of Poverty*. 2d ed. Indianapolis: Pegasus, 1973.

Fried, Joseph. *Housing Crisis, USA*. New York: Praeger, 1971.

Gans, Herbert. *More Equality*. New York: Pantheon Books, 1973.

Harrington, Michael. *The Other America*. New York: Macmillan, 1962.

Hartman, Chester W. *Housing and Social Policy*. Englewood Cliffs, N.J.: Prentice-Hall, 1975.

Jencks, Christopher. *Inequality*. New York: Basic Books, 1972.

Lampman, Robert J. *Ends and Means of Reducing Income Poverty*. Chicago: Markham, 1971.

Levitan, Sar. *The Great Society's Poor Law*. Baltimore: Johns Hopkins Press, 1969.

Moynihan, Daniel P. *Maximum Feasible Misunderstanding*. New York: Free Press, 1969.

Moynihan, Daniel P. *The Politics of a Guaranteed Income*. New York: Random House, 1973.

Solomon, Arthur P. *Housing the Urban Poor: A Critical Evaluation of Federal Housing Policy.* Cambridge, Mass.: MIT Press, 1974.

Steiner, Gilbert. *The State of Welfare.* Washington, D.C.: The Brookings Institution, 1974.

CHAPTER 5 INCOME DISTRIBUTION AND TAX REFORM: THE FAIRNESS TEST

Lampman, Robert. *Ends and Means of Reducing Income Poverty.* Chicago: Markham, 1971.

Nozick, Robert. *Anarchy, State and Utopia.* New York: Basic Books, 1974.

Pechman, Joseph A. *Federal Tax Policy. rev. ed.* Washington, D.C.: The Brookings Institution, 1971.

Rawls, John. *A Theory of Justice.* Cambridge, Mass.: Belknap Press of Harvard University Press, 1971.

Stern, Philip. *The Rape of the Taxpayer.* New York: Random House, 1973.

Surrey, Stanley S. *Pathways to Tax Reform.* Cambridge, Mass.: Harvard University Press, 1973.

Tawney, Richard H. *Equality.* 4th ed. London: Allen & Unwin, Ltd., 1952.

CHAPTER 6 NATIONAL HEALTH INSURANCE: IS THIS THE TIME?

Fuchs, Victor. *Who Shall Live?* New York: Basic Books, 1975.

Kennedy, Edward F. *In Critical Condition.* New York: Simon & Schuster, 1972.

Law, Sylvia A. *Blue Cross: What Went Wrong?* New Haven, Conn.: Yale University Press, 1974.

National Health Insurance Proposals, Washington, D.C.: American Enterprise Institute for Public Policy Research, 1974.

Ribicoff, Abraham. *The American Medical Machine.* New York: Saturday Review Press, 1972.

Schwartz, Harry. *The Case for American Medicine.* New York: McKay, 1972.

CHAPTER 7 CRIME: THE DARK AT THE END OF THE TUNNEL?

Clark, Ramsey. *Crime in America.* New York: Simon & Schuster, 1970.

Committee for Economic Development. *Reducing Crime and Assuring Justice.* New York, 1972.

Gaylin, Willard. *Partial Justice.* New York: Knopf, 1974.

Menninger, Karl. *The Crime of Punishment.* New York: Viking Press, 1969.

Newfield, Jack. *Cruel and Unusual Justice.* New York: Holt, Rinehart and Winston, 1974.

President's Commission on Law Enforcement and Administration of Justice. *The Challenge of Crime in a Free Society.* Washington, D.C.: Government Printing Office, 1967.

Radzinowicz, Leon, and Wolfgang, Marvin E. *Crime and Justice.* New York: Basic Books, 1971.

Reiss, Albert J., Jr. *The Police and the Public.* New Haven, Conn.: Yale University Press, 1971.

Schur, Edwin M., and Bedau, Hugo. *Victimless Crimes: Two Sides of a Controversy.* Englewood Cliffs, N.J.: Prentice-Hall, 1974.

Sherrill, Robert. *The Saturday Night Special.* New York: Charterhouse, 1973.

Wilson, James Q. *Thinking About Crime.* New York: Basic Books, 1975.

CHAPTER 8 THE TWENTY-SEVENTH AMENDMENT AND THE FEMINIST MOVEMENT: A DIALOGUE

DeCrow, Karen. *Sexist Justice.* New York: Random House (Vintage Books), 1974.

Freeman, Jo. *The Politics of Women's Liberation.* New York: McKay, 1975.

Gilder, George. *Sexual Suicide.* New York: Quadrangle, 1973.

Greer, Germaine. *The Female Eunuch.* New York: Bantam Books, 1972.

Jaquette, Jane S. *Women in Politics.* New York: Wiley, 1974.

Maccoby, Eleanor, and Jacklin, Carol. *The Psychology of Sex Differences.* Stanford, Ca.: Stanford University Press, 1974.

Millett, Kate. *Sexual Politics.* New York: Avon Books, 1969.

Tiger, Lionel, and Fox, Robin. *The Imperial Animal.* New York: Holt, Rinehart and Winston, 1971.

CHAPTER 9 PORNOGRAPHY: THE SEXUAL REVOLUTION AND THE STATE

Cline, Victor B., ed. *Where Do You Draw the Line?* Provo, Utah: Brigham Young University Press, 1974.

Clor, Harry. *Censorship and Freedom of Expression.* Chicago: Rand McNally, 1971.

Daily, J. E. *The Anatomy of Censorship.* New York: Dekker, 1973.

Ernst, Morris. *Censorship: The Search for the Obscene.* New York: Macmillan, 1965.

Goldstein, Michael L., and Kant, Harold S. *Pornography and Sexual Deviance.* Berkeley: University of California Press, 1973.

Kuh, Richard H. *Foolish Figleaves? Pornography In and Out of Court.* New York: Macmillan, 1967.

Michelson, Peter. *The Aesthetics of Pornography.* New York: Herder & Herder, 1971.

Oboler, Eli. *The Fear of the Word.* Metuchen, N.J.: Scarecrow Press, 1974.

Sharp, D. B. *Commentaries on Obscenity.* Metuchen, New Jersey: Scarecrow, 1970.

Sunderland, L. *Obscenity: The Court, The Congress and the Constitution.* Washington, D.C.: American Enterprise Association for Public Policy Research, 1975.

Widmer, E. *Freedom and Culture: Literary Censorship in the 70s.* Belmont, California: Wadsworth, 1970.

CHAPTER 10 OUR FEDERAL BUDGET: THE SPIGOT, THE WELL, AND THE AXE

Barnet, Richard J. *The Economy of Death.* New York: Atheneum, 1969.

Bottome, Edgar M. *The Balance of Terror.* Boston: Beacon Press, 1971.

Clemens, Walter C. R., Jr. *The Superpowers and Arms Control*. Lexington, Mass.: Lexington Books, 1973.

Fried, Edward R., et al. *Setting National Priorities: the 1974 Budget*. Washington, D.C.: The Brookings Institution, 1973.

Lambro, David. *The Federal Rathole*. Arlington House, 1975.

Melman, Seymour. *The Permanent War Economy*. New York: Simon & Schuster, 1974.

Middleton, Drew. *Can America Win the Next War?* New York: Scribners, 1975.

Newhouse, John. *Cold Dawn: The Story of SALT*. New York: Holt, Rinehart and Winston, 1973.

Stockfisch, J. A. *Plowshares Into Swords*. New York: Mason and Lipscomb, 1973.

York, Herbert. *Race to Oblivion*. New York: Simon & Schuster, 1970.

INDEX

76 77 78 9 8 7 6 5 4 3 2 1